AF352579

WRITING FEAR

KATHERINE BOWERS

WRITING FEAR

Russian Realism and the Gothic

UNIVERSITY OF TORONTO PRESS
Toronto Buffalo London

© University of Toronto Press 2022
Toronto Buffalo London
utorontopress.com
Printed in the U.S.A.

ISBN 978-1-4875-2692-4 (cloth)   ISBN 978-1-4875-2694-8 (EPUB)
ISBN 978-1-4875-2693-1 (PDF)

Library and Archives Canada Cataloguing in Publication

Title: Writing fear : Russian realism and the gothic / Katherine Bowers.
Names: Bowers, Katherine, author.
Description: Includes bibliographical references and index.
Identifiers: Canadiana (print) 20210347333 | Canadiana (ebook) 20210347511 |
ISBN 9781487526924 (hardcover) | ISBN 9781487526948 (EPUB) |
ISBN 9781487526931 (PDF)
Subjects: LCSH: Realism in literature. | LCSH: Gothic revival
(Literature) – Russia. | LCSH: Russian fiction – European influences. |
LCSH: Russian fiction – 19th century – History and criticism.
Classification: LCC PG3096.R4 B69 2022 | DDC 891.73/30912–dc23

We wish to acknowledge the land on which the University of Toronto Press
operates. This land is the traditional territory of the Wendat, the Anishnaabeg,
the Haudenosaunee, the Métis, and the Mississaugas of the Credit First Nation.

This book has been published with the help of a grant from the Federation
for the Humanities and Social Sciences, through the Awards to Scholarly
Publications Program, using funds provided by the Social Sciences and
Humanities Research Council of Canada.

University of Toronto Press acknowledges the financial support of the
Government of Canada, the Canada Council for the Arts, and the Ontario Arts
Council, an agency of the Government of Ontario, for its publishing activities.

Vivat troika!

Contents

Acknowledgments

When I began working on this project, my father gave me a mug from the National Archives in Washington, DC, with that poster of Rosie the Riveter gamely flexing her arm muscles on it. "We can do it!" the mug proclaimed. My dad commented that writing something so long is a team effort, and he was certainly right about that! As that project has taken shape as this book, countless colleagues, friends, and family members have helped along the way – giving feedback on my research, talking through analytical stumbling blocks, providing mentoring and emotional support – and the end result is that *we* did it. I deeply appreciate everyone who helped this book happen, and I want to thank my key supporters here.

This book was shaped by the three scholarly communities I was a member of while researching and writing it. It began in the Department of Slavic Languages and Literatures at Northwestern University, and I am thankful for the scholars and colleagues I met there, especially Clare Cavanagh, who believed in my weird gothic idea from the start, as well as Susan McReynolds and Nina Gourianova. I thank the community of graduate students in the department during the years I was there, in particular my intrepid writing buddy, Amanda Allan.

I spent three years as a research associate in the Department of Slavonic Studies at the University of Cambridge and was warmly welcomed into the department's research community. I am grateful especially to my postdoctoral supervisor, Simon Franklin, who helped me become a better scholar and researcher. I shared an office with Diane Oenning Thompson, with whom I had many long conversations about Dostoevsky and whose memory remains bright. I am thankful for the friendship and support of Alex Vukovic. Darwin College gave me a Research Fellowship and, with it, an interdisciplinary cohort of colleagues whose conversations have taken this book in new directions. I especially want to acknowledge the support and friendship of Julie Fedor, Vicky Mills, and Dave Blagden, with whom I shared many happy lunches and afternoon coffees.

Now I am a member of the Department of Central, Eastern, and Northern European Studies at the University of British Columbia. I am especially fortunate to have Kyle Frackman, Ilinca Iurascu, and Ervin Malakaj as colleagues and friends. They have been unfailingly there for me throughout the process of finishing this book. Much of the final draft was completed while I was a Wall Scholar in residence at the Peter Wall Institute for Advanced Study, and I am thankful to my fellow 2019–20 cohort members for lively discussions and curious questions about my work. At UBC I have found a warm community outside the department. I especially wish to acknowledge the camaraderie of Alexis Black, Seckin Demirbas, Heidi Tworek, and Elyse Yeager. And I'm grateful beyond words to my writing buddy, JP Catungal, with whom I've shared a seemingly infinite number of "poms" as this manuscript has trundled towards completion.

Research for this book was carried out in libraries around the world, and I owe a debt of gratitude to the librarians who helped with my research queries. Much of the book was completed at Cambridge University Library and the British Library. I am especially grateful to Mel Bach for her help with the Cambridge University Library collections. In 2018 I carried out some research for the book while I was an Associate of the Open Research Lab at the University of Illinois in Urbana-Champaign. Joe Lenkart and the entire staff of the Slavic Reference Service were wonderful to work with and helped me enormously.

Many thanks are due to University of Toronto Press. I am especially grateful to Stephen Shapiro, who has been unfailingly patient and supportive as this book has gone through various stages and I have gone through various revisions. I first began discussing this book with Richard Ratzlaff at UTP, and I'm thankful for his helpful guidance early on. Thank you to copy editor Maureen Epp and Associate Managing Editor Barbara Porter. This book's indexing was supported by the UBC Scholarly Publication Fund. Warm thanks to Jessica Hinds-Bond for her thoughtful work on the index.

Many, many scholars and friends have generously and constructively read parts of this book, and I'm grateful for all of their feedback. I would especially like to thank Carol Apollonio, Alec Brookes, Alex Burry, Yuri Corrigan, Clare Griffin, Ruth Heholt, Hilde Hoogenboom, Katya Jordan, Jenny Kaminer, Alison Milbank (who also taught the class on "God and the Gothic" that I took my first year of university, which clearly sparked a deep curiosity), Eric Naiman, Lynn Patyk, Richard Peace, Vadim Shneyder, Alyson Tapp, Ilya Vinitsky, Claire Whitehead, and Sarah Young for helpful suggestions and conversations over the years.

Several individuals deserve extra-special thanks for generously reading my manuscript in full and for their constructive feedback on it: Kate Holland, Deborah Martinsen, Margarita Vaysman, and the anonymous UTP readers. I'm so thankful to all of them. Ellen Tilton-Cantrell helped me refine and articulate my argument, and Barbara Henry helped me see the places in the text where I needed to push my argument a little further. I am also grateful to my "gothic ladies," the small group of gothic scholars within Slavic Studies who have been a wonderful community over the years, especially Robin Feuer Miller and Valeria Sobol.

This book would not have been completed without the support of my mentors, Lisa Sundstrom and Barbara Alpern Engel, who helped me through a rough time early in my career. I also wish to thank my writing accountability buddy Jessie Handbury and my FSP group members Amy Krings, Jungmin Lee, and Rachel Pang for their unflagging support. Kate Holland also deserves a second thank you for her warm friendship and all of her patient check-ins while I was finishing the manuscript. I'm grateful for all they have done to help me make headspace and time for writing.

I'm thankful to my family for their warm enthusiasm for my work and their support of both my career and this project over the years, especially my mom, Ingrid Bowers; sister, Lisa Lane; and I know my dad, Tom Bowers, is cheering right along with them. My husband, John Ayliff, has been tremendously supportive of this book, although it has disrupted our sleep, given him more than a passing knowledge of both nineteenth-century Russian cultural production and Cyrillic transliteration systems, and been a constant third wheel in our relationship – from our first date, when I brought it up, casually, like you do, to the day I hit send for the last time.

Finally, words are inadequate to express the depth of gratitude I have for my writing group. Connor Doak, Tatiana Filimonova, and I have met nearly weekly for a decade now to talk about our writing, and without them this book would not exist in its present form. Connor and Tanya have helped me conceive of the book's structure, thoughtfully and generously debated and discussed almost every corner of the manuscript, read some parts of it many times indeed, and provided constructive and thorough feedback and, beyond that, warm friendship and emotional support. It is to our *troika* that I dedicate this book.

Note on Transliteration and Translation

This book follows the Library of Congress standard transliteration system for Cyrillic with a few exceptions. Spellings of some names have been adjusted to reflect more familiar North American English spellings (e.g., Dostoevsky and Gogol instead of Dostoevskii and Gogol'). Some proper names have also been adapted to aid in pronunciation (e.g., Alyosha instead of Alesha, Evgeniya instead of Evgeniia, Ol'ga instead of Olga). Russian text in the bibliographic references that appear in parentheticals, notes, or the Works Cited adheres strictly to the Library of Congress transliteration system. Quotes in Russian are written with Cyrillic, however, for ease of reading.

All translations in the text are my own unless indicated otherwise.

Illustrations

WRITING FEAR

Introduction: Russian Realism and the Gothic

Apparitions are frightful, but life is also frightful.
[…] I don't understand life and I am afraid of it.

Anton Chekhov, "Terror"

The whole of the Gothic is the history of realism.

Mikhail Bakhtin, at his dissertation defence

In Anton Chekhov's story "Terror" ("Strakh," 1892), two characters ruminate on the relationship between fear and the unknown. Dmitry Petrovich asks the narrator, "When we want to tell some terrible, mysterious, and fantastic story [что-нибудь страшное, таинственное, и фантастическое], why do we draw our material not from life, but inevitably from the world of ghosts and the shadows beyond the grave?" The narrator responds, "What we don't understand is frightening [страшно]." Dmitry Petrovich's juxtaposition of life, or reality, with the world "beyond the grave" – an unknown, terrifying, and imagined realm – is no surprise; the known and the unknown, life and death are often opposed. However, in this discussion, Dmitry Petrovich also sets two modes of storytelling in opposition. The one – drawn from beyond the grave – maps to fears and anxieties that are the preoccupation of the gothic genre, while the other – drawn from life – is, at its heart, a bare-bones definition of literary realism. Either source could result in a "terrible, mysterious, and fantastic story," and as Dmitry Petrovich continues, he begins to unite these two narrative modes:

Our life and the world beyond the grave are similarly incomprehensible and frightful [страшный]. Whoever is afraid of ghosts should also be afraid of me, and of those lights and of the sky, since all of that, if you think about it, is no less inconceivable and fantastic than apparitions from that other world […] There's no doubt about it, apparitions are frightful, but life is also frightful. My dove, I don't understand life and I am afraid of it.[1]

By the end of this speech, Dmitry Petrovich has brought together the gothic and literary realism, the fearfully imagined and the prosaically lived. His observations speak to a hybrid genre, gothic realism, in which the uncanny and the everyday blur and coexist. Fear is at the heart of this mixing: while fear may be rational or irrational, it is an emotion that is linked with imagination, with the mind's ability to generate terrors based not in what is but in what might be.

As *Writing Fear* demonstrates, the gothic proved a key tool in the project of recreating life in prose. Realism is grounded in the everyday and aims to convey the experience of reality as closely as possible. Gothic writing privileges the affective capacity of fear. The genre relies on the exaggeration of emotions such as fear, terror, and dread, the anticipation of horrors, and moments of hesitation or uncertainty to create its fearful atmosphere. But the gothic also enables an articulation of that fear and, by extension, is uniquely positioned to assuage it. Employing the genre's literary devices within a realist text enables its author to access the narrative suspense that stems from the psychologies of fear, dread, and anxiety, and is a hallmark of the gothic. Additionally, the gothic genre provides a framework for addressing the aspects of human experience within narrative that are often concealed from others: guilt, transgression, fear, and anxiety. Realist writers found the gothic's mobilization of fear within a narrative structure invaluable.

A reaction to both romanticism and technological advances such as photography, realism developed across Europe beginning in the 1830s and 1840s, eventually becoming the dominant literary form. On the one hand, the term realism demarcates a chronological span of writing that corresponds to a new concern, an interest in depicting the results of contemporaneous social, political, and economic change. On the other, realism refers to a trend, a manner of writing that "aims at conveying reality as closely as possible and strives for maximum verisimilitude,"[2] in Roman Jakobson's definition, while still achieving what Ian Watt characterizes as "a full and authentic report of human experiences."[3] In Russia, realism could be said to begin with Vissarion Belinsky's call for a "new literature" in the mid-1840s, a literature that dealt "with life

and reality in their true light."[4] However, while he had some supporters, Belinsky's assessment of the mode drew ire, as critics and authors
alike saw the limitations of his approach to realism.[5] And, furthermore,
all realist writers faced the thorny problem of *how* to go about writing
texts that were both believably grounded in the *realia* of everyday life
and compelling to the reader.

Whereas romantics represented extreme emotional states in such a
way that readers could aspire to experience them, realists wanted to
show the psychological processes of day-to-day life and their effects. In
Peter Brooks's formulation, realism "both appealed to and represented
the private lives of the unexceptional – or rather, found and drama-
tized the exceptional within the ordinary, creating a heroism of everyday life."[6] In René Wellek's discussion, realism "rejects the fantastic,
the fairy-tale-like, the allegorical and the symbolic, the highly stylized,
the purely abstract and decorative. It means that we want no myth, no
Maerchen, no world of dreams. It implies also a rejection of the improbable, of pure chance, of extraordinary events, since reality is obviously
conceived at that time, in spite of all local and personal differences, as
the orderly world of nineteenth-century science, a world of cause and
effect, a world without miracle, without transcendence."[7] Following
Brooks and Wellek, it seems that realism should resist the gothic. Yet
realism has a flexibility and openness predicated in the fact that reality is an inherently subjective experience. As Vladimir Nabokov scepti-
cally observed, "reality" is "one of the few words which mean nothing
without quotes."[8]

Literary realism relies on artful devices in order to render "reality" in a way that believably resonates with readers' own lives. Henry
James famously called nineteenth-century Russian novels "loose and
baggy monsters" because they incorporate "queer elements of the accidental and the arbitrary,"[9] emphasizing this literary need for devices.
Jakobson identifies the inherent tension in the practice of realism as
the ambiguity between the intent of the author and the experience of
the reader,[10] that is, between the author's attempt to portray life with
verisimilitude and the reader's engagement with the literary form of
the text. Realism privileges reality, but, as Irina Paperno has observed,
realism also "affirm[s] the separateness of art and reality and the primacy of life over art."[11] Writers' interventions to enable "art forms to
be experienced as essentially de-aestheticized ('real')," in Paperno's
formulation, lead to the imitation of "a lack of literariness and aesthetic organization."[12] Molly Brunson has called this "desire to transcend the borders of art and life" the "audacity of realism."[13] Brunson
asserts that "the self-consciousness of realism and its wild optimism in

the face of failure" underpin the tradition's triumphs.[14] Indeed, realist works are frequently as much about the process of working out *how* to depict subjective reality as about depicting it. The openness of this self-conscious engagement with form enables literary realism to accommodate the gothic.[15] But which functions of the genre specifically appealed to realists?

As a genre, the gothic is popularly known for its evocative tropes and formulaic plots. Fred Botting provides a list of its associations, including "'tortuous, fragmented narratives,' highly ornamented prose and emotion-driven aesthetics, mysterious or supernatural villains, landscapes which are 'desolate, alienating and full of menace,' and standard loci such as the castle or the old house."[16] Muireann Maguire imaginatively and aptly envisions gothic literature as "an encoded library of buried terrors."[17] When we think of the gothic, we do not immediately think of its psychological impulses or its fascination with transgression. Our first associations are its conventions: ruined castles, incestuous abductions, mysterious strangers, and shrouded secrets.[18] Indeed, gothic novels became known for their ubiquitous collection of props, settings, and conventions that literary critics frequently lampooned, as in this "recipe" for a gothic novel that appeared in a 1797 journal:

> *Take* – An old castle, half of it ruinous.
> A long gallery, with a great many doors, some secret ones.
> Three murdered bodies, quite fresh.
> As many skeletons, in chests and presses [...]
> Mix them together, in the form of three volumes, to be taken at any of the
> watering-places before going to bed.[19]

These lines are intended humorously, but the ruined castle, skeletons, murdered bodies, and secret doors point to underlying anxieties bound up with historical practices such as inheritances and degeneration, social and political oppression, marginalization, and transgression.

Scholars have defined the gothic in terms of its engagement with these practices. Terry Castle defines the gothic as "a decadent late 18th century taste for things gloomy, macabre, and medieval."[20] Botting identifies it as "the writing of excess [...] fascination with transgression and anxiety over cultural limits and boundaries."[21] Rather than specifically defining the gothic, David Punter's study sets out to investigate "[gothic] narratives, insofar as it is possible to isolate them from the surrounding culture."[22] Using Punter's methodology, Maguire identifies three main gothic narratives: "paranoia (metonymic for many forms of madness and the fear of madness), barbarism (including the fear of genealogical degeneration), and taboo (the unclean or unholy)."[23]

Building on these models, I suggest a definition of the gothic that emphasizes generic function:

1) The text must focus on a mystery and its solution. The reader feels propelled to continue reading out of curiosity, anticipating horrors or terrors hinted at but constantly deferred.
2) The text must refer to some transgression or broken taboo, the exploration of the repercussions of which informs the work as a whole.
3) The text is preoccupied with the depiction and/or evocation of emotions such as fear, anxiety, and revulsion, and these psychologies both inform the text and attempt to evoke a strong emotional reaction from the reader.[24]

When these three criteria are all present, a work tends to be labelled as gothic, and, as I will show, realists exploit all three in their appropriation of the genre. While much world literature involves the solving of mysteries or the breaking of taboos, the gothic is unique insofar as it features both and also creates an atmosphere that engages readers on a deep affective level. This is brought out especially in the last point of the definition, which, as the present study emphasizes, is the most important criterion for realism: the genre's preoccupation with the depiction of psychology.

The gothic genre's preoccupation with fear, anxiety, and related emotions sets it apart from other genres that appeared around the same time or shortly after, such as sentimentalism and romanticism. These genres also were concerned with emotional states, but, as Chris Baldick notes, gothic fiction's "distinctive animating principle is a psychological interest in states of trepidation, dread, panic, revulsion, claustrophobia, and paranoia."[25] Gothic writers contrived to depict these states through the genre's conventions: transgressive behaviours, moments of unexpected and horrific discovery, and an atmosphere that anticipates violence at any moment. Significantly, gothic writers also deliberately used lurid or sensational elements to evoke readers' terror, a technique of reader engagement that owes a substantial debt to other forms like drama.[26] But attending a play and reading a novel are radically different emotional experiences. Gothic fiction's utilization of elements of theatrical suspense and melodrama reinforces the affective impact and disturbance of gothic works. As Brooks observes, gothic fiction "reasserts the presence, in the world, of forces that cannot be accounted for by the daylight self and the self-sufficient mind."[27]

In the realist text, the gothic may not appear in the guise of its familiar conventions. Nonetheless, the gothic functionally provokes a similar response using mystery, transgression, and the depiction of psychological states. To see how gothic convention is transformed in realist narrative, let's examine a classic gothic trope – discovery of a corpse – in both modes. Here is one such encounter from Ann Radcliffe's *Mysteries of Udolpho* (1794).

> Beyond, appeared a corpse, stretched on a kind of low couch, which was crimsoned with human blood, as was the floor beneath. The features, deformed by death, were ghastly and horrible, and more than one livid wound appeared in the face. Emily, bending over the body, gazed, for a moment, with an eager, frenzied eye; but, in the next, the lamp dropped from her hand, and she fell senseless at the foot of the couch.[28]

Lurid details of deformed features, grisly lacerations, and the blood-drenched couch contribute to the scene's horror. Emily's immediate reaction – gazing transfixed and then fainting – also gives the reader a deepened sense of the tableau's inherent sensationalism. The description here lacks precise detail. The corpse's features are ghastly and horrible, but what they specifically look like is left to the reader's (ideally overactive) imagination, reinforced by Emily's extreme reaction.

Now compare this scene with another passage, from Lev Tolstoy's *Childhood* (*Detstvo*, 1852), which also describes the reaction of an individual encountering a corpse.

> I climbed onto the chair to look at her face; but in its place appeared to me again the same pale-yellow translucent object. I could not believe that it was her face. I began to stare at it transfixed and little by little began to recognize in it the familiar, dear features. I shuddered from horror, when I realized that this was she. But why were the closed eyes so sunken? Why was there that terrible paleness and on one cheek a blackish spot under the translucent skin? Why was the expression of the whole face so stern and cold? Why were the lips so pale and their shape so beautiful, so majestic

and expressing such unearthly calm that a cold shiver ran down my spine and my hair stood on end when I gazed at [the corpse]? … I looked and felt that some kind of incomprehensible, irresistible power forced my eyes to that lifeless face. I did not take my eyes from it, yet my imagination drew me pictures, brimming with life and happiness. I kept forgetting that the dead body lying before me, at which I blankly stared as at an object that had no connection with my memories, was *her* […] suddenly I was struck by some feature in the pale face, which drew my gaze: I remembered the dreadful reality, shuddered, but did not stop looking. Then dreams would replace reality again, and the consciousness of reality would again destroy the dreams. Finally, my imagination grew weary, it ceased to deceive me; the consciousness of reality also disappeared, and I completely lost all sense of myself.[29]

In the Radcliffe passage, the reader is left to imagine the corpse's features, but Tolstoy describes the corpse in great detail. While an imagined horror can be a source of terror, in adding these specific, arguably naturalistic but seemingly exaggerated details as well as a sense of witnessing through first-person narration, Tolstoy induces his reader's sense of horror in a more visceral way. Even though the narrator explicitly describes the corpse – from its sunken eyes and terrible paleness to the blackened spot under its translucent skin and the object's overall unearthliness – some gothic language underscores the horror of the scene, linking the protagonist's experience to the unknown: the "cold shiver" that runs down the narrator's spine, the "incomprehensible, irresistible power" that forces the narrator to continue looking. These details echo Radcliffe's description of Emily taking in the corpse "with an eager, frenzied eye." There the use of the word "eager" suggests an inability to stop staring, even a kind of attraction, although Emily faints from shock and horror. Both reactions align with Julia Kristeva's theory of abjection, the uncanny experience of being unable to reconcile a living being with a dead *object*, the anxious reminder of one's own mortality, and the perverse mingling of attraction and disgust this experience provokes.[30] Neither protagonist can look away, even as they shudder; both scenes end as the characters become emotionally overwhelmed and lose consciousness.

While both passages describe fear's mechanism and function, drawing on gothic conventions to depict characters' internal experiences, each treats the conventional scene very differently. In the Radcliffe passage, the deformed corpse's abhorrent image shocks Emily, who has drawn back the curtain revealing the corpse thinking she would find her murdered aunt. While this corpse's identity is unknown, the depiction of Emily's terror in the situation results in reader and heroine sharing a common fear. The Tolstoy passage describes a child's growing realization that his loving mother has become a rotting corpse, as framed by an adult narrator. The child's instinctive reaction combines with the adult narrator's questioning internal monologue to convey his fear to the reader. The reader does not feel afraid in the second passage, although the narrator's fear is comprehensible and the lurid descriptions create a cognitively disturbing atmosphere. Despite their authors' disparate writing styles, the two scenes resonate structurally and thematically thanks to their shared gothic elements. Tolstoy's use of gothic tropes here is an example of what I call "gothic realism."

Gothic realism refers to moments when authors writing in what we recognize as a realist style turn to gothic narrative devices, using the genre as a tool to articulate a facet of lived experience through the affective engagement of the reader. A sudden shift in tone directs these sometimes brief but deliberate moments to the reader. Examining gothic realism shows how the gothic functions within realist narrative as a model for depicting elements that do not mesh easily with everyday experience within the bounds of realism. Realist writers use the gothic to highlight a specific transgression, trauma, or injustice, or to engage readers on a deeply affective level through building up fear. The genre's power lies in the implicit relationship forged between writer, reader, and text, a relationship predicated on expectation and familiarity. As Carolyn R. Miller has observed, genre is a social act.[31] In this sense, realist writers use gothic narrative devices, tropes, and themes to harness this relationship of expectation and familiarity. These writers' engagement with the gothic is thus not just a colourful way to describe the gloomy and macabre but a deliberate appropriation of a system of reader expectation and generic convention.

As *Writing Fear* reveals, gothic realism was widespread in nineteenth-century Russian works, and the gothic played a significant role in Russian literature's development. Indeed, as I demonstrate, during the foundational years of literary realism, gothic elements within the realist narrative fabric were broadly deployed. Authors from the 1840s through the early twentieth century and beyond incorporated gothic devices, themes, tropes, and even master plots into their works. Individual realist writers exploited the gothic mode to their own ends. In identifying and analysing some of these incidences, scholars have exposed Russian realist writers' debt to Western gothic fiction.[32] What is compelling about how Russian realists use the gothic is not that the genre – more grounded in Italian monasteries, Spanish prisons of the Inquisition, or English castles than in nineteenth-century Russian reality – unexpectedly crops up in their works, but that many different writers over an extended period consistently use the gothic in similar ways, even to depict differing or opposing philosophical and political positions.

The present study joins a growing trend of scholarship that has begun to address the appearance of the gothic in realist texts of various national traditions.[33] These individual studies are, to borrow Royce Mahawatte's formulation, "in a realm of unchartered ... Gothic. One which hides beneath the consensus of nineteenth-century Realism and so has been largely overlooked or misunderstood."[34] The richness of these studies, both in theme and in scope, demonstrates the productive vibrancy of gothic realism for literary studies, yet they tend to be piecemeal, focused on one author, one text, or one literary device. In one of the more wide-ranging studies, *Gothic Reflections: Narrative Force in Nineteenth-Century Fiction*, Peter K. Garrett connects narrative force in gothic works spanning the long nineteenth century – from James Hogg, Mary Shelley, and Edgar Allan Poe to Robert Louis Stevenson and Bram Stoker – to English novelists more associated with realism, such as Charles Dickens, George Eliot, and Henry James. Garrett terms iterations of the gothic within the realist text "gothic reflections" and argues that they "offer one way [...] of recognizing the unresolved tensions that persist in these novels and qualify the effect of multiple perspectives converging on a shared social reality."[35] The deliberately limited scope of these studies speaks to the enormity of the topic. Gothic fiction played a profound and essential role in shaping nineteenth-century realism, and this influence transcended national literary traditions and borders. While the present study is limited to addressing gothic realism only in the Russian tradition, it takes a more holistic approach than previous studies have, examining gothic realism in Russia from its inception in the 1830s and 1840s to its end as it mingled with modernism and transformed again into a new mode of writing.

Writing Fear tells the story of the gothic's role in Russian realism, from its beginnings as an outgrowth of and reaction to romanticism to its eventual merger with modernism. The first half of the study, "Gothic

Migration," examines the way Russian writers began to use gothic elements outside of gothic works. They engage in a kind of literary alchemy, forging something new from the combination of distinctly different literary modes, during the transition from romanticism to realism. "Gothic Migration" examines the appropriation of the gothic mode of writing into realism, its function and utility, and the specific ways in which it contributed to the realist palette. The first two chapters examine the cultural context of the 1830s and 1840s, a period when romanticism shifted into realism and this nascent realism continued to rely on romantic narrative forms. Chapters 3 and 4 analyse the way the gothic functions within the scope of realist prose, exploring its appearance and significance in sketches of the 1840s and a novel of the 1860s.

Chapter 1, "A Russian Reader's Gothic Library," discusses the literary texts and trends with which a Russian reader in the 1840s would have been familiar, including translations, non-Russian publications, popular fiction, and more aesthetic works, particularly focusing on gothic works but also on works that resonated with gothic themes. While Russian critics of the 1840s panned gothic novels as lurid, sensational frivolity, such works nonetheless dominated the popular literature market in both Western Europe and Russia in the early nineteenth century. Similarly, new gothic-fantastic trends emerged in Russian literary works by writers such as Alexander Pushkin, Nikolai Gogol, Vasily Zhukovsky, and Vladimir Odoevsky. By the 1840s, Western Europeans had been reading gothic novels for more than seventy-five years and Russians had been for fifty. The chapter argues that for Russian readers during this period, the gothic became a culturally familiar concept predicated in a genre ecology, such that the average reader did not need to read gothic novels to understand what gothic was or how to identify gothic tropes or themes. Rather, these elements became commonplace for Russian readers.

The second chapter, "Gothic Transmutations in Pushkin and Gogol," examines the specific use of gothic in the genre repertoire of two important novels that preceded realism: Pushkin's *Eugene Onegin* (1825–32) and Gogol's *Dead Souls* (*Mertvye dushi*, 1842). Each writer incorporates gothic elements, but to different ends. Pushkin imbues his text with gothic sensation in Tatyana's dream, while Gogol exposes Plyushkin's decaying estate through gothic metaphor. In analysing the tension between the gothic's aesthetic, authenticity, and parody in these works, I demonstrate the scope of gothic utility as well as the specific ways that gothic appropriation shaped narrative development in this transitional time in Russian literary history. These novels were deeply influential in the development of Russian realist poetics, and, as the subsequent two chapters illustrate, their use of gothic elements influenced the ways later writers experimented with form and genre.

In the third chapter, "Russian Landscapes in a Gothic Frame," I focus on a specific device, the gothic narrative frame, and its ability to transform realist narrative. In particular, I examine two sketches of the late 1840s and early 1850s, Ivan Goncharov's "Oblomov's Dream" ("Son Oblomova," 1849) and Ivan Turgenev's "Bezhin Lea" ("Bezhin lug," 1851). Whereas Pushkin's and Gogol's novels deploy the gothic with significant irony, the works considered in chapter 3 take a different approach. The gothic in these texts is used to engage readers affectively in a more authentic way. In both works, the gothic frame – by emphasizing reader emotion – forges a connection with folklore and peasant belief systems, making such belief systems viable within a nineteenth-century materialist realist world view. This frame distances sceptical readers from their own perspective, creating a space that allows more room for peasant life and points of view.

The most gothic text by the most gothic Russian realist writer is Fyodor Dostoevsky's *The Idiot* (1869). This novel is the focus of chapter 4's examination of the way gothic realism shapes the novel as a form. In the arc of realism, the 1860s and 1870s are the age of the great novels – great in their philosophical discourse, their engagement with the so-called accursed questions, and, often, their physical size. *The Idiot* is a novelistic experiment, engaging with theology and existential questions, as well as with topics such as legal reforms, social justice, the woman question, and even the rise of mass journalism; the gothic appears prominently in the depiction of each. My reading of *The Idiot* demonstrates the confluence of gothic realism and the realist novel, and exposes the way gothic shapes the novel's form, narrative, plot, and characterization. My study of Dostoevsky's novel concludes the first part of this book because it stands as a benchmark in the narrative of the gothic's migration into Russian realism.

The second part of the book, "Gothic Realism," provides a series of case studies that illuminate the function of the gothic as a formal innovation within literary realism. The chapters in this section include studies of the way gothic poetics – including plot, description, narrative force, and themes – shaped the form of the novel, enabled new forms of critical discourse, articulated moral paradigms, and reflected deep-seated cultural anxieties. The fifth and sixth chapters examine works from the mid-nineteenth century, while the seventh and eighth chapters emphasize realist works of the late nineteenth and early twentieth centuries. Each of these four chapters represents a case study of the way a particular strand of gothic resonated with a specific social anxiety:

urban poverty, the woman question, the threat of revolutionary terrorism, and the decline of the family. Together, they create a broader picture of the gothic's role in both depicting and mediating these anxieties. While my study touches upon social history, my focus is on questions of form and genre, and on how realism engages with gothic poetics. The book thus concludes with a reflection on realism's evolution into modernism and the gothic's role in this process.

Chapter 5, "Physiological Petersburg, Gothic Petersburg," examines the relationship between gothic narrative and the physiological sketch in the late 1840s. The chapter argues that in urban spaces – as seen in works by Nikolai Nekrasov, Vladimir Dal, Evgeny Grebenka, and others, as well as in the early prose of Dostoevsky – the gothic plays a didactic role, exposing the horrors of slum life, the dehumanizing effect of poverty, and the destructive power of modernity. The gothic's acquired associations led the mid-nineteenth-century reader to examine texts more closely, looking for the underlying mystery suggested by such elements. In addition, the feelings of panic, fear, dread, and horror the gothic aroused proved useful in constructing emotionally charged atmospheres for settings likely unfamiliar to the reader, such as urban tenement buildings. In establishing a pervading sense of anxiety and unease through a conscious appropriation of the gothic, early realist writers of the 1840s directed readers to a better understanding of urban issues they sought to expose through gothic frames and gothic description.

The sixth chapter, "Gothic Subjectivity and the Woman Question," analyses the way gothic enables marginalized voices in the realist text by examining the gothic intertext between Evgeniya Tur's *Antonina* (1851), Charlotte Brontë's *Jane Eyre* (1847), and Turgenev's *Diary of a Superfluous Man* (*Dnevnik lishnego cheloveka*, 1850). Gothic narrative elements shape the depiction of women and their inner lives in Brontë's and Turgenev's works, but the writers deploy them in markedly different ways. Tur, engaging with both texts, uses gothic subjectivity both to imagine alternative social models for her heroine and to revise Turgenev's superfluous man paradigm. As this chapter demonstrates, Tur's engagement with gothic subjectivity aligns with her later polemics in *publitsistika* about the woman question.

In chapter 7, "Political Terror and the School of Horror," I focus on what we might term political gothic, looking at representations of nihilism, anarchy, and other revolutionary movements, especially in works by Dostoevsky and Boris Savinkov. In Dostoevsky's *Demons* (*Besy*, 1872), gothic descriptions and narrative force are used to illustrate that the most terrifying aspect of revolutionary terrorists is not their political actions but the moral abyss at the heart of their ideology. While Dosto-evsky exposes the amorality of political terrorists, Savinkov systemati-cally uses gothic realism in *A Pale Horse* (*Kon' blednyi*, 1909) to articulate a moral code. Although the two writers are politically opposed, they deploy gothic narrative in similar ways.

Chapter 8, "The Fall of the House on the Russian Estate," examines the appropriation of a gothic plot through three generational sagas: Sergei Aksakov's *Family Chronicle* (*Semeinaia khronika*, 1856), Mikhail Saltykov-Shchedrin's *Golovlyov Family* (*Gospoda Golovlevy*, 1875–80), and Ivan Bunin's *Dry Valley* (*Sukhodol*, 1912). Across the three works each successive family demonstrates a different phase of decline. Aksa-kov's novel is ostensibly about the establishment of a family line, yet gothic traumas lurk in the family's past. Saltykov-Shchedrin's family is in active decline, and gothic descriptors chronicle each generation's further deterioration. Finally, Bunin's gothic nostalgia-tinged novella retrospectively reflects on a family's fall. This chapter argues that the gothic "fall of the house" plot exposes social anxieties and their connec-tion to political revolution as the nineteenth-century crisis of the family comes to Russia.

Finally, "Chekhov's Ghosts" links late realism with early modernism. The conclusion's analysis of ghosts in Chekhov's stories forges narra-tive links between gothic description, emotion, and psychology within the bounds of the prosaic. Chekhov's ghosts appear when an emotional or psychological fissure opens between the external world and a charac-ter's inner life. The ghosts' appearance is subjective; their manifestation in the text privileges a world view predicated on individual percep-tion rather than objective reality. As the realist novel encounters mod-ernist forms, it transforms. In Chekhov's tales, apparitions result from fevered psychologies and anxious minds that seem exceptional within their realist narratives, whereas in modernism, apparitions exist within the realm of the everyday, animated projections of uneasy minds that come to life. In this sense, Chekhov's ghosts demonstrate the vitality of gothic as a mode of representation for modernism, and gothic realism itself becomes a laden ghost that haunts later literary modes.

Mikhail Bakhtin coined the term "gothic realism" in his dissertation, "F. Rabelais in the History of Realism," but the phrase does not appear in his published works. After his famously contentious dissertation defence, where the concept of gothic realism was attacked, even the

word "realism" was removed from the dissertation's title. In order for
Bakhtin to pass the defence, the examining committee required him to
remove all mention of gothic realism from the dissertation because it
was diametrically opposed to "classical realism," that is, to traditional
critical realism.[36] Committee member N.L. Brodsky explicitly called
classical realism "the antipode of this Gothic method" during the 1946
defence, stating:

> According to your conception there is one kind of realism, Gothic realism,
> and another, classical realism, and your preference is for the Gothic [...]
> I am completely unable to agree with comrade Bakhtin [...] I am a suppor-
> ter of classical realism.[37]

The particular inflexibility of the committee members on what could
be categorized as "realist" and what was outside the bounds speaks
to the particular historical time and place in which the defence took
place – Stalinist Moscow was a dangerous place to assert views that
went against the grain. Bakhtin revised the term to "grotesque realism"
to pass his examination.[38]

At the defence, Bakhtin affirmed, "I believe I have added a new page
to the history of realism [...] I have enriched the history of realism [...]
the whole of the Gothic is the history of realism."[39] "Gothic" in this formulation refers to a concept that is related to the late eighteenth- and
early nineteenth-century gothic literary movement I have described
thus far. Namely, it refers to a relationship to an imagined past. The
first gothic novel, Horace Walpole's *Castle of Otranto* (1764), was sub-
titled "A gothic story" precisely because a significant source of the anxiety within the novel was its "gothic," that is, medieval setting. David
Punter identifies "the Gothic's general opposition to realist aesthetics"
in this imagined medievalism, but further observes that

> time and time again, those writers who are referred to as Gothic turn out
> to be those who bring us up against the boundaries of the civilised, who
> demonstrate to us the relative nature of ethical and behavioural codes,
> and who place, over against the conventional world, a different sphere in
> which these codes operate at best in distorted forms.[40]

Similarly, Bakhtin's conceptualization of gothic realism emerged from
and was predicated on "the idea of the eternal unfinalisedness, 'unread-
iness' of the human being in the world."[41] What Bakhtin advocates
for is a realism that accounts for all aspects of experience, including
those that are concealed, repressed, or unarticulated. Literary realism's

striving for verisimilitude assumes a universality for aesthetic representation of the *realia* of the day to day. However, in its emphasis on the unfinalizability of the human in the world, Bakhtin's concept of gothic realism addresses the limitations of depicting any experience fully through art. For Bakhtin, the gothic adds another layer to realist depiction that enables better representation of the subject.[42]

As *Writing Fear* demonstrates, gothic poetics and realist form are inextricably connected. However, the gothic elements present within realism that are discussed here are invariably a degree or two removed from the original genre; their migration into literary realism is a process of transmutation. An example from Dostoevsky's *Brothers Karamazov* (*Brat'ia Karamazovy*, 1880) illuminates the distinct difference between literary gothic and gothic realism. In the courtroom scene of book 12, Fetyukovich gives a long speech in defence of Dmitry, who has been accused of patricide. He evokes *The Mysteries of Udolpho* in an attempt to cast aspersions on the prosecution's assumptions.

> Why, why does the prosecution not believe the testimony of Alexey Karamazov, given so truthfully and sincerely, so spontaneously and believably? And why, on the contrary, does he force me to believe in money hidden in a crevice, in the dungeons of the castle of Udolpho?[43]

The passage assumes that its reader is familiar not only with Radcliffe's novel but also with the cultural context surrounding it. Fetyukovich is a somewhat ridiculous character and his exaggerations are part of his rhetorical toolkit; he disparages the dungeons of Udolpho as a romantic fantasy that a serious person would not entertain. In this sense, his reading of *Udolpho* chimes with those of many critics before him. Here the gothic is mentioned ironically and the reference evokes a text that is deliberately positioned as removed from both Alyosha's sincere, authentic-feeling testimony and, by extension, the realist narrative fabric of *Brothers Karamazov*.

Yet the novel also aligns with gothic narrative.[44] It contains one of the great gothic realist villains, Smerdyakov, who cold-bloodedly murders his father for the sake of a secret birthright and lives in a room with wallpaper that revoltingly undulates and rustles because of the cockroaches moving behind it. Smerdyakov's narrative arc follows a gothic master plot that maps to my functional definition of gothic. His role in the philosophical fabric of *Brothers Karamazov* is central, and certainly not ironized. But this gothic reading of the text seems significantly removed from Fetyukovich's hyperbolic rhetoric, and even from the clichéd and formulaic conventions of *The Mysteries of Udolpho*.

The gothic narratives in *Brothers Karamazov* – the gothic realist plot about Smerdyakov's rightful inheritance and the gothic metanarrative evoked by Fetyukovich's mention of Radcliffe's novel – coexist, but the novel's intrinsic gothic realism is easy to overlook.

Writing Fear reveals the importance of the gothic for the realist literary tradition. The development of gothic realism requires a recalibration of the narrative of Russian literary history. Smerdyakov's story and this study demonstrate that when gothic elements appear within the bounds of Russian realism, they are not simply grafted onto a realist foundation. Rather, gothic enters the realist tradition from its inception as multiple writers exploit its devices, tropes, and plots. Gothic migrates into realism and then becomes assimilated. As this study shows, gothic realism is a mode, an element in the realist's toolbox that engages readers on an affective level. Its power is its function as a genre that evokes specific affective responses: fear, dread, anxiety. Realist writers continuously sought to overcome the tension between art and life, and gothic realism served as one path to mediate this tension.

PART I

Gothic Migration

Chapter One

A Russian Reader's Gothic Library

"Send me some new novel, only please not one of the newest […]
I want the kind where the hero doesn't strangle his father or mother,
and where there are no drowned bodies.
I'm horribly afraid of drowned bodies."
"That kind doesn't exist nowadays.
Unless […] you wouldn't want some Russian ones?"
"Do Russian novels really exist?"

Alexander Pushkin, "The Queen of Spades"

This exchange between the old Countess and her grandson, Tomsky, in Alexander Pushkin's short story "The Queen of Spades" ("Pikovaia dama," 1833), prompts a number of questions about early nineteenth-century Russian reading habits. Discussing the contents of recent novels, the Countess describes a series of lurid murders, and we wonder what she has been reading, where these strangled parents and drowned bodies are to be found.[1] Tomsky's comment that these sensational episodes (a nod to gothic fiction) are passé except in Russian fiction underscores Russia's somewhat imitative and tardy adoption of Western trends in popular reading. Finally, when the Countess asks if there really are such things as Russian novels, her ironic question pokes fun at early nineteenth-century Russian literature but also emphasizes the rapidly changing literary and reading culture that characterized the period of the 1830s to 1840s. Examining publication records from the time may give us a sense of what Tomsky might be reading, or pretending he has read for the sake of society. The Countess, on the other hand, represents the older generation, although her request for a new novel indicates her interest in fashionable trends. If we were able to look into her library, we would likely see not only recent publications but also books that were popular over the previous fifty years.

The Countess's hypothetical library has a counterpart in Eugene Onegin's library, which Pushkin's heroine Tatyana explores at length in chapter 7 of *Eugene Onegin* (1825–32). As Tatyana discovers, Onegin's reading habits tend towards the Byronic and gothic, but alongside these melancholy, popular volumes there are also books left behind by Onegin's uncle. Like the Countess, Onegin's uncle is from the older generation, and his library – now merged with Onegin's – likely reflected both his taste and the books available outside of Moscow or St Petersburg. The uncle's library might have included once-popular novels such as those by Tatyana's mother's favourite writer, Samuel Richardson, alongside practical works useful for estate management, and perhaps some volumes of history or geography.

My study of Russian realism and the gothic links reader expectation, authorial assumption, generic borrowing, and narrative experimentation. My work's genesis lies not in the blurred beginning of literary realism but in earlier narrative effects and contemporaneous readers' conception of them. This is when the gothic's migration into Russian literature began. What did Russian readers of the 1830s and 1840s understand to be gothic? What tropes were familiar or expected? What associations did gothic novels carry within Russian culture? The answers lie within these imagined libraries. Their hypothetical readers, as seen by writers and critics of the time, evolved, reflecting reading and literary trends.[2] This evolution in turn reveals assumptions about a literary market, popular taste, and the function of genre.

Literary Culture and the Imagined Russian Library

If we were to reconstruct a library from this period, one striking feature would be that few of the books would actually be in Russian. During this period, Russian literature was still a relatively new phenomenon. Eighteenth-century Russia had seen the rise of not only a literary culture but also a *literature*, as writers engaged with Western models argued over and began to develop the Russian literary language, and created the first Russian literary works to appear in the form of novels, plays, poetry, and short stories. The eighteenth century had also seen the development of secular printing, periodicals, circulation libraries, and the inception of popular reading, but at the beginning of the nineteenth century, readership remained small and predominately urban.[3] The early nineteenth-century Russian literary landscape included a significant number of works by French, German, and English authors, with original Russian works being published in smaller numbers.[4]

Nikolai Karamzin points to this trend in his essay "On the Book Trade and Love of Reading in Russia" (1802) when he refers to a German writer in observing that Russian booksellers will sell anything: "a novel, a story, good or bad – who cares as long as the name of the notorious Kotzebue appears on the title page?"[5] For perspective, in 1802 fifty translations of August von Kotzebue's plays were published in Russia, out of a total of 350 Russian publications overall that year.[6] Kotzebue was a celebrity of sorts on account of his misadventures in Russia, which included an arrest as a suspected Jacobin, transportation to Siberia, pardon by Paul I, and appointment to the directorship of the German Theatre in St Petersburg. He also wrote novels and plays popular across Europe and the United States. His works were known for their dramatic effect and exemplify melodrama, which revels in tragic and sensational events. While Kotzebue's works were readily available, they were viewed with some scepticism by critics, as Karamzin's remark demonstrates. Karamzin concludes his essay with the quip, "It's good, at least, that our public is reading!"[7]

In 1800, literate Russians were reading works printed in Russian, French, German, and English, both originals and translations. Although Petersburg and Moscow boasted a fair number of booksellers, circulating libraries in urban centres provided most readers with access to a variety of books.[8] Before 1860, a majority of these were translations from languages other than Russian. After 1860, this trend changed, and more works originally written in Russian appeared. Literary scholar Jeffrey Brooks's study on nineteenth-century literacy and popular literature in Russia begins in 1861, since it was not until the second half of the nineteenth century that the reading public began to represent a broader segment of the population.[9] However, popular literature had existed and been developing in Russia since the eighteenth century. When the Countess asks, "Do Russian novels really exist?" in "The Queen of Spades," Pushkin is poking fun at a line of Russian literary criticism concerned with the importance of aesthetics that had become particularly prominent in the 1820s and 1830s; critic Vissarion Belinsky referred to the same line of criticism when he famously exclaimed in 1834, "We have no literature!"[10]

An often-discussed topic in this critical debate was the journal *Library for Reading*, launched in 1834, which provides an intriguing case study in readers' habits. Alexander Smirdin, a key figure in the establishment of a writing profession in Russia, began the journal. He owned and operated a publishing house, editorial office, bookshop, and circulating library in Petersburg; his authors included many literary celebrities of the day, among them Pushkin ("The Queen of Spades" was first published in the second issue of *Library for Reading*).[11] Smirdin envisioned creating a commercially viable press aimed at a more general audience. Earlier literary periodicals had placed emphasis on the writer as target audience, with critical works engaging in highbrow aesthetic debate. *Library for Reading* appeared just as the orientation of criticism was beginning to shift "from the sort that would be helpful to writers preparing their texts to the sort that would entertain and form a reading public."[12] *Library for Reading* boasted more than 5,000 subscribers and a diverse table of contents that featured "literature, sciences, arts, industry, current news, and fashion."[13] Melissa Frazier's study of the *Library for Reading* phenomenon posits that the journal both contributed to and was a symptom of a "destabilization" of readership in Russia during the second quarter of the nineteenth century.[14] Just as literary criticism underwent an orientation shift, so too did what was being read. Although Belinsky and others claimed a lack of literature, readers continued to read.

The gothic sits at the intersection between highbrow and lowbrow, between aesthetic considerations and entertainment for entertainment's sake. This special liminal state is part of the gothic's power. It carries both market appeal and an affective connection to the reader. However, the dividing line between sentimentalist, gothic, and romantic texts is blurry. Ann Radcliffe's novels rely upon a set of gothic conventions to build suspense, but they also incorporate a sentimental heroine to elicit reader sympathy and feature lengthy landscape descriptions that evoke the Kantian sublime so prized by later romantics.[15] Even in the most lurid gothic works, such as Matthew Lewis's *The Monk* (1796), we can observe "a cohesive and well-structured system, born from preromantic aesthetics and philosophy, which determines the nature of each novel's conflict, the balance of its heroes, the hierarchy of their motives, and the quantity of narrative techniques," as Vadim Vatsuro explains.[16] The gothic's underlying philosophical concerns drive its formulation, which then creates the diverting reading experience associated with the genre.

Gothic Readers and the Power of Fear

Orest Somov's satirical "Mommy and Sonny" ("Matushka i synok," 1833) plays with the notion of generic convention and reading habits.

In this story, a provincial Russian lady's love of gothic novels clashes spectacularly with her son's equally enthusiastic devotion to sentimental fiction. The result is a lampoon of Russian provincial education and life, which nonetheless provides equally valuable insight into reading trends of the time. Somov's narrator takes a didactic tone as he documents literary life away from the capitals. He assumes his own readership will be urban, better read than his provincial subjects, and familiar with the laundry list of titles he mentions somewhat ironically. He describes a peddler who goes from estate to estate selling books, alongside items like soap, "bad" pomade, maps, and chocolate.

> *And the bearded seller of bookish wit* carries in half a dozen crates with printed and other goods. The landowner selects *The Tale of Two Turks*, the adventures of Marquis G***, Sovezdral, and Vanka Kain, *The Midnight Bell, The Cave of Death, The Novels and Tales of Kotzebue*, etc. Sometimes he adds to all this *A Course on Bee Keeping, A Handbook of Equine Medicine, The Lenten Cookbook*, sometimes even *Firmness of Spirit, The Temple of Fame, A Journey to Little Russia*, and *Hamlet*, adapted by Mr. Viskovatov – in a word, all that kind of junk which piles up in Moscow bookstores and is sold to itinerant booksellers by the crate [...] Often the landowner buys all the printed goods by the crateful, unconcerned that in each of them are five or six copies of the same book.[17]

Somov's sample catalogue of provincial titles reminds us of Isabella Thorpe's list of recommended "horrid novels" in Jane Austen's *Northanger Abbey* (1818); one of the titles, Francis Lathom's *Midnight Bell* (1798), is even repeated in both lists! (The novel was published in Russian translation in 1802 but falsely attributed to popular writer Ann Radcliffe).[18] Austen's list amuses readers through the sharp contrast between the idealized sweetness and innocence of the conversing young ladies and the "excessively horrid" and suggestive titles of the books they read: "Castle of Wolfenbach, Clermont, Mysterious Warnings, Necromancer of the Black Forest, Midnight Bell, Orphan of the Rhine, and Horrid Mysteries."[19] Somov's list, on the other hand, pokes fun at provincial readers by naming lurid gothic titles such as *The Midnight Bell* and *The Cave of Death* alongside more practical works, including *A Course on Bee Keeping*, which emphasize the mundane details of daily life.

Whether or not Somov had read Austen's novel,[20] he was familiar with the canon of works that inspired her gothic parody. The same canon inspired his own "Mommy and Sonny" as well as texts like his satirical "Plan for a Novel *à la Radcliffe*," published in May 1816 in the *Kharkov Democritus*:

> Robbers, an underground prison,
> A tower, half a dozen owls;
> Gleaming through ravines the moon has risen,
> Wolves are baying, the wind howls;
> Awful dreams torment my heroes
> Fiery dragons, flying griffins from myth;
> Fear, horror after them flows …
> There you have it, a novel *a la Radcliffe*![21]

Somov's use of gothic convention here plays on the "shared codes" of parody, in Linda Hutcheon's formulation. The humour in his story and poem requires that Somov and his readers have familiarity with the original source material, the gothic genre.[22] Somov is then able to build on contemporaneous readers' assumptions about what gothic fiction is, just as Pushkin's Countess's statements reveal her own expectations about the genre. Both Somov and Pushkin poke fun at the gothic, which simultaneously revels in excess while revealing the conventionality of that excess. Similarly, Somov's heroine loves gothic novels for their conventions, which she finds delightful:

> Margarita Savishna passionately loved robbers' castles, the glint of daggers, the kidnapping of unfortunate heroines, and the secret pacts of murderers under the windows of innocent victims doomed to be killed, meanwhile confined in a tiny room of the east or west tower. In a word, the imagination of Margarita Savishna, a woman of firm character and strong nerves, delighted only in novelistic blood, breathed with the atmosphere of the dungeon, fed on the smell of murder. So to say, she lived on terror.[23]

Gothic fiction appeared as an array of horrors to early nineteenth-century readers. Some of these are fantastic: griffins and dragons. Some are natural, but establish an atmosphere of terror: a rising moon, a flock of owls, wolf cries, howling wind. The details that Margarita Savishna relishes – dungeons, lurking murderers, nefarious plots, kidnappings of innocent victims – appeal not only because of their lurid excess but also because of the delicious sensation of dread that they provoke. All contribute to a feeling of danger lurking just out of sight, and it is this quality of the gothic that sends chills down the spines of Margarita Savishna and other readers, that informs the Countess's dead bodies, and that manifests in Somov's "awful dreams."

Gothic fiction is typically set in the distant (often medieval) past, in an exotic location. Examining Horace Walpole's *Castle of Otranto* (1764) from the perspective of a historical novelist, Sir Walter Scott observed in 1823 that a gothic writer's greater purpose was to "wind up the feelings of his reader till they become for a moment identified with those of a ruder age."[24] Another critical tradition claims that this distance between setting and reader allows for the expression and exploration of anxieties latent in society.[25] One example is the Marquis de Sade's famous observation in 1800 that gothic fiction is "the necessary fruit of the revolutionary tremors felt by the whole of Europe."[26] Sade saw the increasingly excessive array of distant horrors in gothic novels such as Lewis's *The Monk* as a response to the visible horrors of the violent revolutionary period in France.

Austen's, Pushkin's, and Somov's works humorously play on the idea that gothic novels provoke true fear despite the dissonance between the novels' temporally and geographically distant settings and readers' own experiences. Pushkin's Countess admits "a mortal dread of drowned bodies," but the chance of her encountering one in her Petersburg palace is small. In Somov's satirical story, Margarita Savishna is convinced to save her son from an imprudent marriage by a savvy tutor who describes the son's situation in exaggerated gothic language. Using gothic tropes, the tutor moves the mother to action. Moreover, she even begins to conflate the prospective in-laws' wine cellar with a suitably gloomy Italian dungeon, although she quickly returns to reality in formulating an escape plan for her son.

One reason gothic works carry such power is the close relationship between reader and text. One 1830s reviewer observed, "It may be true that [Radcliffe's] persons are cold and formal; but her readers are the virtual heroes and heroines of her story as they read."[27] Austen's young ladies Catherine Morland and Isabella Thorpe discuss Radcliffe's sprawling gothic novel *The Mysteries of Udolpho*, repeating the incongruous word "delight" while discussing a murder victim's skeleton:

"I am just got to the black veil."
"Are you, indeed? How delightful! Oh! I would not tell you what is behind the veil for the world! Are not you wild to know?
"Oh! Yes, quite; what can it be? But do not tell me – I would not be told upon any account. I know it must be a skeleton, I am sure it is Laurentina's skeleton. Oh! I am delighted with the book! I should like to spend my whole life in reading it."[28]

The enticing mix of delight and terror, over which Isabella and Catherine rhapsodize, echoes in Fyodor Dostoevsky's memories of his childhood reading (in the 1820s and 1830s). In 1863 he remembers, "I used to spend the long winter hours before bed listening (for I could not yet read), agape with ecstasy and terror, as my parents read aloud to me from the novels of Ann Radcliffe. Then I would rave deliriously about them in my sleep."[29]

The Gothic Literary Landscape in Russia

The late eighteenth-century Russian book market was flooded with English gothic novels in Russian translation, and Russian gothic works derived their conventions from this flurry of English imports. The initial appearance of a Russian translation of Clara Reeve's *Old English Baron* (1778) in 1792 was quickly followed by translations of William Beckford's *Vathek* (1786) and Sophia Lee's *The Recess* (1785) between 1792 and 1794.[30] Works by authors such as Radcliffe, Lewis, and Scott followed suit. Radcliffe, established as the most popular horrid novel writer in Europe, also gained immense popularity in Russia. In just the year 1802, seven different translations of her novels appeared on the Russian book market, despite the fact that she had only written five![31] Describing Radcliffe's popularity, Alessandra Tosi observes that "[Radcliffe's] name alone on a book cover was perceived as a guarantee of commercial success; hence the number of works by other authors (including Lewis's *The Monk*) attributed to the 'celebrated Radcliffe.'"[32]

Many critics panned gothic novels as lurid sensational frivolity, but the novels nevertheless dominated the literary market in both Western Europe and Russia in the early nineteenth century.[33] During this period, some Russian authors even began writing their own gothic tales inspired by the English models. Karamzin's stories "Sierra-Morena" (1793) and "Bornholm Island" ("Ostrov Borngol'm," 1794) are the earliest examples, and the author himself admits his fascination with Radcliffe's oeuvre.[34] In a nod to the gothic's transfer from English into Russian, in "Bornholm Island" the Russian traveller-narrator sets sail on the ship *Britania*, which bears him from England to Russia by way of a gothic adventure. The titles of other works from this period sound as lurid as Austen's list of horrid novels. They include Vasily Narezhny's drama *The Dead Castle* (*Mertvyi zamok*, 1801); Nikolai Gnedich's novels *Moritz, or the Victim of Vengeance* (*Morits, ili Zhertva mshcheniia*, 1802) and *Don Corrado de Guerrera, or the Spirit of Vengeance and the Barbarism of Spaniards* (*Don-Korrado de Gerrera, ili Dukh mshcheniia i varvarstva gishpantsev*, 1803); and Pyotr Shalikov's *Dark Grove, or the Memorial to Tenderness* (*Temnaia roshcha, ili pamiatnik nezhnosti*, 1801). This last work was set in Russia, marking one of the first transpositions of the gothic onto the Russian landscape. All written between 1793 and 1803, they show the clear influence of Radcliffe, Lewis, Reeve, and other major English gothic writers.

By the early nineteenth century, literary commentators were beginning to critique Russian literature's imitative quality. In an 1806 issue of the journal *Lover of Literature*, for example, one critic remarked: "Many think there is nothing easier than writing a novel according to the new English style where [...] the improbable, based on the impossible, surpasses even miracles and shuns truthfulness."[35] These English gothic imports and their Russian imitations formed a significant part of the way that Russian readers conceived of the genre, by virtue of their runaway popularity in the early nineteenth century. However, a number of other related sources also played a role, including German and French works inspired by or in the vein of the original English gothic novels. Rather than imitating, Russian writers liberally transformed such works, building upon and enhancing or embellishing the gothic strands already extant in popular conceptions of the genre.

Vasily Zhukovsky's literary output allows for an intriguing study of influence. Between 1808 and 1831, the poet engaged in a series of "gothic translations," taking Gottfried Bürger's ballad "Lenore" (1773) and liberally adapting the work into a series of increasingly disturbing ballads: "Lyudmila" ("Liudmila," 1808), "Svetlana" (1813), and "Lenora" (1831).[36] Zhukovsky not only set his gothic ballads in the Russian countryside but also transposed elements from East Slavic folklore into them. In these and other works, such as his novella *Mariya's Grove* ("Mar'ina roshcha," 1809), Zhukovsky operated within a framework of multiple literary influences, including English graveyard poetry, German *Sturm und Drang* works, and English and German ballads, all of which he was translating during this period.[37] While Bürger's "Lenore" itself is not especially terrifying, Zhukovsky's "translations" startled readers. In 1864, Filip Vigel recalled, "We saw something monstrous in [Zhukovsky's] choices. Corpses, visions, demons, moonlit murders; all this belongs to folk tales and even to English novels; instead of Hero demurely waiting for drowning Leander, he gave us a madly passionate Lenore and her lover's galloping corpse."[38] Zhukovsky's reading and translation habits were expansive, more than those of the average Russian reader. However, in lifting gothic tropes and themes for his poetry and prose, Zhukovsky transposed the "low" genre into Russian "high" literature and russified it. In so doing, he lent his own voice to the web of references and conventions that made up the Russian reader's concept of "gothic."

A Gothic Ecology

It is useful to consider the gothic genre as an ecology,[39] a web of independent yet interlinked and constantly shifting or evolving influences and trends structured around specific nodal works. This environment then contributed to a general, palimpsestic, and unconscious sense of "gothic" for a Russian reader of the 1830s or 1840s.[40] Not all readers would have read all works within the network, but an understanding of conventions would have transcended individual reader experience. Whether the Countess in this chapter's epigraph had read novels featuring matricide, patricide, or drowned bodies, she understood these elements to be part of the same strand in fiction, even without the "gothic" label. Genre memory also persists; the Countess makes assumptions about the gothic, creating a list of conventions, even without necessarily having read specific novels that feature them.

More intriguingly, the Countess understood this trend to be popular and "new," even though, both by Tomsky's admission and by historical publication records, Western gothic fiction was no longer in vogue. Reading habits endure after trends have shifted, creating a network of influences that includes works published over a longer chronological span. For example, another library in Pushkin's works can be imagined from Onegin's reading habits, which represent a substantial period of time. The narrator mentions Onegin's reading of Charles Nodier's *Jean Sbogar* (1813), Lord Byron's "The Giaour" (1813) and "The Corsair" (1814), and Charles Maturin's *Melmoth the Wanderer* (1820) as well as works by eighteenth- and earlier nineteenth-century writers including Jean-Jacques Rousseau, Johann Gottfried von Herder, Nicolas Chamfort, and Germaine de Staël. The allure of gothic novels assured their popularity for many years after their original publication. Pushkin was not yet born and Somov still an infant when *The Mysteries of Udolpho* first appeared in print in England in 1794. By the time Dostoevsky was born in 1821, the celebrated Radcliffe had not published a new book in more than twenty years, yet she and other European gothic novelists continued to be popularly read for decades afterwards.

By the 1830s in Russia, this gothic ecology included – in addition to canonically gothic texts – influences that resonated with gothic tropes and themes but that may not have been specifically considered part of the late eighteenth- to early nineteenth-century literary trend that celebrated the macabre, the terrifying, and the medieval. The works of William Shakespeare, John Milton, and *Sturm und Drang* writers such as Friedrich Schiller contributed "the discovery of the dark side of human existence – the sinister, the nocturnal, the demonic, the torn sub-conscious of extreme heroes" to already extant gothic themes.[41] Milton's *Paradise Lost* (1667) was originally translated into Russian in 1745 and quickly ran afoul of the Orthodox Church, which declared it blasphemous. Its status as a scandalous book contributed to its transgressive associations, just as its portrayal of Satan inspired Byron's demonism and, by extension, Mikhail Lermontov's.

Theatrical productions also contributed to a cultural understanding of gothic. The often gruesome and disturbing subject matter of plays by Shakespeare and Schiller resonated with the gothic genre, and they were popular in Russia in the 1830s. The works of Shakespeare were translated into Russian beginning in the eighteenth century, but in the 1820s and 1830s, students at Moscow University produced new translations, which brought the English playwright back into popular consciousness. In 1837, a production of *Hamlet* in Moscow's Petrovsky (Bolshoi) Theatre proved that the tale of ghostly hauntings, vengeance killings, troubled minds, and violent tableaux remained popular. Similar productions of works such as *Othello* and *Macbeth* were staged around this time.

Through the 1820s and 1830s, Russian writers drew inspiration from these theatrical productions, thereby enhancing the sense of gothic by association. Lermontov, for example, was so moved by an 1829 Moscow production of Schiller's *The Robbers* (*Die Räuber*, 1781) that he based his own play *Two Brothers* (*Dva brata*, 1835) on it.[42] This particular production of Schiller's play featured the famous tragic actor Pavel Mochalov playing Karl Moor; Mochalov was well known for his Byronic interpretations of classic roles. The translation of *The Robbers* performed in Moscow also featured a changed ending, in which Karl Moor is stabbed by his own highwaymen, a considerably more sensational fate than his decision in the original to turn himself in to the legal authorities.[43] (Intriguingly, this also influenced young Dostoevsky: in an 1880 letter, Dostoevsky recalls that he was very moved by viewing the same production.)[44] *Two Brothers* emphasizes the elements of Schiller's drama that captured the imagination of Russian audiences: disillusionment and jadedness, doubling, the psychology of power, struggle of conscience, and sensational violence. In Lermontov's play, two brothers love the same woman, who dies tragically. One brother, Alexander, engages in treachery born of his despair, while the other, Yuri, is tormented by grief but ultimately unable to act violently. Alexander broods about free will and his inability to break his fate or feel emotion, all the while becoming increasingly destructive.

The Robbers was a critical success, but Schiller's best-selling work during his lifetime was *The Ghost-Seer* (*Der Geisterseher*, 1787–9), an unfinished three-volume novel that dwelt on the divide between the spirit and real worlds, and which "[opened] a door into the reader's imagination through which fear of the Jesuits, secret societies, and the associated complex of conspiracy theories can enter."[45] Schiller uses startling repetitions in the novel to draw readers in. For example, the appearance of a ghost is revealed to be an optical illusion, but is immediately followed by the apparition of a real ghost with a deadly secret. While the novel purports to engage with the science of spiritualism, its horrors accumulate shockingly, reminding later readers of gothic novels.[46] The work appeared twice in early nineteenth-century Russia: anonymously in 1807, and again ten years later. Although Schiller wrote *The Ghost-Seer* before the gothic wave of works by Radcliffe, Lewis, and Maturin, it appeared contemporaneously with them on the Russian book market. For Russian readers, its themes were part of the literary gothic trend.[47]

In the 1820s and 1830s, nineteenth-century voices from Western Europe appeared increasingly in the Russian reader's library as well. The fame of Byron, whose tormented heroes plumbed the dark depths of human feeling, went so far in early nineteenth-century Russia that reports of it seem to have reached the English poet himself. In *Don Juan* (1819–24) he even refers to his work's circulation in Russia: "and now rhymes wander / Almost as far as Petersburg."[48] Byronic heroes famously populate the works of, for example, Lermontov, Mikhail Bestuzhev-Marlinsky, and Pushkin, but beyond literary influence, Byron's works were enormously popular among readers, in part because of his rebellious heroes' political relevance in the wake of the failed 1825 Decembrist uprising.[49]

Byron's dramatic poem *Manfred* (1817), for example, tells the story of a man tormented by guilt for a past offence never revealed to readers. Not unlike Faust, the eponymous hero calls upon seven spirits and asks them to grant him forgetfulness, but as these spirits' domain is not in the past, they are unable to do so. Eventually, Manfred dies, challenging authority and refusing to submit to the spirits he has summoned. The poem's gothic motifs – supernatural elements, anxiety related to the past, defiance of moral authority, gloomy meditations about death – underscore its debt to the gothic genre (just as its hero's name, shared by the hero of *The Castle of Otranto*, does). Written in 1816–17, the poem was likely inspired by the famous "Gothic Summer," which was shared by Byron, John Polidori, and the Shelleys at the Villa Diodati and saw the origin of *Frankenstein* (1818).[50] *Manfred* was first translated into Russian in 1828, after the Decembrist uprising, during a period when Russian readers were attracted to "an increasingly tragic voice and deeper philosophical significance," "a break with rationalism," and "a growing cult of lyrical emotion."[51]

Inspired by works such as *Manfred*, many authors writing during this time were fascinated by the supernatural's potential for preying on human emotional and psychological states. Following Zhukovsky's model in gothic ballads like "Lyudmila" and "Svetlana," these works were often set in Russian imperial space and incorporated elements from Slavic folklore: Antony Pogorelsky's *A Double* (*Dvoinik, ili moi vechera v Malorossii*, 1828); Mikhail Zagoskin's *Yuri Miloslavsky, or the Russians in 1612* (*Iurii Miloslavskii, ili Russkie v 1612 godu*, 1829); Mikhail Bestuzhev-Marlinsky's "The Traitor" ("Izmennik," 1825), "The Terrible Fortune-Telling" ("Strashnoe gadanie," 1831), and *The Cuirassier* (*Latnik*, 1832); Alexander Veltman's *Deathless Koshchei* (*Koshchei bessmertnyi*, 1833); Alexey Tolstoy's *Vurdalak Family* (*Sem'ia vurdalaka*, 1839) and *The Vampire* (*Upir'*, 1841). Vladimir Odoevsky, sometimes called "The Russian Hoffmann," is the most well-known nineteenth-century Russian gothic writer,[52] whose gothic-fantastic tales satirize modern life using gothic tropes. For example, "The Sylph" ("Sil'fida," 1837) chronicles its hero's obsession with alchemy and resulting decline into madness, and the luridly titled "The Living Corpse" ("Zhivoi mertvets," 1838) satirically recounts the dilemma of a man who wakes up one day and discovers himself a ghost.

"The Living Corpse" echoes Nikolai Gogol's "The Nose" ("Nos," 1836), a fantastic story in which titular counsellor Kovalyov wakes up one day to discover that his nose is not only missing but has actually somehow acquired a higher rank than his own. While Kovalyov's experience discomfits, frustrates, and ultimately terrifies him, Gogol's story does not evoke fear in its reader. However, the ideas Gogol explores through Kovalyov and his nasal extremity's misadventures – estrangement, confusion, grotesquerie, anxiety – take their cues from the swirl of gothic tropes that the genre connoted during this period. Gogol's German influence is so well known as to be a commonplace among scholars, and many of these themes are transposed from his "imaginary Germans," the pantheon of writers such as Friedrich Schlegel and E.T.A. Hoffmann, whom he idolized in his early writing career and who remained influential on his later works. Of these, Hoffmann was particularly important. The German author's popularity across Europe began around 1829–30, but intriguingly, the first Russian translation of his works occurred earlier, in 1822.[53] His tales tantalized with gothic-fantastic elements such as automata, mesmerism, mysterious visitors, and supernatural events that left readers feeling pleasurably uneasy. In a letter from 1839, Gogol reminisced, "To this day, I still love the Germans my imagination created then."[54] Gogol even placed Hoffmann and Schiller directly into the story "Nevsky Prospect" ("Nevskii Prospekt," 1835), albeit in a refracted form. Schiller is "not *that* Schiller, who wrote 'William Tell' and 'The History of the Thirty Years' War,' but the famous Schiller, the master tinsmith on Meshchanskaya street," while Hoffmann is "not the writer Hoffmann, but a fairly good cobbler on Ofitserskaya street, and a great buddy of Schiller's."[55]

Gogol's signature style incorporated folk narratives, romantic tropes, gothic elements, moments of the uncanny, and fantastic hesitation to create new works that quickly gained popularity.[56] In "Viy" ("Vii," 1835), a church overgrown with vines becomes a terrifying prison where a witch holds several students captive. "Nevsky Prospect" concludes with the image of the devil lighting gas lamps along the boulevard in the misty twilight. A demonic portrait terrorizes and ultimately dooms a penniless artist in "The Portrait" ("Portret," 1835). "The Overcoat" ("Shinel'," 1842) ends with a spectral clerk haunting the Petersburg streets, stealing the coats of passers-by. The collections of Ukrainian tales, *Evenings on a Farm near Dikanka* (*Vechera na khutore bliz Dikan'ki*, 1831) and *Mirgorod* (1835), blend folkloric and fantastic elements with depictions of daily life in the countryside. *Arabesques* (*Arabeski*, 1835), which includes the Petersburg stories "Nevsky Prospect" and "The Portrait," intersperses these fictional works indebted to the German gothic-fantastic with essays on history, geography, architecture, and aesthetics.

While the devil or a ghostly clerk gothically haunts the pages of *Arabesques*, groups from the ancient past – Ostrogoths, Visigoths, doomed Pompeiians – contextualize these otherworldly apparitions, adding anxiety from the historical past to the collection's reading experience. This historical anxiety played a significant role in the way nineteenth-century Russians viewed themselves. Bestuzhev-Marlinsky discusses the weightiness of history on contemporary consciousness in "On N. Polevoi's Novel 'Oath at the Tomb of the Lord'" (1833), writing, "Now history is not in deed alone, but in the memory, in the mind, in the heart of the people. We see it, hear it, feel it every minute; it permeates us in all our feelings [...] History is our other *half*, in all the weightiness of the word."[57] Inspired by similar sources, Pushkin's works engage with this anxiety but with gothic undertones. His play "The Stone Guest" ("Kammenyi gost'," 1830) explores the Don Juan legend; drawing its primary inspiration from Mozart's opera *Don Giovanni* (1787), the play also engages with Lewis's *The Monk*.[58] "The Bronze Horseman" (1833) features a terrifying scene in which the celebrated Étienne Falconet statue of Peter the Great comes to life and chases the hapless clerk Eugene through the dark, flooded streets of St Petersburg. Like "The Queen of Spades," "The Bronze Horseman" meditates on the relationship between nineteenth-century Russian reality and the anxieties of the eighteenth-century past.[59]

"To live in the age of Romanticism is to live in the age of history, for in the nineteenth century, history has become an inseparable part of everyone's life," comments Frazier in her reading of *Arabesques*, which exposes the themes of chaos and apocalypse that weighed heavily on Gogol at the time.[60] This historical consciousness draws anxiety along with it, as works from this period demonstrate. Fear, the direct product of the fantastic, not only pervades the chase scene in "The Bronze Horseman" but drives Hermann to madness when the dead Countess appears to him in "The Queen of Spades."[61] Pushkin's and Gogol's works from the 1830s are outstanding examples of the integration of gothic-fantastic, but in their incorporation of the details of everyday life – the drudgery of domestic service, the boredom of working as a copy clerk, the emptiness of society life – they also use the excesses of the gothic-fantastic to offset anxious truths about contemporary experience. Even if the Countess's wink is fantasy, Hermann's mental illness is real, after all.

The trend towards documenting real life also entered the Russian reader's consciousness through Western imports. Charles Dickens's works are an example of realist fiction that owes a substantial debt to the gothic genre for a basic narrative framework and an array of sensational plot elements.[62] *Oliver Twist* (1839) recounts the difficult life of the working classes through the experience of a boy who is born in a workhouse, grimly apprenticed to an undertaker, and recruited into a criminal gang. The novel is a scathing indictment of the hypocrisy of child poverty and labour. While *Oliver Twist* is an early example of socially critical realist writing, Dickens's villain, Bill Sikes, is punished in gothic fashion, hanging himself after being tormented by the apparition of his most recent victim, "a phantom [...] a living gravestone, with its epitaph in blood," whose penetrating, staring eyes follow him everywhere.[63] The first complete Russian translation of *Oliver Twist*, appearing in 1841, established Dickens's permanent celebrity in Russia.[64]

So far, the Russian reader's gothic library includes English, German, and Russian works, but French works must also be included. Before 1830, France was a major influence on Russian culture. Yuri Lotman aptly describes the French language in the eighteenth and early nineteenth centuries as "a bridge for the transfer of ideas and cultural values from Europe to Russia."[65] Most of the gothic novels imported from the West arrived in Russia in French translation. Furthermore, in the 1830s, a new generation of French writers began to gain notice in Russia. Foremost among them was George Sand. Dostoevsky – in *Diary of a Writer*

(*Dnevnik pisatelia*, 1876), remembering Sand upon her death – writes of a "new wave" of writers in the 1830s and 1840s, linking Sand with Charles Dickens.[66] "George Sand [...] at once took virtually first place, here in Russia, among that whole Pleiad of new writers who were suddenly celebrated and trumpeted throughout Europe. Even Dickens, who appeared here almost at the same time as she, came second [...] in the consideration of our public."[67] He recalls of Sand that "everyone was struck [...] by the chaste, supreme purity of her types and ideals, and by the modest charm of the austere, restrained tone of her narrative – and such a woman was going about in trousers and given to debauchery!"[68] Although Dostoevsky remembered Sand's purity of types and ideals, these were offset in novels like *Indiana* (1832), for example, by the lurid, sensational elements of adulterous affairs, suicides, and perilous sea voyages. *Spiridion* (1839), which was particularly popular in 1840s Russia, is a gothic philosophical novel set in an isolated monastery. Its pure hero, Angel, is forced to fight against a slew of corrupt monks. Ultimately, Angel and reason triumph, but not before a visit to a haunted library, the excavation of some mysterious coffins, and even an encounter with secret books encoded with invisible ink. Sand's novels, like others from the 1830s and 1840s, are ostensibly statements about social ills – the rights of women, the corruption of religious institutions – but incorporate melodramatic plot elements, some of which even hint at the supernatural.

The French *école frénétique* was also extremely popular in Russia during the 1830s. The movement was inspired by earlier English and French gothic texts, including *Melmoth the Wanderer* and the works of Nodier, which enjoyed renewed interest among 1830s French readers, as well as the near-cult status of Hoffmann's fantastic tales in late 1820s France. *L'école frénétique* writers included Sand as well as Jules Janin, Eugène Sue, Victor Hugo, Alexandre Dumas, Prosper Mérimée, and Honoré de Balzac. A precursor of the natural school, *école frénétique* writing placed its emphasis on social consciousness but also drew upon lurid plot elements such as murders, incarcerations, affairs, mysticism, and alchemy.

Sue's lengthy, labyrinthine *Mysteries of Paris* (*Les Mystères de Paris*, 1842–3) draws from the sensationalism of earlier gothic narratives and melodrama, as well as earlier physiological writing, to depict life among the lower classes in Paris as seen from the perspective of a disguised nobleman, Rodolphe. Rodolphe meets an assortment of murderers, prostitutes, and others who are driven to crime by the class system, simultaneously raising awareness of the degradations of poverty for readers and entertaining them with sensational escapades and adventures. Balzac's *Eugénie Grandet* (1833) takes a gothic degeneration plot and describes the decline of a noble house as subsequent generations are "infected" with miserliness. As Eugénie's misfortunes pile up, so too do the suicides, corruption, and moral decay. While not overtly gothic, the novel certainly evokes the genre. Dostoevsky's translation of *Eugénie Grandet* modifies its language into a darker lexicon, featuring words such as "gloomy" (мрачный) instead of "pale" or "cold," and liberally adding words like "terrible" (страшный) and "mysterious" (таинственный).[69] Although *Eugénie Grandet* was the only one of his translations published, in the late 1830s and early 1840s Dostoevsky had notably embarked on a series of *école frénétique* translation projects, including Sue's *Mathilde* (1841) and Sand's *Last Aldini* (*La Dernière Aldini*, 1838).

The ecology of influences that contributed to a "gothic strand" in Russian fiction in the early nineteenth century and, beyond this, to the development of gothic within the bounds of literary realism is enormous. "We have all come out of Gogol's overcoat" goes the famous saying. As this chapter demonstrates, while Gogol's influence is arguably present and significant, his "overcoat" is fashioned from a patchwork of other influences. These include earlier gothic imports from England, France, and Germany, Zhukovsky's ballads, the tales of Hoffmann, and the same cultural strands that produced the contemporaneous works of Edgar Allan Poe, James Hogg, the Brontë sisters, and George Sand, among others. The literary landscape this chapter has mapped exposes a gothic network predominately connected through thematic concepts or associations rather than a canon of overtly gothic texts. This uniquely Russian gothic ecology was shaped by publishing culture, translation history, and society fashion. In turn, the Russian reader's gothic library influenced a generation of writers.

Much of early realism took its cues from romanticism, from experimentation with effective and affective manners of narration. Irina Paperno observes that as the movement came into its own, "romantic consciousness [remained] a tangible (though at times vehemently denied) presence, a substratum of the consciousness of a realist."[70] In any one text, intertextual resonance involves, in Laurent Jenny's words, "not a confused, mysterious accumulation of influences, but the work of transformation and assimilation of various texts that is accomplished by a focal text which keeps control over the meaning."[71] Yet in the Russian reader's library, delineations between categories like romantic, realist, and gothic blur, creating a vague, anxious presentiment that manifests in assumptions about what gothic works are like. Pushkin's Countess assumes that gothic novels are brimming with murderous acts, transgressions, and fearful scenes. How Russian writers exploited these assumptions and those of other imagined readers to forge new connections between reader and text is the question the present study seeks to answer.

Chapter Two

Gothic Transmutations in Pushkin and Gogol

There is always something luring me,
something waiting in the distance:
my soul will be bursting and suffering
and where does it get me?

> Vladimir Odoevsky, "The Sylph"

It's now the British Muse's fables
That lie on maidens' bedside tables
And haunt their dreams.

> Alexander Pushkin, *Eugene Onegin*

Everything is dead quiet, and thereafter the becalmed surface
of the unresponsive element becomes
even more dreadful and desolate.

> Nikolai Gogol, *Dead Souls*

In Vladimir Odoevsky's story "The Sylph" ("Sil'fida," 1837), a town gentleman recently transplanted to the country begins to dabble in alchemy after coming across his deceased uncle's stash of books on the subject. He is sceptical at first, but his enthusiasm grows, as does his belief in the experiments, which he charts in a series of letters. The story is made up entirely of letters. The first curated letters are written by the protagonist; later letters are written by others who document the protagonist's fall into a deep alchemical dream state. By combining ingredients, he creates a spirit being who then serves as a muse figure. Urged on by his muse, the protagonist forges a new world for himself, but at the cost of his identity in the real world. When friends intervene and snap him out of the daze caused by his alchemical obsession, he is left a husk, a spectre of his former self, but hopelessly yearning for the world he has lost. Alchemy is a pseudoscience in which disparate elements are combined to create a new substance. However, for the purposes of this chapter's frame, alchemy functions as a convenient metaphor for genre: both alchemy and genre take disparate elements and combine them to create a new type of material, one that does not neatly fit into other categories.

"The Sylph" is an example of gothic-fantastic writing, a subcategory of the gothic genre that engages with the fantastic to build on the tension of the work's gothic narrative force. The fantastic, in Tzvetan Todorov's structuralist definition, is the narrative space of hesitation between the uncanny ("the supernatural explained") and the marvellous ("the supernatural accepted").[1] In the Russian literary canon, gothic-fantastic has become the most visible form of gothic. Other examples of this type of writing include Alexander Pushkin's "Queen of Spades" or Nikolai Gogol's uncanny tales like "The Portrait" and "Viy." Neil Cornwell defines the Russian gothic-fantastic by focusing on its influences: "A certain input from folklore, and such further native medieval ingredients as chronicles and saints' lives apart, Russian Gothic can be said to derive from an amalgam of European influences: the English Gothic novel, the tales of Hoffmann, the French *fantastique* and *frénétique* traditions, and the various schools of European idealist and esoteric thought."[2] While the Russian gothic-fantastic is undeniably important in nineteenth-century literary history, my interest in this chapter is not in its considerable influence but in how gothic narrative, specifically imported from European gothic works, was integrated into and enhanced the development of the Russian novel in the 1820s through the early 1840s.

During the 1820s–40s, the Russian novel was an uncertain category. Victoria Somoff calls it a period "when the exclusive narrative stance of the novelistic author was not an aesthetic given but rather still *in the making*."[3] It was the Golden Age of Russian poetry, when the literary landscape was lit by poetic luminaries, including Alexander Pushkin, Vasily Zhukovsky, Konstantin Batyushkov, Evgeny Baratynsky, and Mikhail Lermontov. Prose was inconsistent, and prose writers faced challenges in sustaining longer narratives.[4] Some novels had appeared on the Russian book market, including Mikhail Chulkov's *Comely Cook* (*Prigozhaia povarikha*, 1770), Nikolai Gnedich's *Don Corrado de Guerrera* (*Don-Korrado de Gerrera*, 1803), and Vasily Narezhny's *A Russian Gil Blas* (*Rossiiskii Zhil'blaz*, 1814). These, however, were mostly inspired by imported literature, such as Daniel Defoe's picaresque novel *Moll Flanders* (1722), Matthew Lewis's gothic horror *The Monk* (1796), and

Alain-René Lesage's picaresque novel *Gil Blas* (1735). A Russian novel that was homegrown, so to speak, was a goal desired by many. As Simon Franklin has observed, this eagerness notwithstanding, "Russian writers themselves […] were often as uncertain as the critics – more uncertain than the critics – as to how this virtually unknown phenomenon should be constructed."[5]

In the present chapter, I examine one facet of the Russian novel's construction, namely, its engagement with gothic narrative. To do so, I analyse the narrative structure and form of two texts that were deeply influential for the development of the Russian novel: Pushkin's *Eugene Onegin* (1825–32) and Gogol's *Dead Souls* (*Mertvye dushi*, 1842). My analysis focuses on the way gothic appears in these novels and the role it plays. In this I have two aims. First, I wish to illustrate the tension between the way the gothic is used aesthetically, authentically, and parodically in these works. Notably, *Eugene Onegin* and *Dead Souls* are not typically read as gothic, although each has a strong gothic trope at its core, and Pushkin and Gogol are also known for their gothic-fantastic writing. Yet as I demonstrate, Pushkin and Gogol do not simply add superficial gothic elements to *Eugene Onegin and Dead Souls*. Rather, gothic narrative force plays a substantial role in the structure of each novel. Second, I aim to explore the utility of the gothic within the array of genres represented in each novel.[6] What is gained by incorporating European gothic models? These novels are self-consciously about literary creation. Their narrators are well aware of their genre, form, and even audience, and this metaliterariness has significantly shaped the notion of novelistic creation since the novels' publication. In particular, the inclusion of gothic tropes proves important for understanding the novels' broader narratives and themes and for understanding the function of novelistic form in these experimental works. The gothic transmutations in these new novels clearly demonstrate the utility of genre and contribute to a literary alchemical experiment in which the writer combines unique generic elements to create a distinctly new form: the Russian novel.

The Machinery of Terror and Pushkin's Imagined Reader

One of *Eugene Onegin*'s key themes is reading: its utility, dangers, and virtues. Many characters' favourite writers are revealed in the novel, each adding to a broader picture of literary cultural connotation and influence in early nineteenth-century Russia: Tatyana's mother is famously a fan of Richardson, and the unfortunate Lensky is fond of Schiller. When Tatyana explores Onegin's library in chapter 7, she learns about his character by reading the annotated and marked pages of novels he has perused: Lord Byron's *Childe Harold's Pilgrimage* (1812–18) and Charles Maturin's *Melmoth the Wanderer* (1820).[7] Pushkin's readers would have immediately recognized these texts, which were extremely popular in Russia as *Onegin* was being published.[8] *Childe Harold* draws significantly on the gothic, while *Melmoth* is one of the genre's most influential texts. Pushkin's reference to these novels would have immediately created an association with the gothic for readers. We can readily identify gothic conventions in *Eugene Onegin*: the midnight chase, the cursed wanderer, the demonic company. The narrator pokes fun at Tatyana's novel reading, but the novels she is reading, as Alessandra Tosi notes, involve "the discovery of the dark side of human existence – the sinister, the nocturnal, the demonic, the torn subconscious of extreme heroes."[9] More interesting, however, is the way Pushkin plays with his imagined reader's reaction to these conventions through formal hybridity: a gothic novel within the bounds of a novel in verse, gothic poetics encapsulated within the Onegin stanza.

In Tatyana's dream, which engages directly with Zhukovsky's gothic ballad "Svetlana" (1813), Pushkin channels gothic generic genealogy. Chapter 5, which includes Tatyana's dream, begins with an epigraph from "Svetlana": "Oh, never know these frightful dreams, My dear Svetlana!"[10] Vladimir Nabokov suggests that Zhukovsky's "marvellous" ballad may have been an inspiration for the Onegin stanza and that the epigraph pays tribute to this ur-stanza.[11] Whether or not this is the case, introducing the dream sequence with Zhukovsky's ballad adds a level of parody. While the terrifying dreams within the ballad are luridly frightful, once removed from their literary context, they lose their horror. This epigraph prompts the reader to recall the act of reading Zhukovsky's ballad, which recounts a young girl's dream of her fiancé's death and his animated corpse coming back to haunt her. Notably, Tatyana's dream episode foreshadows the fatal conflict between Onegin and Lensky at her name-day party later in the same chapter. While gothic terrors hide in the shadows on the first reading of the ballad, there are no unrevealed secrets or surprise endings on second reading, which undermines the narrative's suspense. Although the epigraph suggests gothic cliché or parody, quoting Zhukovsky to introduce the dream chapter also creates an intertextual bond between Tatyana and Svetlana, a bond that persists as the reader continues.

The chapter begins with an idyllic nature scene: Tatyana wakes up to find a new snowfall sparkling in the sunshine. In addition to its descriptions of light and beauty, the passage is sonically charming, featuring sleigh bells, bird song, and a child's laughter. As this bright, merry scene fades into twilight and shadow, the theme of fate is introduced through a discussion of folk beliefs surrounding divination. Tatyana's mysterious midnight encounter then introduces the gothic. While the frosty, clear night initially seems to counterbalance the bright, sparkling day, the scene quickly turns ominous as someone approaches. The imagery of the dark mirror and the vulnerable maiden, as suggested by her *dishabille*, sets the gothic scene. The moon's trembling echoes the initial suggestion of vulnerability, and the ellipses used here emphasize narrative suspense. This gothic mode lurks just under the marvellous and emerges without warning, leaking out through the ellipses in the text.

In the next stanza, stark terror begins to move the narration. We learn first that Tatyana is seized by "sheer terror" (стало страшно вдруг Татьяне), and then, following ellipses, the narrator voices his own fears. He exercises his control of the narrative to pull Tatyana from the scene and send her safely to bed. In confessing his fears in these stanzas, the narrator reveals that he has been reading Zhukovsky's gothic ballad "Svetlana." While "Svetlana" at first might have seemed clichéd, or perhaps only thematically linked on the plot level, here we see its ability to inspire feeling. The passage speaks to the power of reading. Although genre fiction carries a master plot and ending, which are embedded in its conventions, it enables readers to forget its formula and give in to the pure feeling it evokes. As Tatyana goes to bed, the gothic is present but concealed beneath the surface of the text. It threatens the heroine, and then just as suddenly retreats.

Pushkin's vacillation between the mode of terror and the mode of safety echoes Horace Walpole's explanation of the so-called machinery of terror in *The Castle of Otranto*. Walpole holds that positioning tropes in different relationships creates productive new models, and the predictability of surprising and frightening elements assures readers' engagement. Terror is central to this practice and, as a result, to the novel's structure. In the preface to the first edition of *Otranto*, Walpole explains:

> Everything tends directly to the catastrophe. Never is the reader's attention relaxed. The rules of the drama are almost observed throughout the conduct of the piece. The characters are well drawn, and still better maintained. Terror, the author's principal engine, prevents the story from ever languishing; and it is so often contrasted by pity, that the mind is kept up in a constant vicissitude of interesting passions.[12]

Intriguingly, Walpole refers to Aristotle's *Poetics* when discussing the formulation of his story in terms of genre, but rather than keeping pity and fear in equilibrium, the English author privileges terror as "the principal engine." Keeping his reader in a state of affective vacillation between the Aristotelian categories of pity and terror – or, in the terms of eighteenth-century genre, drawing on techniques from sentimentalism and horror (or its forebear, revenge tragedy) – Walpole created a page-turner. In *Eugene Onegin*, Pushkin propels his narrative at varying speeds by using the Onegin stanza and other tools, among them Walpole's gothic machinery of horror. Pushkin's evocation and modulation of the gothic in Tatyana's dream renders it one of the "faster" passages.

The vacillations between terror and the narrator's ironically undermining interventions generate a sense of uneasiness that accompanies the reader into Tatyana's dream. Here the tone, which evokes the world of Zhukovsky's ballad, is highly literary. We see the gothic setting emerge as the stanza continues. The surrounding natural world appears to come alive and propel Tatyana forward into a landscape of gaping chasms and wild torrents. Just then, a pursuer emerges: a bear. And in the following stanzas, Pushkin builds gothic suspense. Tatyana looks behind; we see her footsteps hasten, the pursuer dogged and unshakeable. Although Tatyana is in flight, these verses carry a sense of anxious entrapment: she cannot break free of the chase and she cannot escape her pursuer. Nature again plays a role as the landscape's elements rise up to snatch at her, forcefully tearing out her golden earrings. This painful image is bookended by Tatyana's glimpse of the bear over her shoulder beforehand and by the sound of him following her, ever closer, afterwards. This passage introduces an intertextual node of terror; the gothic machinery of fear encourages the imagined reader's concern for Tatyana, echoing the narrator's earlier fear for Svetlana. At this point, the narrative tension breaks as Tatyana faints and the chase ends.

While the gothic chase builds up a narrative that implies a feeling of terror, this break signals the beginning of a shift away from fear. The gothic narrative continues as the scene moves forward; the mysterious and menacing bear carries Tatyana's limp and vulnerable body through the dark woods. The image of defenceless innocent with fearsome monster is a well-established gothic trope. However, this fearsome tableau is interrupted and ironically undermined when the bear speaks: he cheerfully and politely tells Tatyana that she should warm up at his fire. Throughout chapter 5, the narrative creates waves of suspense and fear; real terror is parodically and continually deflated.[13] The narrator's self-conscious confession that his fears for his heroine are based on his reading of "Svetlana" has the same humorous and layered parodic function as the bear's polite invitation to the unconscious Tatyana to warm

herself by his fire. The shifts between terror and humour disconcert
the reader, allowing for an intertextual space in which gothic narrative
effects can be felt, even by seasoned or jaded readers.

As Tatyana surveys her surroundings, her first impression is of
simultaneous fear and delight at the strange company assembled in the
bear's home. The narrator describes the various strange and grotesque
creatures present, including a dog's face with horns and another with
a rooster's head. The group is notably jolly; there are festive sounds
and some of the creatures are spinning or even dancing a jig. When
Tatyana recognizes Onegin amid the guests, he is himself, not a hybrid
creature with grotesque additions. In the next stanza, after Tatyana is
discovered and Onegin's rage unfolds, he again appears as himself,
recognizable and yet distanced, even as his rage spurs the demonic
company to deconstruct into a number of grotesque parts. Tatyana recognizes Onegin, but his performance of self in this company terrifies
her. His motivations and feelings are unknown, and he acts increasingly demonically.

As chapter 5 continues, Tatyana wakes up, the guests begin to arrive
for the name-day celebration, and the tone again vacillates from gothic
terror to merriment. Tatyana's guests recall the strange company, but
whereas in the dream, witches had goatees and spinning skulls wore
red hats, here rotund local squires wear pince-nez and unnaturally
coloured wigs. The group is described as engaging in acts that evoke
the same carnivalesque atmosphere: gluttony, drunkenness, wild
dancing, buffoonery. Just as Onegin's appearance in the dream struck
Tatyana with confusion and dread, here his appearance elicits a similar
response: she pales and trembles. During the name-day party, the main
characters' emotions are obscured by the narrator's detailed discussion
of the ball. However, like the gothic undercurrent in the beginning of
chapter 5, these emotions emerge suddenly and fatally at the end of the
chapter when Lensky gallops off. While Onegin's ploy to distract Olga
and Lensky's subsequent duel challenge seem like society tale fodder,
the emotions described in this scene notably echo the earlier dream
sequence and thus take on sinister overtones.

The playful gothic – at times ironically terrifying, at times parodic –
gives rise to a metaliterary self-consciousness as the reader becomes
aware of the generic palimpsest at work here. Onegin's acceptance of
Lensky's challenge provokes authentic feelings of fear in Tatyana, as
she has been discomfited by her nightmare. The chapter's opening discussion of divination and Tatyana's consultation of a dream dictionary
both suggest her belief that her nightmare may have been a supernatural revelation of fate. After all, she dreamt of Lensky's death by

Onegin's hand. For the reader, references to Zhukovsky's "Svetlana" in both the chapter's epigraph and narrator's exclamation add a layer of gothic irony. Yet this gothic reference also contextualizes Tatyana's moment of fantastic hesitation as she grapples with the fatal potential of her nightmare.

In the gothically tinged world where fictional events from "Svetlana" reverberate in Tatyana's subconscious, the reading scene in Onegin's library in chapter 7 takes on added importance. The library is coded with intertextual clues to Onegin's true self: the portrait of Byron, the bust of Napoleon, and the traces of Onegin's own reading of gothic novels. As Tatyana searches for Onegin's true self, the reader remembers chapter 5, in which Onegin's vacillation between a variety of selves was a source of gothic terror that later played out in the party and duel. The narrator's question, "Who is Onegin, really?"[14] reveals the emptiness and ghostliness of a character who imitates without genuinely revealing his sensibility. Onegin's lack of a fixed self is dangerous, as he has as much divine as demonic potential. In his ambiguity, he acquires petty yet fiendish attributes: he is an "arrogant devil" (надменный бес), a "worthless ghost" (ничтожный призрак), and perhaps most damning of all, a Muscovite in Childe Harold's cloak.[15] For Tatyana, the realization that Onegin has draped himself in Byronism destroys the myth of his individuality, which had prompted her pursuit of his affection. The imitative quality in Onegin's performance of self enables Tatyana to project both her girlish romantic dreams and her terrified nightmares onto him. Onegin becomes a blank slate, ripe for Tatyana's creative impulses.

In projecting the mysterious gothic hero onto Onegin, the narrative openly engages with another gothic work, one suggested early on in the novel: Maturin's *Melmoth the Wanderer*. Published in 1820, this convoluted novel depicts the travels of a seventeenth-century scholar who sells his soul to the devil in exchange for an exceptionally long life. The wanderer then spends the ensuing 150 years searching for someone to take over his pact. In the course of these travels, he has various adventures, tempting many to take his place, but is ultimately unsuccessful and does not recover his soul. Onegin, too, searches for true feeling, for a way to access his soul and feeling, as we see in his early *ennui* and later pursuit of and pining after Tatyana in Petersburg. Like Melmoth's, Onegin's story is a series of framed episodes from different perspectives, each highlighting different aspects of his character but none able to answer the question, "Who is he?" Onegin's emptiness, so unfathomable to deep-feeling, sensitive Tatyana, may simply be a symptom of his status as a cursed wanderer.

The empty, wandering figure of Melmoth frames *Eugene Onegin*'s main events, first in chapter 3, appearing again in the library scene in chapter 7, and again in the final chapter.[16] In chapter 3, as the narrator muses on the popular power of the gothic, he mentions Melmoth by name:

> It's now the British Muse's fables
> That lie on maidens' bedside tables
> And haunt their dreams. They worship now
> The Vampire with his pensive brow,
> Or gloomy Melmoth, lost and pleading,
> The Corsair, or the Wandering Jew,
> And enigmatic Sbogar too.
> Lord Byron, his caprice succeeding,
> Cloaked even hopeless egotism
> In saturnine romanticism.[17]

Melmoth thus joins the ranks of notable romantic heroes, which range from the fictional to Lord Byron himself. At the novel's end, Onegin is left to wander onwards, the final scene providing no closure. The reader, too, is left wondering, "Who is Onegin?," just as Tatyana was left in the library with only the traces of Onegin's fingernails on his books to show who he might be.

Eugene Onegin is a metafictional work that reveals the narrative strategies that are calculated to make readers "feel." By incorporating gothic narrative in *Eugene Onegin* and engaging readers in "vicissitudes of terror," Pushkin thus follows Walpole's design. The so-called machinery of terror invites readers to transcend their own consciousness of the artificiality of reading fiction and feel afraid. As this fear is transmuted from a generalized fear of the unknown in Tatyana's dream to a more specific anxiety related to the horror of Onegin's lack of a true self, opportunities for genuine feeling are opened in the narrative's fabric, as per Walpole's formula.[18] In this sense, the gothic within the text functions similarly in the shift from the irony of Lensky's fledgling verses to the poetic authenticity of the narrator-poet's tribute to him after his death. Both examples represent deliberate systems of building and undermining strong feeling, which in turn serve as one method of infusing the narrative with vibrancy and urgency.

The Gothic Infection of Gogol's Wordscape

Dead Souls carries the subtitle *poema*, or narrative poem; Gogol's poem in prose thus declares from its title page that it is from the same lineage as Pushkin's novel in verse. Where Pushkin's novel demonstrates the virtuosity of the Onegin stanza, Gogol's novel privileges and showcases the Russian word in all its variety and forms. In *Dead Souls*, the word is potential. In the text, a tapestry of words generates a cacophony of images, a chaos that is controlled by the narrator's manipulation of words and the images they evoke. Arguably, Chichikov's journey is not one through the Russian landscape so much as it is through what I would call the Russian *wordscape*, the spatial plane generated through the system of vividly imagined words that serves as the text's setting. Gogol ends chapter 5 with a celebration of the word: "There is no word so sweeping, so bold, so torn from under the heart itself, so bubbling and quivering with life, as the aptly uttered Russian word."[19] Here the utterance of the word acts as a catalyst for a series of transmutations: the word becomes each of these actions as they are uttered by the narrator – sweeping, bold, torn out, bubbling, quivering. The word comes alive and undulates through this progression and it shimmers through the rest of the text.

In Gogol's text, words are liberated, breaking free of their prescribed functionality through their transfiguration. As Robert Maguire suggests, "Words are inadequate to the phenomena they purport to betoken."[20] The wordscape correlates to poetics, not to reality. Thus, the word is both the foundation of the text and its most unreliable formal aspect. Susanne Fusso has argued that Gogol's poetics are informed by two opposed desires: "the urge toward order, system, and clarity, and wholeness and the urge toward disorder, disruption, obscurity, and fragmentation."[21] The tension between these two urges is apparent in *Dead Souls* on a structural level, where the rogue word plays and transforms joyfully but chaotically, creating the narrative's wordscape, which is held in check through the text's formal architectonics. Because of the unreliability of its base element, the word, Gogol's novel has a tightly organized structure, which orders the reader's experience in the narrative.

The novel was modelled on Dante's *Divine Comedy* (1308–20) and planned in three parts, with part 1 serving as a metaphor for *Inferno*.[22] Subsequent volumes would ascend à la Dante through *Purgatorio* and into *Paradisio*; in the third volume, never written, Gogol planned to reveal a solution to Russia's problems. The first part of *Dead Souls* is thus structured in a way that mirrors the spatial configuration of Dante's narrative poem. *Inferno* chronicles the journey of Dante and his guide, the ghost of Virgil, into hell. Hell is laid out in nine concentric circles, each more terrible than the last, in which the souls of the damned are eternally tormented for progressively worse sins. As Sandro Botticelli's

Figure 1. Sandro Botticelli, *Chart of Hell* (1480–90).

Chart of Hell (1480–90) illustrates, Dante's hell is an inverted cone, with each concentric circle leading incrementally deeper down. *Dead Souls* also chronicles a journey, one in which Chichikov drives to a series of estates in the neighbourhood to buy deceased enserfed peasants (the dead souls of the title) as part of a scheme to pass himself off as wealthier than he is.

The novel is divided into eleven chapters, and following the first chapter, in which Chichikov arrives in the town of N, the subsequent five chapters each detail an estate visit. Just as Dante and Virgil encounter sinners whose faults are increasingly serious, Chichikov encounters a series of landowners who are each worse than the last. The frontispiece that Gogol designed for the novel's first edition (see figure 2 on p. 50) suggests the shape of Dante's hell as well. Here the face on the scroll at its base corresponds to the image of Satan in the lowest level of Botticelli's chart. In the centre of hell, Dante and Virgil encounter Satan frozen in a lake of ice, eternally gnawing on the three most offending sinners of all time: Judas, who betrayed Jesus, and Brutus and Cassius, who betrayed Julius Caesar. In the centre of *Dead Souls*, in chapter 6, is Plyushkin's estate. It is here, the last of the estates Chichikov visits, where the novel's vibrant wordscape becomes infected with the gothic.

As chapter 6 opens, the narrator meditates on the excitement of visiting an unknown estate. He asserts that it does not matter what kind of estate it is, as there are always pleasant surprises in store. The homes he imagines are different – one made of stone, one clad in whitewashed metal with a cupola on top, one with a red roof and white chimneys hidden behind leafy green trees – but all enticing in their own ways. He wonders whether the landowner is "a jovial sort" or whether he is "as gloomy as September in its final days."[23] The narrator's tone shifts as he concludes his commentary by reflecting, "Now I drive up, indifferent, to any unfamiliar estate, and I look, indifferent, at its ordinary exterior […] it offers no hospitality, I am not amused […] and my motionless lips preserve an apathetic silence."[24] He ends with a lament on his past youth. This long meditation on the potential of the visit raises both narrator and reader expectations, leading into Chichikov's arrival at the next estate. The narrator is transformed, through words, into his youthful self again, with excited anticipation at the visit. The reader understands two opposing scenarios: an exciting visit or an indifferent one. As the narrator describes Chichikov's arrival at Plyushkin's estate, both narrator and reader are confronted with a space that defies and undermines the expectations established by the preceding wordscape; as if to signal this disjunction, Chichikov is "compelled to take notice by a healthy jolt" as his *brichka* rolls over uneven logs paving the road.[25]

Plyushkin's estate is described in degrees, as Chichikov notices it. In this way, the gothic creeps into the narrative's wordscape incrementally. It is not a sudden leap but a gradual degeneration of the word from the vibrant utterance that ends chapter 5 to the moment when Plyushkin and Chichikov meet, in which words fail.

> Plyushkin had been standing for several minutes without uttering a single word, and Chichikov was still unable to initiate a conversation, distracted as he was by the appearance not only of the proprietor himself, but of everything in the room. For a long time he could not find words to explain the reason for his visit.[26]

This wordless scene interrupts the long descriptive passage that catalogs Chichikov's observations of Plyushkin's estate. This perusal takes

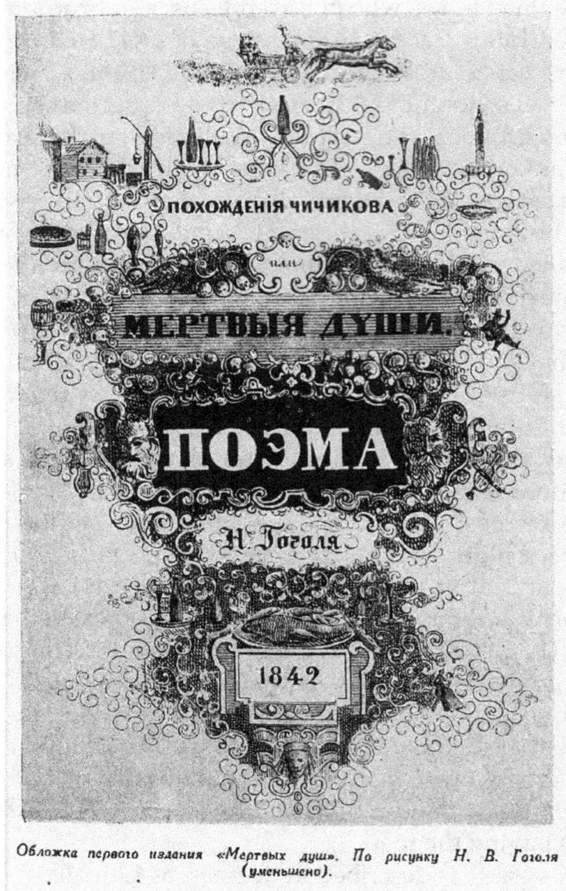

Обложка перваго изданія «Мертвых душ». По рисунку Н. В. Гоголя
(уменьшено).

Figure 2. The frontispiece for *Dead Souls, Part 1* from Gogol's
original drawings (1842).

in several vivid gothic images that are linked to specific affective cues
buried in the text's wordscape. Tracing the gothic images through the
web of references that occurs before and after them in the text reveals
an embedded and encoded web of signs and associations that trigger
an emotional response.

Chichikov first notices the dilapidated houses of the estate's peasants, "with beams that look like ribs" (в виде ребр).[27] The image of the
collapsing cottages stripped of materials by their own former inhabitants immediately dispels all of the narrator's illusions. These structures

suggest the decay of Plyushkin's estate, but Chichikov's observation of them comes between two other views of the estate: the functional estate, reflected in the narrator's introduction to the passage as how he would have imagined it in his youth, and the positive memory of the estate in its heyday, revealed in Plyushkin's backstory later in the chapter. Ever since the novel's initial publication, critics have argued that Plyushkin's miserliness is redeemed through this biographical discussion.[28] However, the positive image of the estate exposed in Plyushkin's biography is not the final image in the chain of linked images exposed by tracing the gothic language through the text's wordscape.

The description of the peasants' houses appears in the middle of a long paragraph that begins with Chichikov laughing to himself about the nickname the local workers call Plyushkin: "the patched ——." This name was introduced at the end of the previous chapter, but incompletely, its final indelicate noun omitted. In the same passage, however, Chichikov himself gives another epithet to Plyushkin: "the one who feeds his people so badly." The narrator's meditation on the power of the Russian word that concludes chapter 5 also includes the observation that "if [the Russian people] bestow a particular epithet on someone, it will become part of his lineage and posterity, he will drag it around with him into his place of work, and into his retirement, and to Petersburg, and to the ends of the earth."[29] On the estate, the houses "with beams that look like ribs" immediately evoke the skeletal – a corpse on the ground with an exposed ribcage. Tracing the textual clues back to the word's origin adds an additional layer of meaning. The cottages are empty and derelict because of starvation caused by Plyushkin's miserliness. This is the traumatic secret that lies buried behind the estate's various facades.

The second aspect of Plyushkin's estate that Chichikov notices is the manor house itself. As the house comes into view, wordplay transforms it: "Parts of the manor house began to show themselves […] This strange castle, which was long, inordinately long, looked like some disabled veteran who was on his last legs."[30] This "strange castle" (странный замок) has historically been the sole focus of discussions of gothic influence on Gogol's novel.[31] As Bakhtin discusses in his essay on time and the chronotope, the castle is a primary gothic convention. Bakhtin identifies the connection between the image, "the time of the historical past," "human relationships involving dynastic primacy and the transfer of hereditary rights," and "legends and traditions" that constantly remind readers of past events.[32] In Bakhtin's formulation, it is this last element, "legends and traditions" and their mimetic link to the past, that "gives rise to the specific kind of narrative […] that is then worked out in gothic novels."[33] Thus the chronotope of chapter 6, at this point in the narrative, takes on a gothic tinge by association, colouring readers' interpretation of Plyushkin, his estate, and what Chichikov will find there.

Yet the castle is not just a castle. The narrator's words are unreliable, and the shifting wordscape provides a stage between the decaying manor house as it appears to Chichikov and the strange castle, a "disabled veteran on his last legs" or *driakhlyi invalid* (дряхлый инвалид). The castle may be the outcome of this transformation, but its semantic connotations – derived from its prime place in gothic convention – immediately strike the reader. Tracing the transformation of *logos* across the novel's wordscape again emphasizes gothic mysteries. Why a decrepit veteran? Four convalescent veterans appear in the text: this one, the two minor characters in chapter 7, and Captain Kopeikin. Each adds a new facet to the narrative of banal evil that emerges from the wordscape after the gothic chronotope of chapter 6.

In chapter 7, Chichikov and Plyushkin are again united through their transaction when Chichikov projects imaginary past adventures onto the dead souls he has purchased. The two veterans appear in a lengthy episode in which Chichikov imagines the possible fate of Popov, one of Plyushkin's runaway peasants. The detail of Popov offering snuff to the two veterans who are fastening his leg irons when he is caught seems inconsequential, but it again emphasizes Plyushkin's and Chichikov's connection, as well as a connection to the "strange castle." Plyushkin enters the scene through Popov, and through the mention of the "invalid," Chichikov imagines the scene, and the snuff evokes the sneeze of his name.

The final "invalid" reference occurs when "The Tale of Captain Kopeikin" is recounted in chapter 10. "Captain Kopeikin" tells the story of a Napoleonic War veteran who has lost an arm and a leg and gets bogged down in bureaucracy in his efforts to gain recompense for his injuries. This penultimate chapter examines Chichikov's potential identities. He is paired with Kopeikin, and the townsfolk of N even suggest that Chichikov is actually Kopeikin in disguise. The townspeople imagine that Chichikov transforms into a forger of banknotes, an official of the governor general's chancellery, a disguised brigand, a man of violent behaviour, Captain Kopeikin, and Napoleon, who then becomes the Antichrist.[34] The episode connects Chichikov and Kopeikin, and – through the image of the *driakhlyi invalid* – Plyushkin as well.

Tracing these gothic word-image genealogies through the novel's wordscape reveals a significant relationship between the narrator, Chichikov, Kopeikin, and Plyushkin. In his investigation of the "demonic-picaresque mode" in the novel, Adam Weiner argues that Kopeikin,

Chichikov, and the narrator function together "as a kind of infernal triad."[35] Missing from this paradigm is Plyushkin, who sits in his castle at the centre of the novel, infecting its wordscape with gothic imagery. In discussing the role of the miser in *Dead Souls*, Jillian Porter concludes, "The old miser haunts the new man of money like a ghost."[36] Examining the gothic-infected wordscape that radiates out from the first meeting of Plyushkin and Chichikov, we can see that Plyushkin does not just haunt Chichikov transactionally, but also morally. Initially, Chichikov was the most morally repugnant character. In chapter 6, Plyushkin, who has starved his peasants out of miserliness, supplants him. Their transaction in the gothic chronotope means that Chichikov takes on the burden of Plyushkin's moral abyss, but by the end of the semantic chain, Chichikov's unrepentance makes him demonic, the Antichrist.

The word *driakhlyi* (дряхлый) appears twice in *Dead Souls* – in the description of Plyushkin's house and in the ensuing description of the gothic garden. This is the next stop on Chichikov's progress through Plyushkin's estate.

> In places green, sun-struck thickets parted to reveal a hollow between them, untouched by light and gaping like a dark maw; it was cast all in shadow, and its black depths afforded but the faintest glimpse of a coursing narrow path, the ruins of a railing, a tumbledown gazebo, the hollow, decayed [*driakhlyi*] trunk of a willow, and from behind the willow a grey thicket which thrust out a dense bristle of leaves and twigs, entangled and enmeshed, withered by the fearsome wild, and finally, the young branch of a maple that had stretched forth from one side its green paw-leaves, beneath one of which the sun had made its way, Lord knows how, and was turning it suddenly transparent and fiery, a wondrously shining thing in this thick darkness.[37]

The garden was once landscaped – evidenced by the path, ruins, and gazebo – but has since run wild. The shifting oppositions of light and darkness, youth and decay, thrusting out and being entangled create a chaos of imagery. The young branch, its leaf glowing in the fiery sunlight in spite of the gloom of the overgrown garden, contrasts with the hollow, decrepit trunk of the willow, which has been exhausted of life. As the passage continues, the space is described as "somehow desolate and splendid" (как-то пустынно-хорошо), neither natural nor artificial, but some hybrid of the two.[38] The ambivalence and indistinctiveness of the language here presents two paths forward through the wordscape: into the darkness or into the sublime. Each has an intertextual connection, the former with Dante's *Inferno*, the latter with the gothic novel.

Plyushkin's garden first provides a nodal link with *Inferno*. Canto 13 opens with the description of a forest:

> Nessus had not yet reached the other side
> When we made our way into a forest
> Not marked by any path.
>
> No green leaves, but those of dusky hue –
> Not a straight branch, but knotted and contorted –
> No fruit of any kind, but poisonous thorns.[39]

The forest of hell's Seventh Circle is characterized by only the gloomy aspects present in Plyushkin's garden. The hint of a path there becomes no path here. The contrasting green leaves of the maple become the dull decay of the willow. The protruding branches are gone; here only the knotted and contorted prevail. Through the intertextual node, following this path from Plyushkin's garden leads to suffering: poisonous thorns and, several stanzas later, tree branches that bleed when they are broken. In this part of the Seventh Circle, the cries of the suffering souls are heard but invisible, encased in the trees. Following this intertextual path, as Chichikov progresses forward from the garden towards Plyushkin, he becomes Dante travelling towards Satan.

This reading places Plyushkin at the centre of *Dead Souls*, its Lucifer trapped in an icy lake. Of all the horrors described on the journey into hell, the image of Satan is the most horrifying, described in a manner calculated to disgust.

> Out of six eyes he wept and his three chins
> Dripped tears and drooled blood-red saliva.
>
> With his teeth, just like a hackle
> Pounding flax, he champed a sinner
> in each mouth, tormenting three at once.
>
> For the one in front the gnawing was a trifle
> To the clawing, for from time to time
> His back was left with not a shred of skin.[40]

Similarly, when Plyushkin is described, he transforms into images calculated to evoke disgust: a grotesque protruding chin covered in spittle, eyes that become mice "thrusting their sharp little snouts from their dark holes."[41] While Satan appears in *Inferno* as an obvious symbol of evil, eternally gnawing on the worst sinners, Plyushkin's evil qualities are more banal, less visible. Where Satan's chins are wet with tears, drool, and blood, Plyushkin hides his chin under a handkerchief.

When Plyushkin and Chichikov meet, words fail. Yuri Mann describes moments like this in Gogol's works as the "poetics of petrification" and links this formula to a feeling of horror.[42] The moment of petrification in chapter 6 carries a link to the icy core of Dante's hell, in which Dante and Virgil stand frozen in horror just before encountering Satan frozen in the lake of ice.

> Then how faint and frozen I became,
> Reader, do not ask, for I do not write it,
> Since any words would fail to be enough.
>
> I did not die, nor did I stay alive.
> Imagine, if you have the wit,
> what I became, deprived of both.[43]

This phrasing, "I did not die, nor did I stay alive," resonates with the implication that Plyushkin is neither dead nor alive. The intertext here invites Gogol's reader to imagine what Chichikov might become after Plyushkin's gothic infects him.

The word "frozen" implies a lack of motion, but in both *Dead Souls* and *Inferno*, these scenes culminate in necessary motion. Just as Dante and Virgil must climb down to the frozen Satan in order to emerge out of hell and journey onward to purgatory, so too must Chichikov make a deal with Plyushkin in order to carry out his fraudulent scheme and move onwards, disentangling himself from Plyushkin's dilapidated estate and overgrown garden. In finalizing the transaction, however, Chichikov sets off on the path that transforms him within the word-scape first into Kopeikin, then Napoleon, and finally the Antichrist. Yuri Lotman argues that in *Dead Souls*, "evil is given not only in its pure form, but also in its insignificant forms."[44] His example is the transformation of Chichikov from Kopeikin into the Antichrist – a path that destroys the paradigm of the romantic villain, who could have been redeemed. At the end of Dante's journey is purgatory, where he has the chance to bathe in the River Lethe, lose his memories, gain salvation, and join Beatrice in paradise. Following the intertextual path onwards in *Dead Souls*, Kopeikin also bathes in the River Lethe at the end of "The Tale of Captain Kopeikin," but the word-propelled transforming Chichikov is not redeemed; rather, he continues on his evil path.

Plyushkin's garden offers an alternative path, however, through its gothic intertextuality. The garden description provides the most extended gothic passage in the text, reminiscent of descriptions of sublime nature in Ann Radcliffe's novels. Compare it with the following passage from *The Romance of the Forest* (1791).

> His chateau stood on the borders of a small lake that was almost environed by mountains of stupendous height, which, shooting into a variety of grotesque forms, composed a scenery singularly solemn and sublime. Dark woods, intermingled with bold projections of rock, sometimes barren, and sometimes covered with the purple bloom of wild flowers, impended over the lake, and were seen in the clear mirror of its waters. The wild and alpine heights which rose above were either crowned with perpetual snows, or exhibited tremendous crags and masses of solid rock, whose appearance was continually changing as the rays of light were variously reflected on their surface, and whose summits were often wrapt in impenetrable mists. Some cottages and hamlets, scattered on the margin of the lake, or seated in picturesque points of view on the rocks above, were the only objects that reminded the beholder of humanity. On the side of the lake, nearly opposite to the chateau, the mountains receded, and a long chain of alps was seen stretching in perspective. Their innumerable tints and shades, some veiled in blue mists, some tinged with rich purple, and others glittering in partial light, gave luxurious and magical colouring to the scene.[45]

Here the same oppositions of light and darkness, protrusion and valley, barrenness and growth exist, but the passage emphasizes the play of light, the reflection of water, the beauty of an array of jewel-like mists, mountains, and flowers. While Plyushkin's castle garden has just a single glow of sunlight through a leaf, the gothic chateau is surrounded by still more sublime landscapes. The only peaks surrounding Plyushkin's castle are the mountains of goods Plyushkin has hoarded, which rot and gather dust on his dormant estate. Yet in *Dead Souls* there are sublime mountains. They appear in chapter 11, in the narrator's celebration of the road as Chichikov flies along in the bird-troika towards the truth of his identity, away from N with its gothic infections and horrors and into the unknown future. In this sense, although the gothic chronotope of Plyushkin's castle infects the wordscape of the novel, the gothic intertext provides an alternative path and a possible escape, just as moments of the sublime add a sense of exhilaration and terror of the unknown in gothic narratives.

Alchemical Transmutation and Generic Hybridity

In its inception, the gothic was the product of generic mixing. Walpole reflected on his process of writing *The Castle of Otranto* in the preface to its second edition: "It was an attempt to blend the two kinds of Romance, the ancient and the modern";[46] that is, to create a work that fused the superstition, violence, adventure, and supernatural fantasy of the medieval romance with the eighteenth-century English novel set in the familiar and realistic present. The medieval setting was a key part of this formula: it enabled the author to draw on "miracles, visions, necromancy, dreams, and other preternatural events," which he saw as absent from contemporary fiction but embedded in both the literature of the past and the beliefs associated with it (for example, Catholic mysticism).[47] The formalist critic Yuri Tynianov observed that "the sensation of form is always the sensation of the flow (and, consequently, of the alteration) of correlation between the subordinating, constructive factor and the subordinated factors [...] Art lives by means of this interaction and struggle."[48] Tynianov's view of form is a dialectical one, but he argued that although these elements may be hierarchical in nature, the ordering of that hierarchy remains in flux in the literary work, able to shift, mutate, and transform. In this sense, generic mixing can forge new literary forms, and this kind of hybridity is characteristic of Russian works published before the 1850s, the decade that marked the rise of the novel.

Eugene Onegin and *Dead Souls* are not gothic novels. They are, rather, novels that draw from the gothic tradition. As this chapter has demonstrated, gothic borrowing not only changes them on a formal level, it also provides clues to solve textual mysteries and to derive additional layers of meaning. The midnight chase and gloomy castle are steeped in gothic convention and cliché, but in Pushkin and Gogol's novels, these tropes are transmuted. In this alchemical equation, gothic narrative and novelistic form are combined, and as they merge, gothic becomes part of the fabric of the developing Russian novel.

Chapter Three

Russian Landscapes in a Gothic Frame

The moist earth springs up under your feet;
The tall dry blades of grass are silent [...]
And a strange anxiety enters your soul.

Ivan Turgenev, "Forest and Steppe," 1849

Many works written in the 1840s demonstrate their authors' efforts to work out new literary techniques for representing life with verisimilitude. As Elizabeth Cheresh Allen, analysing the narration in Ivan Turgenev's prose cycle *Sketches from a Hunter's Album* (*Zapiski okhotnika*, 1852), notes: "[Turgenev's narrator] is not merely hunting for game, or even simply hunting for new experiences, but [...] hunting for a manner of *narrating*, that is, for a way to comprehend and communicate those experiences."[1] While this statement specifically refers to Turgenev, it essentially applies to nearly all works from this period. Early realist writers relied on devices drawn from older generic models such as romanticism, sentimentalism, and the gothic to "pass the facts of reality through [their] imagination[s] and imbue them with new life," as Vissarion Belinsky observes.[2] The narrative framing device was one such useful tool in early realist works.

A framing device is the incorporation of a story that serves predominately as a vehicle for another, primary narrative. In Alexander Pushkin's *Tales of the Late Ivan Petrovich Belkin* (*Povesti pokoinogo Ivana Petrovicha Belkina*, 1831), for example, the five tales are accompanied by a fictional editorial note, which serves as the framing device. This note explains that Belkin was a secretive landowner who enjoyed collecting stories, and that the stories presented were ones told to him. In each story, then, the origin of the tale is recounted, which lends a sense of authenticity. In "The Shot" ("Vystrel"), a romantic story about a deferred duel and a mysterious character called Silvio, for example, the reader learns that the story was told to Belkin by I.L.P., a colonel who had been stationed near Silvio many years before. This framing device connects all the stories in the collection, which would have otherwise seemed somewhat arbitrary.

In gothic fiction, framing devices are particularly important. Clayton Carlyle Tarr observes that they "blur narrative and cognitive boundaries, producing a destabilizing effect that challenges rational epistemology and suggests a deeper 'reality' than the realist novel can possibly achieve."[3] Tarr's study examines the way framing devices function in gothic fiction to anchor the text's gothic core to the reader's reality, "draw[ing] out the horror of the diegetic tale and plac[ing] it systematically closer to the everyday world of the reader that the editor inhabits."[4] In gothic fiction, narrative frames are not just boundaries but also thresholds that create a conduit between the external, real world and the interior, gothic narrative, which tends to eschew realism.

In this chapter, I consider the way early realist writers used gothic framing devices to create narrative spaces that enhance the realism of their texts. First, I examine Ivan Goncharov's sketch "Oblomov's Dream" ("Son Oblomova," 1849), and then I turn to Turgenev's sketches "Bezhin Lea" ("Bezhin lug," 1851) and "Loner" ("Biriuk," 1848). Gothic framing devices are employed to different effects in these three works, but their function is similar across all three. While chapter 2 examined gothic narrative techniques intended to engage the reader on a deep emotional level, the gothic frames I discuss here create a sense of distance between the reader and the narrative. This distance provides a narrative space in which new meanings can be grafted onto the core text's verisimilitude and in which new impressions can emerge from what at first might seem like a depiction of mundane daily life.

Oblomov's Nightmare

"Oblomov's Dream" is a sketch that describes Oblomovka, protagonist Ilya Oblomov's childhood estate, in a framed dream narrative. The dream was published first in 1849 as a stand-alone sketch, and then again in 1859 as part of the novel *Oblomov*. There are two competing voices in the dream. First, an ironic narrator who pokes fun at Oblomov and existence in Oblomovka. Second, Oblomov himself, the dreamer who idealizes his childhood and his family. The frame is entirely narrated by the first voice.

The first-person narrator describes Oblomovka for the reader first in terms of what it is not:

> Where are we? In what blessed little corner of the earth has Oblomov's dream transferred us? What a lovely spot! It is true there is no sea there, no high mountains, cliffs or precipices, no virgin forests – nothing grand, gloomy, and wild.[5]

These opening lines are only one example of a phenomenon that occurs multiple times in the dream when the narrator clearly differentiates his landscape from that which his reader may be expecting. In provincial European Russia, a flat, bucolic, and pastoral region, there is no expectation of a grandiose, wild, or menacing landscape. The irony of the difference between the landscape of the everyday (*byt*) and a more exotic romantic landscape creates humour. But then we must ask, why frame the dream in this way? Is irony the only goal? Christopher Ely has observed that, particularly during the 1840s, the view of the Russian countryside that rose to national prominence "made a virtue of its would-be deficiency […] The very lack of picturesque scenery […] became a prized attribute of Russia's national landscape."[6] "Oblomov's Dream" may be part of this trend, but in its use of gothic framing devices, landscape becomes more complicated.

The narrator's descriptions of this non-landscape suggest a gothic landscape through absence. Ann Radcliffe's *Mysteries of Udolpho* (1794) includes a typical gothic landscape description:

> Leaving the splendour of extensive prospects, they now entered this
> narrow valley screened by
> *Rocks on rocks piled, as if by magic spell,*
> *Here scorch'd by lightnings, there with ivy green.*
> The scene of barrenness was here and there interrupted by the spreading
> branches of the larch and cedar, which threw their gloom over the cliff,
> or athwart the torrent that rolled in the vale. No living creature appeared,
> except the lizard, scrambling among the rocks, and often hanging upon
> points so dangerous, that fancy shrunk from the view of them.
> This was such a scene as SALVATOR would have chosen, had he then existed,
> for his canvas; St. Aubert, impressed by the romantic character of the place,
> almost expected to see banditti start from behind some projecting rock,
> and he kept his hand upon the arms with which he always travelled.[7]

Comparing a gothic description like this to the landscape described in "Oblomov's Dream," we can see that the gothic informs

Goncharov's idyll. The narrator ostensibly denies any connection between Oblomovka and gothically charged space, but he nonetheless evokes a specifically gothic landscape in describing what Oblomov's dream's setting is *not*. The underlying anti-pastoral casts its shadow over the idyllic Oblomovka that the narrator describes in such detail. The dream's gothic narrative frame serves to undermine and ironicize its pastoral idyll, but I argue that it serves an additional purpose: it introduces a negative Oblomovka, an anti-pastoral threat, into the reader's imagination. In "Oblomov's Dream," this gothic frame enables a deeper realist vision. In differentiating his pastoral landscape from the romantic vistas that his reader may be expecting, Goncharov not only establishes the imagined landscape of Oblomov's estate for his reader but also plants the thought of another, more dangerous and gloomy landscape in the reader's mind, an *anti-pastoral* setting that essentially links the work to the gothic tradition.

What is the nature of the gothic frame? In every subsequent landscape description that follows within the dream, the imagined wild landscape appears in detail, although the narrator is careful to specify that this terrain is *not* present in Oblomovka. Take the following passage, for example:

> But what is the good of the grand and wild? The sea, for instance? Let it stay where it is! It merely makes you melancholy: looking at it, you feel like crying. The heart quails at the sight of the boundless expanse of water, and the eyes grow tired of the endless monotony of the scene. The roaring and the wild pounding of the waves do not caress your feeble ears; they go on repeating their old, old song, gloomy and mysterious, the same since the world began; and the same old moaning is heard in it, the same complaints as though of a monster condemned to torture, and piercing sinister voices. No birds twitter around; only silent sea-gulls like doomed creatures, mournfully fly to and fro near the coast and circle over the water.[8]

Here gothic elements abound, from the fearful reaction of the observer ("The heart quails at the sight") to the anxiety that pervades the scene. Anxiety is implicit in the imagined soundscape of the sea, which includes not only the "gloomy and mysterious" song but also moaning, a tortured monster's cries, and "sinister voices." In this seascape, even the gulls are "doomed" and "mournful." This lexicon projects gothic emotions onto the landscape: anxiety, trepidation, and fear.

These anti-pastoral landscapes are gothic, not simply romantic. To differentiate between a romantic seascape and Goncharov's gloomy and violent seascape, one need only compare it to another romantic

seascape depiction, one that is not influenced by the gothic. In this
excerpt from a poem by Fyodor Tyutchev, for example, we see all the
passion of a romantic seascape but none of the gothic elements that
characterize Goncharov's imagined seascape.

> Как хорошо ты, о море ночное, –
> Здесь лучезарно, там сизо-темно …
> В лунном сиянии, словно живое,
> Ходит, и дышит, и блещет оно …
>
> На бесконечном, на вольном просторе
> Блеск и движение, грохот и гром …
> Тусклым сияньем облитое море,
> Как хорошо ты в безлюдье ночном![9]

> (How wonderful you are, o night sea,– / Here radiant,
> there slate gray … / In the moonlight, as though alive, /
> you shimmer, and breathe, and shine … /
> On an infinite, uninhibited expanse / Shine and
> movement, rumble and thunder … / A sea bathed
> in dim radiance, / How wonderful you are
> in nocturnal solitude!)

The poetic voice contrasts the sea's radiance with its dullness. It anthro-
pomorphizes the sea, but the sea also thunders and rumbles. Although
similar in content to Goncharov's seascape, in Tyutchev's poem, the
narrator revels in the sea's splendour. The elements that characterize
Goncharov's seascape are absent.

   In juxtaposing a gothic landscape, with its psychological connotations, to the pastoral, sleepy setting of Oblomov's dream, Goncharov
decisively informs his reader that the Russian landscape depicted in
his novel is not picturesque, neither in the eighteenth-century sense
nor in the romantic sense. While these passages serve to introduce the
idyllic world of Oblomov's childhood, they also set a sharp contrast
between what the reader expects in an idyll (based on eighteenth-
century modes) and what is, in fact, depicted in the dream. Furthermore, evoking this violent landscape in such a vivid way before shifting to the bucolic depictions of Oblomov's dream nonetheless leaves an
implicit association of violence and transgression with the reader. By
associating the hyperbolic descriptions of the countryside – filled with
beautiful produce and livestock, happy peasants, rolling hills, sparkling
waters – with the anxiety-filled gothic landscape, Goncharov meditates
on the look and experience of the Russian landscape without resorting to

earlier pastoral modes.[10] However, in depicting Oblomovka, Goncharov paints a picture of a society where there is no need for action or even planning; every task is done for the estate family by enserfed peasants.

"Oblomov's Dream," which depicts a comfortable but dull life on the family estate, has been the subject of discussion since its publication. Many scholarly readings of the dream examine its historical basis as a critique of serfdom and stagnation, but I am more interested in a line of scholarship analysing the dream's temporal dimension. Dmitry Likhachev was the first to identify the temporal changes in Oblomov's dream, and Christine Borowec's work builds on his analysis. Likhachev observes that "Oblomov's Dream" is "not a story about what was [было], but about what existed [бывало], happened, and perhaps continues somewhere."[11] The overwhelming feature of the village and surrounding fields, which the narrator moves on to describe, is their lack of vibrancy, their continuity. Borowec argues that the temporal ideology of Oblomov's dream and dreaming elsewhere in the novel *Oblomov* is cyclical. She writes, "His dream, centering on his past, affords him no future that is not also a part of his past."[12] In this sense, while the chronicle time of the dream connects with an ahistorical past, the dream also represents entrapment. Life there is calm, until finally death comes like sleep – no different than the sleepiness of daily life. As Likhachev writes, "Oblomov doesn't sleep – nature sleeps, Oblomovka sleeps, daily existence [быт] sleeps."[13]

This deadly languor is everywhere: from the babbling brooks that lull one to peaceful sleep to the variations in weather patterns that all seem to induce perpetual napping. The village itself is described as sleepy, the fields as peaceful and profoundly silent. Everything, while idyllic, is referred to in terms associated with death. As such, Oblomov's dream is not just a meditation on a child's life in the Russian countryside but also begins to take on a new guise, becoming, as Amy Singleton puts it, "an anxiety-provoking land of the dead."[14] The dream becomes a nightmare. Oblomov's nightmare points to the stagnation of the Russian countryside, and by extension its people, revealing a landscape described by what it is not and containing only stagnation and lifelessness.

When Likhachev links temporal slowness to dreaming in the novel, he concludes, "Thus the realist relationship to artistic time went far afield from the naturalist time of the physiological sketch, and, similarly, from the real time of didactic literature of medieval Rus."[15] The gothic, however, is tied to a specific historical timeline, even though gothic novels may include a timeless quality, as when, for example, a heroine becomes trapped in a labyrinthine castle. Ideologically, gothic novels always emphasize forward motion, the progress of time.

In framing Oblomovka with an imagined gothic landscape, even ironically so, Goncharov creates a narrative temporal vortex in which two timelines simultaneously exist – one pastoral, one anti-pastoral – and influence the reader's understanding of the text. For the reader of Goncharov's novel, the potential exists for the Oblomov family to be cursed, the landscape to be haunted, and the dream to be a nightmare.

Independently, "Oblomov's Dream" also provides a glimpse into life on a Russian estate, framing its depiction with hints of the gothic. In the larger context of the novel *Oblomov*, the chapter is, at times, called the core of the novel. It serves to explain the origin of the title character's passivity and psychological hesitation, providing a background for these behaviours. The chapter implies not only that *oblomovshchina*, or oblomovism – an idea that sparked great debate in the later part of the nineteenth century – stems from inherent traits. It also implies that these traits originate in a landscape that is fundamentally lacking in vibrancy, in life, and (by extension) in momentum. In using gothic landscape depictions to stage Oblomov's dream, Goncharov is able to emphasize this perceived flaw more pointedly and attach a sense of unease to it, immediately casting Oblomov's lifestyle in an ambiguous light elsewhere in the text. Goncharov's gothic framing device gives the reader a negative association that conflicts directly with the positive descriptions of happiness, family, and coziness that typically inform Oblomov's daydreaming. Similarly, Turgenev's sketches showcase the way that gothic frames can be used to exploit the evocation of negative emotions such as fear, dread, and anxiety to assert social critique.

Sketches from a Gothic Wanderer's Album

Perhaps the most famous rural landscape descriptions of the 1840s and 1850s appear in Turgenev's *Sketches from a Hunter's Album*. During their serial publication in the journal *The Contemporary* between 1847 and 1850, Turgenev's *Sketches* received great critical acclaim, especially as Belinsky and his circle saw in them a new voice for social criticism. Turgenev's depictions celebrate the Russian countryside's natural beauty, and the work consists of equal parts lyric effusions describing landscapes and sociological commentary on the characters encountered by the narrator in his travels. German idealism heavily influenced Turgenev's earliest writing, which was in verse, and this lyrical sensibility comes to the fore in the *Sketches*.[16] "Bezhin Lea," for example, begins with a description emphasizing the beauty of natural elements: a meditation on the sun rising from behind a cloud, a comparison of clouds in a blue sky to islands in a flooded river, and a lyrical sunset depiction.[17] Nonetheless, the gothic intrudes at key moments in the *Sketches*.

The few gothic moments in the cycle seem at odds with the narrator's typical descriptive tone. These intervals demonstrate how writers used gothic conventions to create a new, realist aesthetic. As "Bezhin Lea" continues, night falls and the narrator realizes that he is lost. The surrounding landscape description becomes harsher and less lyrical: "I saw completely different places which were unknown to me. At my feet there stretched a narrow valley; directly ahead of me rose, like a steep wall, a dense aspen wood."[18] The narrator feels physically trapped by this topography, and his relationship to its individual natural elements also changes: "The tall, thick grass on the floor of the valley was all wet and shone white like a smooth tablecloth; it felt clammy and horrible to walk through."[19]

As the narrator becomes increasingly uncomfortable in the setting, the night noises that seem so explicable and common in other stories, such as birds calling or bats crying, become "mysterious." The entire landscape is transformed by the narrator's feelings:

> Meanwhile, night was approaching and rose around me like a thunder cloud; it was as if, in company with the evening mists, darkness rose on every side and even poured down from the sky [...] Everything quickly grew silent and dark; only quail gave occasional cries. A small night bird, which hurried low and soundlessly along on its soft wings, almost collided with me and plunged off in terror [...] It was only with difficulty that I could make out distant objects. All around me the field glimmered faintly; beyond it, coming closer each moment, the sullen murk loomed in huge clouds.[20]

The transformation itself is not unexpected: the narrator's feelings and moods constantly shape the landscape in the *Sketches*. Turgenev uses this description to influence his reader's feelings here as well: as the narrator feels lost and frightened, so, too, the reader – used to picking up on gothic cues in popular fiction – begins to feel anxious for the narrator. The terrified animals, sudden surrounding darkness, and looming "sullen murk" all promote this heightened anxiety.

Further on in the passage, the narrator looks to his hunting dog for comfort, but even this familiar creature serves only to discomfit him. The depicted landscape shows how the narrator's fears intensify:

> I felt ill at ease in front of her and strode wildly forward, as if I had suddenly realized which way to go, circled the knoll and found myself in a

shallow hollow which had been plowed over. A strange feeling took pos-
session of me. The hollow had the almost exact appearance of a cauldron
with sloping sides. Several large upright stones stood in the floor of the
hollow – it seemed as if they had crept down to that spot for some mysterious consultation – and the hollow itself was so still and silent, the sky
above it so flat and dismal that my heart shrank within me.[21]

The narrator's impression that the landscape participates in some mysterious, dark meeting clearly derives from the fear he feels. The passage
serves to emphasize further the gothic elements in the earlier passage
and to distance this unfamiliar landscape from the objective, known
countryside described in the story's opening. This part, however, is
mainly introductory. The narrator's experiences while lost in the woods
frame the sketch's core.

Lost in this environment, the narrator stumbles across the cheerful
sight of a group of peasant boys exchanging stories around a camp-
fire. Turgenev specifically juxtaposes the frame with the boys' tales,
contrasting the traveller-narrator's literary language with the peasants' folkloric narratives. As he tells their stories back to his reader, he
reveals the complicated web of folk and Christian beliefs that informs
their world view. Kostya tells of a village carpenter in the forest who
encounters a *rusalka*, a folkloric female spirit who lures men to their
deaths, and saves himself from drowning by crossing himself. Fedya
recounts the tale of a discontented squire who haunts a nearby village
after his death. Each of the stories has elements of fear related to the
contemplation of death, but only Ilyusha's stories evoke real fear in the
boys. Ilyusha shares his terrifying encounter with a goblin or possibly a
demon, then later tells of a mysterious demonic lamb that appeared on
a drowned man's grave. In these tales, the supernatural is mysterious
and lies outside of the boys' well-ordered belief system. By contrast,
in Kostya's tale, the carpenter encounters a *rusalka* but is able to save
himself through ritual. In Fedya's tale, the squire's death and ghostly
afterlife seem natural and the spectral squire benign, discontented in
death as he was in life. Ilyusha's tales, in engaging with elements that
go beyond the conventions of folk belief, show the boundaries of the
peasants' belief system and the terror that the inexplicable evokes.

For the boys, the spirit world has its rules and explanations, just
like the material world. Ilyusha frames the story of his grandmother's
death omen with the explanation that "you can see dead people at any
time [...] but on Parents' Sunday you can also see the people who're
going to die that year."[22] Within this frame, his tale of real deaths foretold is accepted by the boys; his grandmother's encounter with her

own foretold death merely elicits the remark that her death has not yet come to pass. Similarly, when Pavlusha reports that he has just heard a drowned boy calling his name from a nearby river, the boys take it as an omen. Rather than reacting with fear, Pavlusha "declare[s] resolutely" that "you can't escape your own fate."[23] In this belief system, death is a transitional process that separates life and afterlife, one mapped through experience, the other through ritual.

A later exchange similarly and more explicitly exposes the fluid boundaries between the spirit world and the boys' world. It also highlights the tension between the sketch's gothic frame and folkloric core. The boys hear a sudden noise, which is described as "strange, sharp, sickening" (странный, резкий, болезненный).[24] Kostya fears the unknown sound, while Pavlusha calmly identifies it as a heron's cry. This prompts Kostya to tell a story:

> So, mates, I walked past this tarn an' suddenly someone starts makin' a groanin' sound from right inside it, so piteous, piteous, like: Oooh – oooh … oooh – oooh! I was terrified, mates. It was late an' that voice sounded like somebody really sick. It was like I was goin' to start cryin' myself … What would that have been, eh?[25]

Kostya's colloquial description of his terror at encountering an unfamiliar and unidentifiable sound recalls the narrator's gothic descriptions of the forest at night that introduce the boys' stories. There, however, the literary gothic descriptions play to the readers' expectations, reflecting the narrator's fear and dread, whereas here Kostya's story relates a gothic trope in colloquial, somewhat jovial speech. Both gothic and colloquial descriptions emphasize aspects of the psychology of fear, but Turgenev's reader, attuned to gothic convention, recognizes that fear as a result of the narrator's description. Kostya's account discloses his fear, but in mimicking the heron's cry becomes almost comical. The scene continues:

> "The summer before last, thieves drowned Akim the forester in that tarn," Pavlusha remarked. "So it may have been his soul complaining."
>
> "Well, it might be that, mates," rejoined [Kostya], widening his already enormous eyes. "I didn't know that Akim had been drowned in that tarn. If I'd known, I wouldn't have got so terrified."[26]

The subsequent discussion, in which the boys suggest both natural (frogs) and supernatural (wood demon) causes for the sound, shows that in their world, the supernatural is natural. Pavlusha's calm identification of the unfortunate Akim's soul complaining and Kostya's reply, "If I'd known, I wouldn't have got so terrified," underscores this belief structure. While within the bounds of the gothic, a tarn haunted by a drowned man would be a catalyst for dread, for the boys it is a natural explanation for a frightening sound, like frogs or wood demons.

The narrator's tendency to delve into a gothic mode of description frames the boys' stories. Ultimately, the gothic mode gives a fatalistic, frightening context to Pavlusha's foretold death when he concludes the story with the note, "I have, unfortunately, to add that in the same year Pavlusha died," and with prosaic details about his demise.[27] Pavlusha's reaction to hearing his name called by a drowned boy seems nearly ambivalent, an acceptance of his fate; this type of omen is an aspect of peasant belief, at least in Turgenev's depiction. Mark Simpson argues that Pavlusha acts as a gothic hero, "a kind of Melmoth, a sign of the dangers inherent in skepticism." "Only the Gothic hero," Simpson notes, "aims to explain the many unknowns and the many fears which confront us."[28] While Simpson's reading identifies this boy as a gothic hero, surely the narrator, as voyeuristic observer, more directly embodies this role. The narrator contextualizes Pavlusha's words and the boys' beliefs. His nocturnal explorations enhance the sketch's gothic atmosphere. And ultimately, the narrator's description of Pavlusha's untimely death gives the sketch its fatalistic connotations.

Even though the narrator's addendum to the sketch adds an element from everyday life that disrupts the gothic and folkloric modes of narration, the sketch's gothic frame leaves the reader feeling uneasy. Within a realist framework, the boundaries between life and death are clearly delineated, but the gothic frame emphasizes dread and mystery and hints at the possibility that Pavlusha's death omen may have a basis in reality. The gothic framing device brings the peasants' belief system into the bounds of a realist structure. In this way, Turgenev legitimizes a belief system that perhaps offers a more comforting view of death than his own positivist and materialist views allowed. For the peasants, death is merely another facet of life, entrance into a world that exists parallel to – and at times overlaps with – ours, whereas Turgenev viewed death as a definitive end, a state of non-existence.

In many of Turgenev's other sketches, the narrator depicts death or danger matter-of-factly – reinforcing the idea that these extraordinary moments are just another aspect of life. For example, in "Farmer Ovsyannikov" ("Odnodvorets Ovsiannikov"), when a group of peasants tries to drown a teenaged French soldier by forcing him to jump into a hole in an iced-over lake, the narrator depicts the event without fanfare, although peasant mobs do not attempt to kill Frenchmen on a daily basis. In the story "Death" ("Smert'"), the narrator describes a contractor's death and compares it to a forest's death. The narrator sees both events as "natural," even though the contractor, Maksym, dies as a result of an untimely accident. In "Forest and Steppe" ("Les i step'"), the final story in the collection, the narrator meditates on life:

> In the meantime there come to mind beloved images, beloved faces, the living and the dead, and long-since dormant impressions unexpectedly awaken; the imagination soars and dwells on the air like a bird, and everything springs into movement with such clarity and stands before the eyes [...] The whole of life unrolls easily and swiftly like a scroll; a man has possession of his whole past, all his feelings, all his powers, his entire soul.[29]

Death, here, is simply a part of the cycle. Everyone eventually experiences it as part of the whole of life.

Furthermore, events elsewhere in the cycle that one would expect to be conflated with gothic exaggeration or anxiety are also described matter-of-factly and can almost be brushed aside. In "Chertopkhanov and Nedopyuskin," the narrator describes a dilapidated farm but glosses over a pack of mangy dogs ripping apart a horse carcass behind the barn. In "My Neighbour Radilov" ("Moi sosed Radilov"), the titular character describes his wife's death in detail, right down to the flies walking over her open eyes. This incident becomes merely another detail of Radilov's description, however. Radilov is appropriately horrified, but the narrator offers no reaction:

> "Suddenly I saw ..." (At this point Radilov shuddered.) "What d'you think? One of her eyes wasn't completely shut and over this a fly was walking ... I collapsed [...]" Radilov stopped. I looked at him and then at Olga and I'll never forget the expression on her face.[30]

The narrator does not describe the expression on Olga's face. Clearly both Radilov and Olga respond viscerally to this memory, but the narrator's reaction remains unknown. Even ruminations on life's transience, sure to bring about reveries in the sense of a *memento mori* in gothic novels, are treated as mere episodes. The narrator, coming upon gravestones in the story "Lgov," claims that he has fallen into "reflections" but only describes the graves and their inscriptions for the reader, without embellishment or lyrical tangent.

Whereas the narrator takes care to underscore death's ordinariness elsewhere, in "Bezhin Lea," he accentuates its mystery and extraordinariness. Although peasants in other sketches accept death as simply a part of life, the narrator of "Bezhin Lea" portrays the peasants more spiritually: they do not see death as an end, but they also do not fully understand it. Their *dvoeverie* – mixture of pagan and Orthodox beliefs – helps them explain the unknown and irrational aspects of life, as the boys demonstrate with their stories.

Turgenev, seeking to describe the peasants' entire world, cannot omit an element as important as their belief system, but he frames it carefully so that his readership can understand it without condescension. To this end, he uses gothic motifs. The irrational fears of the narrator, lost in the woods at night, precede the boys' irrational fears, which prompt their stories about foretold deaths, ghosts, and place spirits. Relying on his readership's familiarity with gothic conventions, Turgenev exploits them to foreground the peasants' complex beliefs about death and afterlife. This technique bridges the divide between the upper classes reading these sketches and the peasants, who are the sketches' subjects.

"Loner" ("Biriuk"), another sketch in the collection, evokes the gothic in a similar way. The gothic mode appears almost immediately in this sketch, as the narrator describes a storm. Elsewhere in the *Sketches*, the narrator describes storms simply as natural phenomena to be enjoyed, as in "Forest and Steppe," for example. The description of a fierce gathering storm in "Loner," however, differentiates the story from others in the collection:

> A thunderstorm was threatening. Straight ahead an enormous lilac cloud rose slowly beyond the forest and long grey lengths of cloud hung above me and stretched towards me. The willows rustled and murmured in alarm. The muggy heat was suddenly replaced by moist cool air and the shadows thickened [...] A strong wind suddenly began roaring on high, the trees began thrashing about, huge raindrops started pounding sharply on the leaves and splashing over them, lightning flashed and thunder exploded [...] [S]uddenly by the light of a lightning flash I thought I saw a tall figure on the road. I began looking intently in that direction and saw that the figure had literally sprung from the earth just beside my droshky.[31]

The storm's violence in this description has two functions. It terrorizes both the narrator ("long grey lengths of cloud hung above me and stretched towards me") and the landscape itself ("The willows rustled and murmured in alarm"). Drawing on this terror, the description provides a memorable introduction for the forester called "Biryuk," or "lone wolf," as he suddenly and mysteriously seems to materialize out of nowhere.

Jane Costlow identifies "Loner" as a quintessentially gothic tale, pointing to this passage as an initial indicator to the reader that the gothic is at work: "[Here] Turgenev takes the gothic as his point of departure – working from the almost hackneyed landscape of the opening to the more complex moral structure of the ending."[32] Costlow interprets Biryuk as a throwback to Slavic folklore figures such as the *leshii*, the often violent and vengeful forest spirit. According to Costlow, this allusion implies that "the order of modernity is always threatening to slip back into an anarchic and violent past, in which passions – rather than reason – rule the day."[33] While Costlow's reading highlights elements clearly at work here – for example, the underlying violence that Biryuk symbolizes in his role as forest regulator – it does not fully explain why this description seems gothic. After all, violence and justice are themes that run throughout Russian folklore – from the legend of the *bannik*, the bath house spirit, who, when his rules are violated, steams offenders to death or flays them alive with his claws, to the *polevik*, the field spirit, who punishes those who sleep in the fields by giving them diseases or trampling them with his horse.[34]

In fact, "Loner" describes an untenable cycle of transgression, a key concept in gothic texts. Biryuk is a loner because he is a peasant who sides with the landowner when carrying out his duties. In punishing and reporting those who illegally fell wood, he threatens the abjectly poor peasants who live nearby. However, if the forester were to sympathize with the peasants, his peer group, he would shirk his responsibility towards the landowner. Ostracized either way, Biryuk himself becomes a symbol of society's transgressions against the lower classes. He represents both the oppressive policies of the upper classes and the harsh social conditions that require him to injure his own people simply to assure his small family's livelihood.

The initial landscape description serves to frame this sense of transgression for the reader. The threat felt by both the narrator and the "alarmed" willows sets the stage for Biryuk's entrance, evoking the gothic in such a way that the reader associates the forester with its dark heroes – Melmoth, or Matthew Lewis's monk Ambrosio – who appear in similar fashion. Biryuk, materializing suddenly as though conjured from the threatening storm, seems wrapped in an aura of unnatural and transgressive events from the sketch's outset. "Loner" thus serves not only as a meditation on the violence inherent in the feudal system but also as a means of underscoring particular problems within the system. By using a gothic frame to alert his reader to the sketch's underlying genre, Turgenev covertly suggests that something is awry with the situation his narrator encounters.

Because an important defining feature of the gothic mode is its connection to transgression, although the narrator does not name any specific transgression in the sketch, the gothic's use implies a moral wrong. These gothic elements provoke a strong reaction from the reader attuned to them, allowing Turgenev to convey his social criticism within a sketch that merely describes an encounter between a forester and the narrator. In using gothic tropes, Turgenev's narrator invokes gothic transgressions, highlighting the psychological and sociological implications of a realist landscape that is much more complex than a simple depiction of trees and fields.

Gothic Migrations into the Realist Text

Typically linked to a very specific landscape characterized by crumbling castles, gloomy forests, wildernesses, and oppressive mountains, the gothic takes its descriptive cues from its protagonists' anxieties and fears. While "the city, a gloomy forest or dark labyrinth […] became a site of nocturnal corruption and violence, a locus of real horror,"[35] writers also used these locales as reflectors of the corruption, violence, and horror already present in society. Writers like Turgenev and Goncharov who focused on the Russian countryside strove to find ways to depict landscape without relying on "picturesque" models. For them, gothic frames provided a tool to exploit the reader's assumptions, establishing a perspective that was deliberately distanced from the reader and yet provided the reader with an additional layer of information to understand characters or situations. In accommodating the hyperbolic language and extreme moods of the gothic in their writing, early realist authors continued the work done by Pushkin, Gogol, and others to translate the genre into the Russian literary language. More importantly, these early realists effectively embedded gothic within literary realism.

Goncharov and Turgenev were not alone in their use of gothic framing narratives. "Oblomov's Dream" was published in 1849, at the end of a decade that saw the rise of the naturalist physiological sketch and a shift away from romanticism. Chapter 5 of this study will analyse gothic framing narratives in urban physiological sketches of the 1840s and the ways realist writers used them to expose moral wrongs and social injustices to their readership. During the 1840s, gothic realism emerged as a method of addressing perceived social ills such as poverty, injustice, squalor, and domestic abuse. How gothic realism migrated into the novel's structure and why gothic narrative force held such attraction for realist writers is the topic of the next chapter.

Chapter Four

The Idiot: Dostoevsky's Gothic Novel

Like a bat, some trouble is hovering;
and I'm afraid, afraid!

Fyodor Dostoevsky, *The Idiot*

"The gothic novel is a cohesive [целостная] and well-structured system," states Vadim Vatsuro in his posthumous study of the gothic novel's inception and reception in Russia.[1] By contrast, Fyodor Dostoevsky's 1869 novel *The Idiot* is considered one of the author's messiest. The novel's plan was thrown out multiple times. It was already being serialized when Dostoevsky changed course, and as a result, in part 2, some characters whom we expect to play a leading role are marginalized, while others become more prominent in the text. There are gaps in the plot, and several plot threads have no resolution. The seams of Dostoevsky's creative process are on display throughout the novel. Yet reading *The Idiot* as a gothic novel imbues the work with structure and cohesion. Dostoevsky's gothic novel demonstrates the power of gothic realism, the intersection of gothic and realist poetics within the form of the novel.

In the previous chapter, I examined the way early realists of the 1840s and 1850s used gothic framing devices to enhance the meaning of their sketches. Dostoevsky also incorporated gothic narrative force into his texts of the 1840s, as chapter 5 will discuss. In the present chapter, I argue that Dostoevsky adopts a gothic master plot in *The Idiot*, building on the gothic poetics that had already begun to shape realist aesthetics in the preceding decades. In addition to an overarching gothic narrative force, the novel includes many other gothic structural elements, such as a gothic narrative voice and a series of linked gothic narrative arcs.[2] *The Idiot* showcases Dostoevsky's use of gothic poetics to address the philosophical questions that are foundational for his writing, and as such represents a key work in the development of a Russian gothic realist aesthetic.

The gothic's appearance in *The Idiot* is not surprising. Dostoevsky himself confesses to an early love of gothic novels in *Winter Notes on Summer Impressions* (*Zimnye zametki o letnikh vpechetleniiakh*, 1863).[3] Elsewhere, in a July 1861 letter to Yakov Polonsky, he meditated, "How many times since childhood I have dreamed of travelling to Italy. Ever since I read Radcliffe's novels ... various Alfonsos, Catherines and Lucias have been whirling around in my mind."[4] Beyond Radcliffe, Dostoevsky is known to have read *Melmoth the Wanderer*, *The Monk*, *The Old English Baron*, and other works from the British gothic canon.[5] Dostoevsky's gothic aesthetic comes in large part from the British gothic fiction that he had read and loved as a child, but also has its roots in his fondness for Balzac and Dickens and in his genealogical debt to Gogol.

This gothic influence has long been discussed by scholars, from Leonid Grossman's influential study on low genres in Dostoevsky to more recent publications such as Robin Feuer Miller's comparative study of *Brothers Karamazov* and *Melmoth the Wanderer*.[6] Vladimir Nabokov dismissively describes Dostoevsky as "a much overrated, sentimental, and Gothic novelist of the time"[7] and famously criticizes his use of gothic (and sentimental) generic elements as "a shoddy literary trick."[8] Joseph Frank observes that both Dostoevsky's novels and gothic works feature "a plot based on mystery and suspense; characters who always find themselves in situations of extreme psychological and erotic tension; incidents of murder and mayhem of various sorts; and an atmosphere calculated to impart a shiver of the demonic or supernatural."[9] Although Dostoevsky was not writing conventional gothic novels, gothic elements run throughout his works, from his earliest Petersburg tales to his final novel, *Brothers Karamazov*.

The Idiot, however, holds a special gothic place in this oeuvre, as Miller underscores when she identifies a gothic voice that "employs techniques of arbitrary disclosure and heightened terror"[10] among the novel's four narrative voices. Thanks in large part to this narrative voice, a specifically gothic sensibility saturates the novel. Gothic motifs with violent, anxious, or fearful psychologies reminiscent of those from Ann Radcliffe, Matthew Lewis, or Charles Maturin lend terrifying atmosphere to the characters' interactions. These strands are bound by a gothic master plot that drives the novel's narrative. Narrative arcs such as the fall of a noble house, the implied quasi-incestuous seduction of an underage ward by her guardian, and the uncanny figure of the Idiot who unconsciously causes violence when he tries to do good underlie the main action. Similarly, gothic influence is seen in the novel's leitmotifs, such as the many instances of torture, anxiety accompanying sublime transfiguration, and the constant discussions of violent death. Indeed, the gothic-inspired narrative structure of *The Idiot* builds to such a pitch that the reader is hardly surprised when, in one of the novel's final scenes, Myshkin and Rogozhin spend the night with Nastasya Filippovna's corpse. It seems easy to simply compare *The Idiot*'s various apparent traits to the qualities that make up a gothic novel, note that all are met, and label Dostoevsky's novel "gothic." However, I want to demonstrate here that a gothic structure pervades the novel on a much deeper narrative level, prompting individual characters' actions and enabling interactivity between reader and text.

The Gothic Master Plot

From the novel's first paragraph, the reader enters a world of mystery. A train approaches Petersburg in the dim morning light, and the reader learns that all the passengers have pale, yellow faces that match the damp fog surrounding the train, blocking the morning light from permeating the car. We meet Rogozhin and Myshkin, and from the start, the narrator links the two together and establishes them as opposites: Myshkin's fair complexion, light hair, and placid blue eyes counter Rogozhin's deathly pallor, dark hair, and fiery gray eyes. Similarly, Myshkin appears robustly healthy, although his sunken cheeks and something in his eyes suggest lingering illness, whereas Rogozhin's mocking, malicious smile belies the inner torment suggested by his sickly appearance and exhausted demeanor.

From this first meeting, Myshkin and Rogozhin enter into a binary opposition that propels the novel's narrative.[11] A cycle of mutual torment binds the two, revolving around their shared fascination with Nastasya Filippovna. Myshkin's compassionate, idealistic attitudes and actions unintentionally provoke Rogozhin to violent behaviour against himself and others.[12] Rogozhin, similarly, acts as a catalyst for Myshkin's extreme self-sacrificing behaviour. In this sense, Myshkin's inability to break out of this struggle causes Nastasya Filippovna's death as much as Rogozhin's knife does. Nastasya Filippovna is a strong character, but her role in the Myshkin-Rogozhin binary is decidedly external, although her role in the novel is crucial to its narrative trajectory.[13] On a structural level, this struggle is the key to understanding *The Idiot* as an essentially gothic text.

In the original eighteenth-century gothic novels, a mystery may drive the narrative, but an age-old plot device constitutes the fundamental basis for the narrative's trajectory: the battle between good and evil. This struggle is so common in world literature that it seems obvious, but the way it plays out in *The Idiot* is uniquely gothic. In a basic gothic master plot, an essentially good but naive character begins to learn self-reliance, independence, and courage as s/he works to find the solution to the text's inherent mystery. An essentially evil character serves as a foil. Not necessarily an inherent tendency, evil in gothic fiction can manifest as a lack of control over excessive passion, a predilection for extremes. The good character's well-intentioned actions prompt the evil character into ever more severe excesses. Similarly, the good character's interactions with the evil character are necessary for his or her own positive development; without the evil character, the good character would remain a naive innocent, unsuited to life in the broader world. Eventually the good character finds salvation, and some moral authority justly punishes the evil character. The arbiter of punishment for the wicked sometimes appears in human form, as in Horace Walpole's *Castle of Otranto*, where the rightful heir of the castle metes out justice to a usurper, and sometimes divinely, as in William Beckford's novel *Vathek* (1786), where – after many years of accumulated sins – Vathek is mysteriously pulled into hell while still alive.

Despite what one might assume, the gothic is not emphatically didactic. These novels do emphasize education but more in the sense of a *Bildungsroman*, underscoring the virtues of broadening one's mind through experience and exploration rather than morally teaching readers why it is a poor idea to have carnal relations with one's sister or murder one's brother. Instead, the drama of behavioural extremes preoccupies gothic fiction. "Sources of intense fascination" in the gothic tradition, according to Chloe Chard, these behavioural extremes can be identified "precisely by virtue of the expressions of horror and censure which are directed towards them."[14]

Gothic novels are typically divided by scholars into two schools – the school of terror and the school of horror – and the gothic master plot can play out in different ways in each. Kim Ian Michasiw describes the difference between the two schools thus:

> Terror seems to evoke by suggestion, by suspense; horror displays in the hope of producing disgust. Terror veils a potentially ghastly unknown and tempts the reader to peer through, to pull up a corner; horror marches readers through catacombs filled with violated nuns, with the rotting corpses of infants, with entombed lovers turned cannibal. Terror remains discrete and seeks a unity of tone; horror has an appetite for sudden variation, for the blackly comic, for the grotesque.[15]

In the school of terror, plots frequently echo the basic plot of Ann Radcliffe's novels, in which a young, naive heroine finds herself isolated from her friends and in the power of an older man. The young lady slowly comes to realize the dangers of her situation through a series of fearful discoveries. In the end, the entire truth is revealed, the heroine is rescued, and the villain is suitably punished. The school of horror presents a variation on the same master plot, placing more emphasis on the villain's spiral into ultimate evil. In this school, the positive character acts as a catalyst for the negative character's violence and unwittingly prompts increasingly excessive behaviour. The school of horror dwells on the unrestrained passion of the negative character, who aspires to a greater position than he should. In fact, the representative of good is often a victim of the hero's increasingly extreme violent behaviour, as in Beckford's *Vathek*. By contrast, the school of terror is more focused on the positive development of an individual, placing its protagonist in a series of frightening situations that serve as tests. Sublime anxiety – an anxiety that stems from the tension between the protagonist's fears and desires, and from which he tries repeatedly to break free – characterizes these works.

The Idiot effectively follows a positive character's development through the Radcliffe line. Myshkin's traits are ideal for such a hero: he is humble, naive, trusting, loyal, and incapable of cruelty. When he feels anxious, Myshkin even retreats in his own imagination to a sublime Alpine landscape, which features a gloomy ruined castle and towering snow-capped peaks:

> At moments he dreamed of the mountains, and especially one familiar spot in the mountains that he always liked to recollect, to which he had been fond of going when he still lived there, and from which he used to look down on the village, on the waterfall barely gleaming like a white thread below, on the white clouds and the old ruined castle.[16]

Yuri Corrigan has described Myshkin as "a wounded individual who struggles to distinguish between a projective world, populated with reflections of his own psyche, ... and the actual world of people."[17] In this scheme, the imagined Swiss landscape comforts Myshkin and becomes a safe space when reality and society become too dreadful to bear.

Similarly, when wicked villains in Radcliffe's archetypal gothic novel *The Mysteries of Udolpho* oppress heroine Emily St Aubert – seeking to corrupt and harm her – she finds moments of comfort in sublime landscapes that provide interludes of mental relief in an otherwise fraught existence. One such moment occurs, for example, as she travels with her uncle, the villainous Count Montoni, to an unknown location:

> The charming scenery soon withdrew Emily's thoughts from painful subjects [...] Emily often lingered behind the party, to contemplate the distant landscape, that closed a vista, or that gleamed beneath the dark foliage of the foreground; – the spiral summits of the mountains, touched with a purple tint, broken and steep above, but shelving gradually to their base; the open valley, marked by no formal lines of art; and the tall groves of cypress, pine and poplar, sometimes embellished by a ruined villa, whose broken columns appeared between the branches of a pine, that seemed to droop over their fall.[18]

Emily may feel oppressed by her situation, but the landscape enables her mental release, just as it lifts Myshkin's anxiety.

The gothic novel heroine finding solace in a sublime landscape is a common motif in the literature of terror, and Myshkin's parallel search for succor in the remembered landscape of his Swiss sojourn fits neatly into this pattern. Earlier, when discussing Switzerland with the Epanchin sisters, Myshkin remembers how anxious he felt there at first, and how the landscape both provoked this anxiety and then resolved it:

> It was in those moments that I was sometimes overcome with great [anxiety] [доходил иногда до большого беспокойства]. Sometimes [...] you stood by yourself in the middle of the mountain, pines all around you, ancient, big, full of sap; up above on the cliff, an old medieval castle, ruins [...] the sun bright, the sky blue, the stillness terrible. Well then, indeed, I would feel drawn away somewhere, and I kept fancying that if you went straight ahead, walked a long, long way, and got beyond that line, the very one where the sky meets the earth, that the whole key to the mystery would be there, and directly you would see a new life, a thousand times more vivid and tumultuous than ours.[19]

In the far-away blue line, Myshkin is able to transcend his troubles in a moment of sublime revelation, although this moment pales in comparison to his brilliant epiphanic visions just before he falls into a fit. The landscape he describes closely echoes the landscape Emily traverses with her family:

> The solitary grandeur of the objects that immediately surrounded her, the mountain-region towering above, the deep precipices that fell beneath, the waving blackness of the forests of pine and oak [...] these were features

which received a higher character of sublimity from the reposing beauty of Italian landscape below, stretching to the wide horizon, where the same melting blue tint seemed to unite earth and sky.[20]

Hero and heroine share both sensibility and sense of the sublime in these passages. Myshkin's view results in a sublime vision in which his questions are resolved, his mysteries solved. Even if both Myshkin and Emily search for solace in sublime beauty, they also both react to it with fear, as does Emily's aunt. We understand Myshkin's unease in his observation of "terrible stillness," while Emily and her aunt both react with a shudder.

While Emily begins her adventures surrounded by family, she loses all early on. Similarly, compared to the other characters, Myshkin is strikingly isolated, his parents unknown and his guardian dead. Thrust into the society of two interconnected families, the Epanchins and the Ivolgins, upon his return to Russia, Myshkin has only tenuous connections with them; he boards with the Ivolgins and may be a distant relative of Madame Epanchina. Nearly every other character has a blood or legal connection to one family or the other. Dostoevsky's first two notebooks for the novel chart a debate as to whether Myshkin should be illegitimate or legitimate. Dostoevsky vacillated on this point, ultimately eschewing the question in favour of the simple solution that "there are no *relations*" (нет *родни*),[21] deliberately alienating his hero from the two families. Myshkin expresses fears of becoming trapped in this society:

> [The prince] suddenly had a terrible longing to leave all this here and to go away, back where he had come from, somewhere quite far, to some remote region, to go away at once without even saying good-bye to anyone. He had a foreboding that if he remained here even a few days longer he would certainly be drawn into this world irrevocably, and that this very world would then be his lot from then on.[22]

Myshkin's fear is at odds with his attempts to fit in the Epanchins' and Ivolgins' social circle. As an outsider, he has spent considerable time establishing himself as a relative of Madame Epanchina and working to help the various members of the circle. Why, then, does he feel such anxiety about assimilating?

In Marilyn Butler's description of the Radcliffe heroine, she presents this isolation as an important feature: "The Radcliffe heroine is isolated and surrounded by strangers, enemies or equivocal friends. Her parents are dead, possibly dead, or not certainly known – the last, an equally

powerful, more suggestive indicator of her alienation."[23] Butler continues: "At the nodal point or points in her story she comes to a building
which may provide a seeming refuge by day but becomes a threatening, haunted maze by night: 'a mystery seems to hang over these cham-
bers, which it is still, perhaps, my lot to develop.'"[24] Rogozhin's house
serves as this space in *The Idiot*.

> Without and within, the house is somehow inhospitable and frigid,
> everything appears to be hiding and secreting itself away, and why it
> seems so from the mere physiognomy of the house – it would be hard to
> explain. Architectural lines have, of course, a secret of their own.[25]

The description of the house alerts us to its mysteries, if not to their
solutions, which it is Myshkin's task to discover.[26]

Myshkin visits Rogozhin's house in parts 2 and 4. His first visit occurs
just before he begins to experience epileptic seizures again, before his
circle of acquaintances in St Petersburg begins to spiral out of control.
The second visit concludes the novel. Myshkin feels excitement and
dread approaching the house; his journey to its second floor, where
Rogozhin lives, is no less fraught with mysteries and secrets:

> The staircase was dark, made of stone, coarsely designed, and its walls
> were covered with red paint [...] The servant who opened the door to
> the prince led him in without taking his name, and led him a long way;
> they passed through a grand parlor, the walls of which were "faux mar-
> ble," with an oak block floor and furnishings from the twenties, coarse and
> heavy; they passed also through some little cells, winding and zigzagging,
> mounting two or three steps and going down as many, till at last they kno-
> cked at a door. The door was opened by Parfyon Semyonovich himself;
> seeing the prince, he turned so pale and was so frozen to the spot that for
> a time he resembled a stone idol, looking with his fixed and frightened
> gaze and twisting his mouth into some kind of utterly bewildered smile.[27]

The perilous and mysterious ascent through zigzagging hallways and
up and down stairs that fit no architectural plan, as well as the strange
encounter with Rogozhin at the end of it, mirrors the exploration of a
medieval castle in a gothic novel. As Butler notes: "Always at midnight,
in fear of discovery by the other people of the house, in fear of ghosts
and whatever else she may find, she unlocks hidden doorways, feels
her way down dark passages, and finds the equivocal keys to the past –
a familiar-looking portrait, a blood-stained dagger, a scroll of paper
or a chest big enough to hold a human skeleton."[28] Rogozhin's rooms,

similarly, could have been taken directly from a gothic castle, from the strange old furniture to the suspicious and gloomy portrait of his father hanging in its dusty frame, although the faux marble and painted walls add a sense of modern artificiality to the scene. At the end of this passage, Myshkin remarks to Rogozhin:

> Your house has the physiognomy of your whole family and your whole Rogozhin way of life; but ask me how I concluded that – I have nothing to explain it. It's raving nonsense, of course. I'm even anxious that it troubles me so. Before, I would have never even imagined that you live in such a house, but as soon as I saw it, it occurred to me at once: "Why, that's just the sort of house he ought to have!"[29]

This reflection of a character and his family legacy in the form of a house is common in gothic novels, stemming from *The Castle of Otranto* and including all of the famous works by Ann Radcliffe, as well as Clara Reeve's *Old English Baron*, and others. This is not to say that this technique is only used in the gothic tradition, but its placement here, following Myshkin's ascent to Rogozhin's chamber, signals gothic narrative force.[30] Building upon this initial exploration of the space, Myshkin's second visit to the house and discovery of Nastasya Filippovna in Rogozhin's study echoes Emily's discovery of what lies behind the black veil in *The Mysteries of Udolpho*.[31]

Ostensibly the gothic villain character of the work, Rogozhin, not surprisingly, serves as the dark counterpart to Myshkin's wholly good character. Rogozhin lives a life of extreme passions, committing infamous acts, frequently because of his passion for Nastasya Filippovna. His actions become increasingly extreme and immoral as the novel continues. In the beginning he steals from his father. Rogozhin then beats Nastasya Filippovna and attempts to purchase her for money. Rogozhin swears eternal brotherhood with Myshkin, exchanges crosses with him, and then attempts to murder him. After engaging in an orgy with Nastasya Filippovna, he chases her until she agrees to marry him, then, following their marriage, murders her. At the end of the novel, Rogozhin is struck by delirium, then arrested, tried, and sent to Siberia for his crime.

Analysing gothic elements in Dostoevsky's *Idiot* reveals that the complex plot of the novel actually draws from both the school of terror and the school of horror, using both variants of the gothic master plot simultaneously. Through the characters of Myshkin and Rogozhin, both the progress of the good character and the downward spiral of the bad character are captured in the novel. These two plotlines play

Figure 3. Illustration of the black veil scene from *The Mysteries of Udolpho*, 5th edition (1803).

off each other, informing the trajectories of each. Myshkin's so-called mission to spread goodness through the example of active love is increasingly ineffective, while Rogozhin, with his countering obsessive passions, sets events in motion that lead to the moral downfall of other characters. In this sense, Dostoevsky's realist novel echoes a gothic one.

To a certain extent, *The Idiot* makes use of a binary narrative model of a good Myshkin and evil Rogozhin, but the novel proves considerably more complicated. At times, Christ-like Myshkin seems like a stock character, endlessly good, patient, and self-sacrificing. There are moments, however, when he admits that the stress of such behaviour is wearing on him, and certainly, his eventual relapse into idiocy is not an expected fate for a virtuous positive character in either gothic model. Additionally, Myshkin's behaviour constantly underscores his tendency towards a lack of restraint. His inability to control his passion for self-sacrifice prompts other characters to make poor decisions. Meanwhile, Rogozhin follows the classic gothic pattern of spiralling into increasingly extreme behaviours, but he is tightly self-controlled elsewhere in the text. While on the surface *The Idiot* appears to fit well within the eighteenth-century gothic novel master plot's confines, Dostoevsky's realist characters explode the boundaries of gothic stock characters. This in turn prompts us, like the Radcliffe heroine, to dig deeper to solve the mystery of the novel's gothic facade. What is the function of the gothic in *The Idiot*? Why do these characters follow gothic models? To answer, we must turn to the notebooks.

A Gothic Laboratory: The Notebooks

The notebooks Dostoevsky wrote while formulating *The Idiot* provide a unique look at the way he conceived the structuring of the novel and the purpose of his characters, throwing their origins into bold relief. As we read Dostoevsky's notes, we can see precisely which questions he grappled with most as he constructed the novel's narrative plan. Furthermore, in charting the characters' development as he plotted eight versions of the novel, Dostoevsky's fascination with the themes of violence, redemption, family, isolation, and love, among others, come to light. The notebooks to *The Idiot* do not contain the information necessary for a decisive statement about the text's formulation. By tracking the changes that the characters and plots of the notebooks undergo, however, we can draw tentative conclusions about Dostoevsky's particular narrative and character choices for the final form of the novel.

The most striking part of the plan in its early stages is Dostoevsky's obsessive use of details from the Olga Umetskaya case, widely reported in the Russian press, especially in mid-September 1867 as the trial took place.[32] Olga Umetskaya's parents had abused and starved their children, including Olga. Oppressed and terrorized by her parents, Olga had several times set fire to her family home and other estate buildings, sometimes remorsefully waking her family before they were trapped by the fire. In the trial, Umetskaya's parents were sentenced for the cruel abuse of their children, but Olga, too, was sentenced for her arsonist tendencies. Olga Umetskaya's story incorporates several classic gothic motifs: child abuse, the terror of torture, the abuse of power, and the innocence and moral conscience of a tormented heroine. The Umetskaya case points to the gothic as a key component in the realist depiction of contemporary Russian society during Dostoevsky's time.

Troubled by the Umetskaya case, Dostoevsky incorporated its basic elements into his working model for the novel, embellishing or changing them as he built his narrative.[33] In the notebooks, Umetskaya becomes a rape victim, a victim of incest, or in some versions, both. The Idiot character is her rapist and tormenter in some instances, and her accomplice in arson and other forms of revenge in others. In every case, however, the Olga Umetskaya character of the notebooks loves the Idiot character and shows him compassion, even going so far as to forgive or conceal the rape in some versions. She struggles with indecision; she cannot forgive her tormenters and desires to burn things, but nonetheless seeks redemption on some level. Her mental anguish turns to madness in some versions. In several, she becomes a Holy Fool. In other versions she marries. In all, the ultimate fate of her soul remains unknown.

While Dostoevsky describes the Idiot character in the notebooks as an "enigma" or a "Sphinx," the Umetskaya character is the real mystery. She does not appear in the novel's final version, but she appears in every plan in the notebooks. Her origins are unknown, her reasons for committing violence are unknown, and her eventual fate is unknown. She passes from the notebooks into oblivion, although some facets of her character emerge in other characters in the final novel. Nastasya Filippovna's gothic-inspired story is part of Olga Umetskaya's legacy from the notebooks. Like Olga Umetskaya in some of the notebook plans, Nastasya Filippovna is seduced by her guardian as a minor, then abandoned. Like Olga Umetskaya, she feels violently angry, and we can blame her irrational and self-destructive tendencies on humiliated pride. Her inability to choose between Rogozhin and Myshkin represents her inability to reconcile her conflicting ideas of self. She torments Myshkin because she fears the burden of being good, as he sees her. Conversely, she torments Rogozhin because she hates being thought wicked, as he sees her. This dual nature appears in the description of her portrait in part 1:

The face, extraordinary in its beauty and in something else, astonished him even more now. There was something like immeasurable pride and contempt, almost hatred, in that face, and at the same time something trusting, something wonderfully simple-hearted; these two contrasting elements aroused a feeling almost of compassion at the sight of these features. Her dazzling beauty was positively unbearable, the beauty of a pale face, almost sunken cheeks and glowing eyes; a strange beauty![34]

Nastasya Filippovna's beauty is couched in gothic language. Dazzling beauty masks a dual nature, one aspect of which is a fierce hatred, while the features that characterize this beauty are corpse-like: a pale face, almost sunken cheeks. The glowing, or burning (горевших) eyes, in this sense, seem nearly unnatural rather than complimentary. Here beauty is external rather than internal, but the narrator links Nastasya Filippovna's beauty to the "two contrasting elements." This becomes a metaphor for her struggle of conscience as she decides whether to forgive and accept humiliation or commit evil acts in revenge. Like Olga Umetskaya, Nastasya Filippovna's potential for violence as a result of humiliation is an inherent part of her character, just as her potential for redemption and forgiveness is.

The larger theme of love's duality that characterizes the Idiot character in the notebooks echoes Umetskaya's struggle with forgiveness. Dostoevsky writes several times of the idea of love that he hopes to expand upon in the novel. In Dostoevsky's plan, the excessive, ego-driven love associated with torment gives way to the redeeming power of love as true compassion and forgiveness. The Idiot as described in versions of the novel prior to the seventh notebook is vengeful, angry, and cruel. Like a gothic villain, his pride and humiliation drive him to commit violent and malicious acts, but he also commits crimes out of boredom, or purely from spite. His excessive passions cause him to love, but the objects of his affection fear him; his love is a manifestation of his ego.

Dostoevsky clearly sought to have the Idiot redeemed through love. He wrote several times of love's transformative power once it has progressed through three stages: revenge and self-love, obsessive passion, and finally, the lofty love of true compassion and feeling. He was unable to realize this transformation in the novel plans, however. At first, Dostoevsky suggests that this saving love must be spontaneous, unpremeditated. However, by the seventh notebook he abandons this plan, deciding to have the Idiot appear as a Christ figure from the start and setting him up to interact with those around him who, like Olga Umetskaya, struggle with violent or excessive passions caused by personal history.

In establishing the Idiot as a Christ figure from the outset, Dostoevsky solves the problem of how the character achieves redeeming love, but some aspects of his former character remain. The Idiot of the later notebooks, like Myshkin in the novel, is isolated. Additionally, although Dostoevsky creates a Christ figure in Myshkin, Myshkin proves unable to redeem other characters. Humiliated pride drives characters who encounter the Idiot's forgiving compassion to commit violent or vindictive acts against others. This constant stream of violence drives the narrative in both the notebooks and the final version of *The Idiot*.

The Idiot shares with *Crime and Punishment* (1866) a fascination with the motivation and causation of violent crimes, and both have a journalistic origin.[35] As Louise McReynolds observes, "Dostoevsky, a fan of Poe's, found *why* a significantly more compelling question than *who*."[36] Dostoevsky did not conceive of *The Idiot* as a crime novel,[37] but its experimentation with the impact of a "positively good man" on society brings into sharp relief other characters' anxieties, traumas, and – in their psychological reactions – ability to wound others, both metaphysically and physically. The notebooks become a "laboratory" for Dostoevsky's experiment, in Jacques Catteau's formulation.[38] Indeed, the violence caused by humiliated pride in the final novel is a direct consequence of the Christ-like Myshkin's actions. However, in the notebooks, Myshkin only appears as a Christ figure in the seventh plan. Before this, senseless and random violence alone drives the narrative. The plans provide each character's backstory as a cause for his or her behaviour, but the frequency and shocking excess of violent and transgressive acts suggests the stream of horrors invented by gothic novelists to provoke readers' fear and anxiety.

Dostoevsky, too, writes of his readers several times throughout the notebooks, noting that he must be sure to put in "questions and enigmas"[39] or "episodes and denouements" for the benefit of the reader.[40] These vague but suggestive remarks demonstrate the particular influence that the lowbrow genre fiction he loved wielded over his narrative style. Miller observes:

> Dostoevsky here consciously rejected the comic mode as a means of depicting his hero. But a straightforward presentation of a virtuous character could be extremely boring. As an avid reader of gothic and adventure novels, Dostoevsky knew how entertaining an air of mystery was. His many directives to himself to recount only the facts without explanation and to make use of rumor and enigma reflect his awareness that he had to counteract the potential dullness of a perfectly good man.[41]

The episodes and mysteries that he planned to embed in the novel include a wide range of transgressions, from incest, rape, illegitimate children, and murder, to suicide, secret debts, secret marriages, arson, and cannibalism. Like gothic villains, the characters in the notebooks by and large commit these acts without apparent motivation.

Despite this apparent lack, the actions' extreme violence prompts Dostoevsky to seek motivations for them in his characters. In his early notebooks he obsessively tries to establish the Idiot's particular character. Early on he writes, "*An enigma*. Who is he? A terrible villain or a mysterious ideal?"[42] This question continues to drive his formulation of the Idiot throughout the notebooks, until in the eighth plan he finally establishes that the Idiot should simply be "a Sphinx." Dostoevsky continually vacillates between establishing his Idiot as a Holy Fool with the naivety of a child or as a vengeful, jealous man, the same difficulty he has with Olga Umetskaya's character.

Dostoevsky's lengthy deliberation on this point across the notebook plans suggests that he felt the need for an embodiment of evil in the novel. This element of evil would serve both to test his hero, the Christlike Idiot, and to explain the motivations for some of the violent actions that characterize the novel's narrative. On 10 April 1868, in his notes for the novel's second part, Dostoevsky writes, "Gradually showing *the Prince in action* will be sufficient. But! For this is needed the *plot of the novel*. In order to set forth the character of the Idiot (more sympathetically) it is necessary to think up for him a field of action."[43] This "field of action" projects the entire novel back into the realm of an experiment. Having established what kind of character he desires for a hero, Dostoevsky now seeks to highlight the hero's unique qualities against a backdrop of contrasting qualities. For this effect, he turns to the gothic master plot and attendant gothic conventions.

Dostoevsky's experiment in *The Idiot* was to place a "positively beautiful" hero into contemporary Russian society as a way to explore the redemption of humanity.[44] Through his use of the gothic, Dostoevsky is able to frame this great theological experiment, staging a theoretical war between good and evil. He uses the gothic to highlight his hero's Christlike outlook, compassion, and actions, but also to reveal the extent of Myshkin's failure. The gothic mode offers the powerful rhetoric Miller describes but also contains the *possibility* of the experiment's ideal outcome: a happy ending. For Dostoevsky, the ending of the novel was crucial: "The ending will decide everything," he wrote in a December 1868 letter to Apollon Maikov.[45] The ending was the point on which the experiment's outcome – and the novel's purpose and meaning – rested.[46]

Gothic Trappings and the Reader

While *The Idiot* incorporates a gothic master plot, the most apparent gothic elements to readers are its gothic trappings; these are what initially strike readers and convey the atmosphere of anxiety that permeates the novel, but they also add humour and irony. First, and perhaps most obviously, Dostoevsky constantly repeats lexemes that contribute to the generic atmosphere. For example, gloomy (*мрак* or *мрачн-*) appears sixty-seven times in the novel; horror (*ужас* and adjectival/adverbial variations) appears 296 times, and terror/fear (*страх* or adjectival/adverbial variations of *страшный*) ninety-eight times. Second, and most provocatively, brief gothic moments appear in the narrative's course. These moments appear so suddenly, without context, that they seem out of place or are easily overlooked. Often, they are at first humorous, but taken together, they inform the novel's broader atmosphere of anxiety.

In the beginning of part 3, for example, Alexandra Epanchin has a dream about a monk:

> Once, and only once, she managed to see something in a dream that seemed to be original – she saw a monk, all alone, in some dark room that she kept on being afraid to enter.[47]

Alexandra's dream features a classic, clichéd gothic scene that might have been lifted directly from *The Monk*, *Melmoth the Wanderer*, or any of a number of other works: a heroine fears to enter a monk's dark chamber. The dream is hardly original, although it may seem so to Alexandra's mother, who, we learn, prefers English romances to horrid novels. For Dostoevsky's reader, the derivative, clichéd nature of the dream would have been apparent. At first, the episode seems in keeping with Alexandra's previous dream, a humorous flight of fancy about poultry. However, the scene also serves to hint at a darker gothic subtext. While the dream is ironically tongue in cheek, we wonder why a young girl's subconscious is engaged with such a dark and implicitly frightening subject. Even though the dream's content is funny, Alexandra's terror is real. Never mentioned again, this dream feels like an aberration.

However, the dream prefigures the cannibalistic monks who feature in Lebedev's outlandish stories. These apocalyptic and cataclysmic tales evoke the gothic again, although more in the sense of a humorous interlude meant to poke fun at a character. Lebedev begins by discussing the apocalyptic star Wormwood, but his manner of speaking lends an air of absurdity to the discussion. This sense of the absurd continues as he tells the story of an order of cannibalistic Catholic monks. In addition to cannibalism's inherent sensationalism, the moral depravity of both Catholic monks and cannibals are well-known themes in gothic fiction. Lebedev imbues them with humour in his story:

For then [...] famines visited the human population once every two years, or at least every three years, so that with such a state of affairs men even took recourse to anthropophagy, though they kept it secret. One of these cannibals, approaching old age, announced of his own accord, without being compelled at all, that in the course of his long and wretched life he had killed and eaten, by himself and in dead secret, sixty monks and a few layman infants, a matter of six, but not more, that is to say, extraordinarily few compared with the number of ecclesiastics he had consumed.[48]

The story of a man eating sixty-six people, if true, represents such excessive transgressive behaviour that it is difficult for a casual listener to process. Preceded by Lebedev's discussions of apocalyptic imagery and followed by one of Myshkin's recurring descriptions of ruined castles in the Alps, the tale's gothic cloaking contributes to its comedic effect. Lebedev's tendency towards hyperbole shows him to be ridiculous as well, not unlike the defence lawyer Fetyukovich in *Brothers Karamazov*.

As Lebedev continues his speech, he begins to discuss the torments of the medieval justice system, arousing pity and indignation in his initially sceptical and merry audience:

Now I ask you, what tortures awaited him in that age, what wheels, stakes, and fires? [...] Why not simply [...] keep the secret till his dying breath? [...] There must have been something stronger than stake and fire, or even twenty-year-old habit! There must have been an idea stronger than any misery, famine, torture, plague, leprosy and all that hell, which mankind could not have endured without that idea, which bound men together, guided their hearts and fructified the springs of life! Well, then, show me anything like such a force in our age of vices and railways [...] Show me an idea binding mankind together today with even half the power it had in those centuries![49]

This sudden serious note is at odds with Lebedev's earlier riotous tale of cannibalistic monks. While "the fanaticism of the twelfth century" is far removed from the novel's present, Lebedev here, through his gothic tale and subsequent speech, introduces the idea that medieval torments resonate more closely with the present day than one would think. Moreover, in linking Myshkin's and Ippolit's vague fears with this gothic tale and one of the very real mysteries of the novel – namely, what this binding element is and how it can be achieved – Lebedev sets the stage for Ippolit's tortured monologue to follow. This combination of comedy and terror creates a black humour that adds an edge to the narrative. This edge then easily mutates into Ippolit's dark bitterness, apparent throughout his subsequent tale.

In these episodes, Dostoevsky exploits the gothic's comic, parodic potential for readers, as well as its predilection for shock value. Alternating humorous ironic jibes at characters' originality or rhetorical inability with glimpses of baldly serious or genuinely terrifying moments creates a disorienting atmosphere in which unease creeps up on the reader, enabling an overwhelming sense of anxiety to permeate the text, engulfing both characters and reader.

Miller's study posits that Dostoevsky uses the gothic narrative voice strategically, which also enables the novel's dialogic structure:

> Dostoevsky raises the themes and techniques of the Gothic novelists to new heights, for he forges a metaphysical system out of a language, which, in the hands of lesser novelists, remains merely a style, an effective fictional point of view. The language of the Gothic novel and its themes offered Dostoevsky a powerful rhetoric for describing modern man's predicament.[50]

This gothic voice plays a significant role in the relationship between the novel's narrator and its reader, the target of Dostoevsky's "powerful rhetoric." This link between reader and text was key for Dostoevsky, for whom the novel's importance lay not only in its idea but more importantly in that idea's reception by its intended audience.

Malcolm Jones takes Miller's argument one step further, arguing that the gothic narration in *The Idiot* plunges the reader into a gothic mindset:

> Readers, so long as they go on reading, are in the same predicament. They are imprisoned in this world of barely structured dialogue and emotional provocation [...] they are overcome by vaguely apprehended ideas which seem momentarily to offer an explanation for what they have not grasped.[51]

Jones describes the experience of reading the novel as one of entrapment, and I would argue that it even positions the reader as an active player in its action. The narrator "provokes increasing anxiety in readers";[52] the reader becomes mystified and confused as the text continues, until eventually the narrator "reveals indirectly and by way of repeated hints that he knows his readers' guilty secret."[53] Jones's language recalls gothic novels, and we recall that one of their key features is a focus on mystery and its solution. In reading *The Idiot*, in Jones's view, the reader becomes complicit in this relationship, playing an active if unconscious role in the text. Jones suggests that this strategy results in greater reader investment in the novel, either because readers are lured into "individual consciousness," which perpetuates the novel's realism, or because readers are able to connect and sympathize with the emotional underpinnings of the text.[54]

The reader's unease and the novel's anxious atmosphere unite, creating a viable mode in which gothic conventions that should be clichéd or parodic still carry a sensation of fear with them. Voyeuristic watching is one of the most frequent manifestations of anxiety in the text, often represented as two eyes, staring.[55] The uncanny feeling discomfits Myshkin, Nastasya Filippovna, and others. In part 2, Myshkin feels Rogozhin's eyes on him at the train station:

> No one met him at the station; but as he got out of the carriage he suddenly fancied that he saw the strange, fervent gaze of two eyes belonging to someone in the crowd that surrounded the passengers arriving with the train. When he looked more attentively, he could not discern anything more. Of course, he had only fancied it; but it left an unpleasant impression.[56]

Myshkin does not know if he is truly being watched. The feeling could be a manifestation of his own anxieties, or Rogozhin could be covertly observing Myshkin. Either way, the scene provokes an uncanny fear in Myshkin, described above as an "unpleasant impression," and contributes to the underlying anxiety various characters feel throughout the novel.[57]

These eyes appear again in Nastasya Filippovna's three letters to Myshkin at the end of part 3:

> I have almost ceased to exist and I know it; God knows what lives within me in my stead. I read that every day in two terrible eyes that are always gazing at me, even when they are not before me. Those eyes are *silent* now (they are always silent), but I know their secret. His house is gloomy and dreary, and there is a secret in it. I'm sure that he has, hidden in a drawer, a razor, wrapped in silk like that murderer in Moscow; he too lived in the same house with his mother, and also wrapped a razor in silk to cut a throat with. All the time I was in their house, I kept fancying that somewhere under the floorboards there might be a dead man hidden there by his father, perhaps, wrapped in oilcloth, just like that Moscow one, and surrounded in the same way with jars of Zhdanov's fluid.[58]

Like Myshkin, Nastasya Filippovna feels Rogozhin's eyes upon her, even when she knows that he is not present. They provoke an uncanny feeling of fear, which she then associates with basic gothic conventions: a gloomy, dreary house and a dead body under the floorboards. Nastasya Filippovna's anxieties manifest themselves through these voyeuristic eyes. The cycle of anxiety and fear creates a sense that horrors lurk beneath society's surface facade, contributing, again, to the novel's gothic narrative.

A third voyeuristic scene is described more like a tableau, with more detail than just a description of disembodied staring eyes. In part 3, chapter 5, Ippolit wakes up suddenly, pales, and looks about in alarm; the narrator notes that "there was almost a look of horror on his face when he remembered everything and collected his thoughts."[59] As Ippolit prepares to read to the assembled guests, he infects all with this fear, although the others cannot understand precisely why they are afraid:

> "What is it? What's going on here? What's he going to read?" some people muttered gloomily; others were silent. But everyone sat down and stared inquisitively. Perhaps they really did expect something unusual. Vera caught hold of her father's chair, and was almost crying with fright; Kolya was almost in the same state of fright as well.[60]

From this opening, we expect another scandal scene. The anxious anticipation of characters echoes the atmosphere before Nastasya Filippovna's name-day party. There, however, the anxiety is merely social; party guests are looking forward to a scandalous scene. Here the anticipatory anxiety is genuinely terrifying to a degree out of proportion with the event – a young man doing a reading.

Just as this fear begins to wane, Rogozhin begins interacting with the company and once again stirs up these feelings of fear and a general aura of mystery. Ippolit's recognition of and reaction to Rogozhin as the man who was in his room late one night adds to this atmosphere:

> On Ippolit these words made a terrible impression; he trembled so much that the prince started to put out his arm to support him, and would certainly have cried out if his voice had not evidently failed him. For a whole minute he could not speak a word, and stared at Rogozhin, breathing painfully. At last, gasping for breath, with an immense effort he articulated: "So it was you … you … It was you?" […] "Why did you frighten me? Why did you come to torment me? I don't understand it, but it was you." And there was a sudden flash of boundless hatred in his eyes, despite the shivers from his fright, which had still not subsided.[61]

Rogozhin does not wield thumbscrews or a rack in this scene, but Ippolit reacts as though he is being tortured. We can understand

Ippolit's reaction; his diagnosis of terminal illness (a condemned state) leaves him vulnerable to fear. In this scene, however, his reaction does cast Rogozhin as a villain, and we must wonder why. The image of Rogozhin watching the sleeping Ippolit from the shadows in the middle of the night should be alarming. Ippolit has, until now, been a peripheral character. Largely unexplored within the novel, this new link between the two adds a sinister undertone to their relationship, however, exposing a fundamental difference in authority. The sleeping state renders Ippolit his most vulnerable. Rogozhin, awake and observing, could hurt or even kill the defenceless Ippolit. Secretly watching, after all, constitutes a typical gothic tableau; it subtly incorporates multiple gothic conventions – voyeurism, an authority willing to exploit its victim, the uncanny feeling of being watched, paranoia, and imprisonment.

By building up fearful anxiety, Dostoevsky creates a gothic Petersburg. The fine gentlemen and ladies who inhabit the fair city and its summer neighbourhood in Pavlovsk are, on the surface, living lives taken from society tales. Mothers seek to marry off daughters. Heads of families are engaged with the business of official life. Connections are made and nearly all the action occurs through conversation, in carefully staged social settings. Behind this veneer, however, these same fine ladies and gentlemen are not what they appear to be. Guardians seduce wards. Daughters dream about monks and do not know why. Gentlemen die, and death is not gentle, but agonizing and sometimes violent. And underlying all of this, a basic anxiety, the cause of which remains unknown, drives society. In part 2, chapter 11, General Epanchin confesses to Myshkin: "Yes, yes … but I'm afraid, after all! I don't understand what of, but I'm afraid … It's as though there's something darting about in the air; like a bat, some trouble is hovering; and I'm afraid, afraid!"[62] The characters – General Epanchin here, and also Alexandra after her dream, Lebedev, Ippolit, Nastasya Filippovna, and Myshkin – are aware, on some level, of this fear. Society's veneer cracks for them at times, and this gothic foundation shows through in the manifestations of their anxiety, in the hovering bats and voyeuristic eyes, the creeping monsters and strange monks, the cannibals and apocalyptic stars, and the corpses under the floorboards.

The Potential of Dostoevsky's Gothic Poetics

Ultimately, despite the novel's gothic trappings, Myshkin's inability to develop as a character causes the abrupt and ignominious end of the gothic master plot's positive trajectory. Vladimir Zakharov observes that "the 'idea' of Myshkin persists as the main concept" in *The Idiot*, while later novels develop multiple ideologies conveyed through multiple characters.[63] Perhaps, then, the gothic master plot's denouement is a symptom of the narrative experiment with its reliance on one character. Elizabeth Dalton presents a terrifying reading in this vein:

> The character of Myshkin himself is somehow an absence or negation: his personality is defined in large part by what he does *not* do, by what he is *not*, and thus not only evokes a vision of its opposite, a shadowy double embodying all that is missing and yet somehow contained by its absence in Myshkin, but also suggests in him a sort of gulf or abyss, the possibility of a terrifying fall into a negative realm of being where the very forms of personality might be annihilated.[64]

Dalton's psychoanalytic reading brings into question Dostoevsky's claim to have created a "positively good man." Bruce French argues that Myshkin's isolation from a predictable narrative trajectory results in his inherent goodness: "It is the prince's lack of storiness, made possible by his dialogical relationship with the world, that is fundamental in his being able to live fully, morally, and religiously."[65] In this chapter's gothic reading of *The Idiot*, Myshkin's narrative trajectory is unique in that it does not continue to its conventionally predicted conclusion as Rogozhin's does; in French's terminology, it defies its own storiness. However, the question remains: if Myshkin is wholly good, why is he unable to effect positive change?[66] Instead, Myshkin acts blindly, without considering the destructive consequences of his actions: as Dalton observes, "his gentle passage through the lives of the other characters has laid waste to them with a kind of apocalyptic destructiveness."[67] According to Dostoevsky's experiment, the tension and inadvertent destruction unleashed by Myshkin's innocence, humility, and truthfulness expose both the insufficiency of his idealism and society's greater spiritual emptiness in its inability to accommodate him. Perhaps Dostoevsky means that Myshkin's inner beauty as a man without sin, with a naive, childlike outlook and compassionate love for all, will save the world by standing as an example for all.[68] However, Myshkin fails to save even one of the doomed characters he encounters in Petersburg and Pavlovsk, including himself.

Can beauty save the world?[69] In gothic novels, it can. In *The Mysteries of Udolpho*, Emily St Aubert is a truly beautiful person – steady, compassionate, kind, morally decent, and courageous. She faces a slew of fearsome trials as she attempts to extricate herself from the situation at Udolpho and succeeds, emerging as a better, more mature person for it. Her courage and reason shine in the face of all who seek to destroy her, and at the end, the novel finds her morally whole, living out her days in peace and tranquility with her loved ones, the evil foes vanquished and her ancestral estate saved. This is one reason this genre works especially well as a backdrop for Dostoevsky's "positively beautiful man"; the desired outcome is at least possible within the gothic's realms, even though beauty does not save the world in *The Idiot*.

Dostoevsky showcases gothic realism's full potential in *The Idiot*. Gothic poetics in the novel create a strong and subtle bond between reader and text. This connection lends Dostoevsky's experiment and its philosophical message greater impact. As realist writers continued to develop narrative techniques, they drew on the gothic models put forth by Dostoevsky without realizing the extent of his debt to the schools of horror and terror. By the 1860s, the vogue for gothic novels had waned in Russia, but the original genre's memory remained relevant precisely because it was embedded in gothic realist works like *The Idiot* and their readers' subconscious. In the readings that make up part 2 of this study, gothic realism proves a powerful tool for writers to engage with social and political discourse, just as the gothic realist poetics of *The Idiot* do in the realm of philosophy and in the novel's form.

PART II

Gothic Realism

Chapter Five

Physiological Petersburg, Gothic Petersburg

A sad and uncomfortable feeling fills one's soul,
and an inexpressible melancholy possesses one's entire being.
One enters a remote, dark alleyway,
and the heart contracts more powerfully than before.
Dmitry Grigorovich, "Petersburg Organ Grinders"

He stopped for a moment and cast a penetrating glance
along the river into the smoky, frost-deadened distance,
which had suddenly flared with the last purple of a blood-red sunset
that was burning itself out on the smudgy horizon.
Fyodor Dostoevsky, "A Weak Heart"

The visual lies at the heart of literary realism. As writers of the 1840s turned to depictions of life more grounded in reality, in verisimilitude, vision took on new importance. Peter Brooks's study of the stakes of realist representation is predicated on the fact that "realism more than almost any other mode of literature makes sight paramount – makes it the dominant sense in our understanding of and relation to the world."[1] In the 1840s, the novels of European writers such as Charles Dickens and Honoré de Balzac influenced a general shift away from the romantic-fantastic in favour of depictions of life more grounded in reality.

This shift coincided with the rise of early commercial photography following Louis Daguerre's announcement of the daguerreotype process in early 1839. The process was introduced in the Russian Academy of Sciences in the summer of that year, and in October 1839 the first successful daguerreotype in Russia was reported in the journal *Son of the Fatherland* with the note that "even at 60 degrees latitude, in the fall, the daguerreotype does not lose its effect!"[2] Photography had arrived

in Russia. As the 1840s began, daguerreotype studios became commonplace on the streets of St Petersburg. This new technology, which placed
emphasis on representing life with accuracy, was associated with vision,
"with the lens imitating the retina to reproduce the world."[3]

In Russia, the 1840s witnessed the birth of the so-called Natural
School. This literary movement, championed by critic Vissarion Belinsky, was dedicated to a new literature that – inspired by Nikolai Gogol's
Dead Souls – aimed to represent reality. The movement initially carried
with it a moral focus on social improvement.[4] Literary works of this
period partly represent the efforts of writers to work out new literary
approaches for representing life with verisimilitude, for mimicking the
effect of the "objective" camera. To achieve this aim, however, writers
turned to earlier literary models, drawing on genres such as the physiological sketch and the gothic novel. Focusing on 1840s depictions of
St Petersburg in Nikolai Nekrasov's edited collection *The Physiology of
Petersburg* (*Fiziologiia Peterburga*, 1845) and Fyodor Dostoevsky's early
prose (1845–9), this chapter considers how early Russian realists used
and repurposed earlier styles, especially the gothic, to develop new
modes of urban representation.

The physiological sketch's prevalence as a useful canvas for 1840s
realist depictions is not surprising, but the gothic's role seems peculiar,
as its basic conventions appear diametrically opposed to realist aims.
The physiological sketch – which describes what its narrator sees as
precisely as possible – appealed to realists as an attempt to reproduce
everyday life experiences in prose. This prose mirrored, to some extent,
the new advances in photography developed during this period. Physiological sketches held great promise for the new realist aesthetic but
lacked a strong narrative force, relying more on exposition than plot.
In contrast, gothic writing was typically heavily plotted and included
manifold narrative twists and turns.

Depicting Urban Life in the Gothic Mode

The gothic's associations and themes, as well as its focus on narrative
force, proved ideal for communicating the perceived tragedy and horror of the social problems associated with urban poverty to the readers
of early realists works. Typically linked to a landscape characterized by
crumbling castles, gloomy forests, wildernesses, and oppressive mountains, the gothic takes its descriptive cues from the anxieties and fears of
protagonists. While in gothic novels "the city [...] became a site of nocturnal corruption and violence, a locus of real horror,"[5] urban locales
were also used in early realist fiction as reflectors of the corruption,

violence, and squalor already present in society, particularly in the Petersburg slums. The Russian reader of the 1840s, already attuned to cues from the gothic fiction read popularly for nearly fifty years, was well able to recognize gothic generic markers planted in non-gothic texts.

While sometimes used parodically, or to give texts an emotional, humorous tone, these markers simultaneously evoked the trappings of the genre – secrets, violence, and transgressions – and suggested an underlying sense of mystery. In addition, the feelings of panic, fear, dread, and horror the gothic aroused were useful in lending a charged atmosphere to settings most likely unfamiliar to the reader, like dark alleys or decaying tenement buildings. In establishing a pervading sense of anxiety and unease in their texts through gothic markers and themes, writers were able to direct readers to a better understanding of the injustices and issues they sought to highlight. As authors took on the mammoth project of depicting St Petersburg life, they turned to the gothic to help convey a sense of the city's unique atmosphere, ultimately embedding the gothic within the complex of tropes characteristic of what scholars call the Petersburg Text.[6]

Petersburg is a city particularly suited to the gothic mode. Even Belinsky, who generally championed St Petersburg in his writing, observed in the 1845 essay "Petersburg and Moscow" that

Petersburg was built in an instant. Things that should have taken a year were done in a month. The will of one individual triumphed over nature itself. It seemed as though fate itself, despite all right and reason, wanted to hurl the capital of the Russian Empire into this wretched region – a place where the sky is greenish white; where nature and the climate are hostile to humankind; where the plants of the north are thick grass, crawling heather, dry moss, gray tussocks, and swampy verdure; where sickly birch trees add to the pervasive monotony of prickly pines and sorrow spruce; and where the fumes from the swamp and the dampness of the air penetrate stone homes and human bones. Petersburg does not have spring or summer or winter; rather, it is host to a rotten and rainy fall which rages through the city all year long and which parodies first spring, then summer, and then winter.[7]

Belinsky's St Petersburg description shows just how closely the city's basic features correspond to gothic landscape tropes. Correlations with the gothic exist between the natural features of the environment such as swamps, poor weather, and gloomy light. However, the discrepancy between the city's regions also evokes the genre: an imported neoclassical fantasy set among artificial waterways, Petersburg houses the opulently wealthy but is surrounded by dimly lit tenements where residents live in squalor and destitution. Even the city's longstanding association in literature with empire – from Peter the Great's initial autocratic command to build it to the bureaucratic Table of Ranks that defines its social interactions – evokes the gothic's preoccupation with authority and its themes of entrapment and anxiety. Perhaps the best example of this theme in the Russian literary imagination is Alexander Pushkin's poem "The Bronze Horseman" ("Mednyi vsadnik," 1833), which culminates with a monument to Peter the Great coming to life and chasing a hapless clerk through the capital's flooded streets. Indeed, the appearance of the gothic in 1840s depictions of St Petersburg seems an intuitive method for writers to represent a psychologically and sociologically charged urban Russian landscape.

Other depictions of urban life from this time showed gothic influence, although not on the same scale. Led by Belinsky, who considered French physiological works to be at literature's forefront at this time, Russians became enamoured with Eugène Sue's *Mysteries of Paris* (*Les Mystères de Paris*, 1842–3), which took Petersburg by storm in the 1840s. Part gothic novel, part journalism, and part romance, Sue's novel describes how a disguised nobleman, Rodolphe, encounters the city's lower classes and chooses to live among them. He is accompanied by an assortment of socially conscious companions. However, the power of Sue's work relies not on its characters so much as its setting, which incorporates gothic details into the Parisian cityscape. Sue sought to play upon his reader's emotions through his depiction of Paris's grimy underbelly; indeed, he was so successful at this that his novel was credited with sparking the 1848 revolution.[8] Additionally, Sue's novel directly inspired works like Nekrasov's innovative edited collection, *The Physiology of Petersburg*.

Physiological works of the mid-to-late 1840s used Sue's feuilletons as a model for the portrayal of day-to-day life in Petersburg. Sue's style, in turn, drew on low, sensationalistic genres, including the gothic, which encouraged a more fraught, descriptive narrative. While most physiological sketches do not have a plot per se, Sue infused sensational plot turns into a predominately descriptive work, thus rendering it a compelling read. As literature became increasingly linked to movements for social awareness and reform, writers began to experiment, using Sue's newly reconceived physiological version of the feuilleton in *Mysteries of Paris* to describe lower-class life in St Petersburg. A physiological writer would in great detail note what his narrator perceived, for example, as he descended into a slum courtyard or a squalid tenement. Liberal use of sensational language was necessary in these instances to create an impression of horror for the reader. A combination of horror and pathos then compelled the reader onward.

The Physiology of Gothic Petersburg

Thomas Gaiton Marullo sets *The Physiology of Petersburg* apart from other Petersburg depictions of the period in his introduction to the 2009 English translation of Nekrasov's volume:

> The urban mapping-topologies in *Petersburg* bypass sinister melancholy, existential indifference, and tomblike claustrophobia; they also eschew yawning abysses, shadowy underworlds, and specters of death-in-life. Nowhere does the comic draw from the tragic, the melodramatic from the mundane, or the supernatural from the trivial. Nowhere is there a blurred line between the animate and inanimate, the true and false, the vulgar and sublime.[9]

Works like Pushkin's "Bronze Horseman" and "Queen of Spades" (1833) and Gogol's urban tales such as "Nevsky Prospect" (1835) and "The Nose" (1836) exemplify the romantic-fantastic meditation on St Petersburg life that Marullo contrasts with the physiological tradition, as exemplified by Nekrasov's volume. He goes on to note: "The writers of *Petersburg* see the northern Palmyra as the realest of real places. [...] Here the imperial city is hero, not antihero; here it is unity, not atmosphere. Self-conscious rationality and reality are triumphant, the order of the day."[10] Marullo's point – that these writers were crafting works distinct from the romantic-fantastic depictions of Petersburg that came before them – is well taken, but I disagree with his assertion that no elements from the earlier Petersburg can be seen in these texts. In Nekrasov's volume, writers use the gothic mode to capture elements of the anxious mood created in earlier romantic-fantastic texts. Furthermore, these gothic elements frequently emphasize the irrational fears and anxieties of the sketches' narrators.

Earlier, the Petersburg Text concept had built up a cityscape characterized by fantastic incidents: the devil strolling along the capital's boulevards, a monument coming to life and chasing a terrified clerk, a mysterious gambling secret driving men to ruination and madness, a missing nose running amok among famous landmarks, and even the ghost of a mild-mannered copyist sneaking up behind citizens and pulling their overcoats over their heads. In addition to these extraordinary happenings, however, these earlier works associated a certain mood with the city: anxiety, nervous and frenetic behaviour, violence, want, and oppression were its main characteristics. As I argue, this atmosphere persists in *The Physiology of Petersburg*, in descriptions of citizens and depictions of space. In particular, the melancholy and "tomb-like claustrophobia" already noted come to the fore again and again.[11] Furthermore, the blurring of the melodramatic and the mundane, of the animate and the inanimate, of the vulgar and the sublime are established gothic tricks employed in Nekrasov's volume.

In "Petersburg Organ-Grinders" ("Peterburgskie sharmanshchiki"), author Dmitry Grigorovich concludes his pseudo-ethnographic essay on the customs of various Petersburg organ-grinders with an affecting scene. A man, overcome with melancholy because of the grim Petersburg weather, hears an organ-grinder's music and feels momentarily cheered. This scene relies on a specifically gothic tone to describe the narrator's state of mind and its relationship to the city in order to project this experience onto the reader:

> The high walls of homes, illuminated from time to time by the dim light of streetlamps, seem even bleaker than the sky. In places the buildings and the gray clouds merge into a single mass, and the small lights in the windows shine like moving stars. The rain falls on roofs and pavements with a monotonous tone. A cold wind blows forcefully and wails mournfully through the gates. The streets are empty. Here and there, a rather late pedestrian makes his way, or a night cabbie drags himself along, cursing the bad weather. But soon all quiets down. Now and then one can hear only the prolonged whistle of a watchtower or the creaking of a barge, swaying in the gusting wind [...] A sad and uncomfortable feeling fills one's soul, and an inexpressible melancholy possesses one's entire being. One enters a remote, dark alleyway, and the heart contracts more powerfully than before [...] Suddenly, one hears a street organ amid the silence. The sounds of *Luchinushka* reach the ear, and, very shortly, the figure of the organ-grinder passes by. You somehow come to life. Your heart begins to beat strongly. The anguish momentarily disappears, and you set out cheerfully for home. The mournful sounds of *Luchinushka*, though, continue to hover over you. For a long time there flashes before you the pitiful figure of the organ-grinder.[12]

The vulgar songs of a street organ inspire the narrator's sublime state.[13] Inanimate objects appear and disappear, or become other things altogether in this landscape. Not only is gothic narrative at work here in descriptions that incorporate mournful sounds, violent action, and mysterious objects, it also figures prominently in the narrator's "haunting."

Like the technique of second-person narration, the gothic appears in this episode to give the reader a more personal understanding of the experience of cheerfulness in the face of abject poverty and grim daily life.[14]

Gothic tropes reappear throughout the rest of the collection. In Vladimir Dal's "The Petersburg Yardkeeper" ("Peterburgskii dvornik"), Grigory, the yardkeeper in question, delights in the squalor of his filthy basement apartment. The narrator describes the space evocatively: "Go down about half a dozen steps, stop, and blow away the heavy air and clouds of steam. If, by the third step, you have not fainted from the sour and rancid fumes, you will catch a glimpse of the various objects lying amid the endless gloom of the cellar."[15] Dal wants us to understand his yardkeeper's character, an Everyman of Petersburg yardkeepers, and by extension, his motivations, choices, and secret pleasures. While the yardkeeper's life is hard, he remains in good spirits. However, Dal adds small gothic elements: the gloomy basement, a twisted hag who stops by the yard, the yardkeeper's secret financial transactions, characters that smell of mould and rot. The elements juxtaposed with the cheerful yardkeeper's day-to-day business create the impression of lingering unease.

Evgeny Grebenka's vibrant "Petersburg Quarter" ("Peterburgskaia storona") uses this same gothic mode more overtly than other sketches. It celebrates the various lives that make up the city's Petersburg Quarter region. While discussing theatres and other entertainments in the area, Grebenka breaks the work's cheerful overall tone to observe an abandoned wooden arcade, described as "ruins," a particularly gothic image:

The building [...] still stands to this day. It is surrounded by a colonnade and still preserves its grandeur from the outside. The building, however, gives one a sad feeling. It stands (or better to say, is collapsing) amid small hovels and dirty streets. Everything in it is dead and black. The windows and doors have darkened terribly and look like the socket hollows of a dead skull. Inside it is terribly blackened, run down, and stripped to the frame. One finds neither life nor sound in these ruins. Sometimes, however, when the wind passes through, one will hear a cautious breathing or a quiet rustling. Sometimes, from behind a door, a girl in tatters appears, stealthily pulling out a half-rotten plank or log; or, from under a floorboard, a dog begins to bark at a passerby.[16]

This strange interlude emerges between a lengthy description of theatre history in the Petersburg Quarter and a discussion of the neighbourhood's carriages and cabs. The *memento mori* suggests a bleak outlook for the little girl's future, as does the evocative image of the dog barking under the floorboards, reminiscent of Edgar Allan Poe's "Tell-Tale Heart" (1843).[17] Here again, just as elsewhere in the volume, the gothic exposes the sad state of life among the lower classes for the sympathetic reader.

The centrepiece of *The Physiology of Petersburg* is Nekrasov's own offering, "Petersburg Corners" ("Peterburgskie ugly").[18] Nekrasov plunges readers into the dark and seamy underworld of a Petersburg tenement, introducing a host of desperate characters. The lives of these people may be the main focus, but certain details describing place clearly establish a gothic-inspired setting. As the narrator descends into the tenement, he compares the space with a tomb: "The room was about three and a half arshins in height and had its own special air, the likes of which is met with only in wine cellars and burial vaults."[19] Gothic exaggeration comes to the fore as the narrator absurdly describes the marks on the walls as human blood stains:

> The chief adornment, however, was neither the decorations nor the remnants of plaster but the oblong, bloody (but innocent) stains that bore the traces of fingerprints as well as the thin and brittle shells of sacrifices that had perished long ago. Thick spiderwebs hung in curtains and garlands about the room. Their strands went out in all directions, entangling my face and even getting into my mouth.[20]

Only after this first impression does the narrator reveal that the stains are, in fact, the remains of dead flies. The cobwebs decorating the room further add to the atmosphere, suggesting death and decay. While the narrator pokes fun at these gothic clichés, they serve to set the scene, emphasizing the subtler anxiety built by the narrative as the piece continues.

As the narrator progresses further into the tenement, each knock on the door is terrible and each new visitor mysterious. The narrator represents the other inhabitants as cruel and the tenement as crypt-like. These descriptions sharply contrast with brief mentions of the beautiful Petersburg daylight to create an overall sense of claustrophobic terror, as though these people have been driven to desperation by their unbearable surroundings. Here Nekrasov uses detail in the same way it would be used in a gothic novel: to amplify horror through setting.

Even at the structural level, we can see that gothic narrative force drives Nekrasov's "Petersburg Corners." First, the text revolves around the solution of a mystery plot, building on the reader's curiosity (as well as the protagonist's). Second, the text focuses on taboos and transgressions, which in this case introduce the physiological writers' social agenda: drawing attention to the unspeakable poverty of Petersburg's lower classes. Belinsky's circle viewed these poor people's plight as a transgression against human decency. Finally, the text uses urban space to emphasize the protagonist's anxious psychological state. Nekrasov anticipates readers' familiarity with gothic conventions and uses them to enhance the sketch's background in order to communicate his indictment of Russia's social ills more forcefully.

The Physiology of Petersburg marked a turning point in Russian literature and stood as a manifesto of sorts for the burgeoning early realist movement. The depiction techniques used here were borrowed from French physiological models, but writers fine-tuned them to meet the sociocultural specificities of the Russian capital. Following Sue's example, the writers who worked together on the volume incorporated gothic elements into their texts to establish atmosphere, engage the reader in the narrative, and communicate the urban poor's plight. Their work stands as testimony to early realist innovation.

Dostoevsky's Gothic Cityscape

Dostoevsky's early works present an intriguing contrast when read with reference to Nekrasov's volume, *The Physiology of Petersburg*. While his writing of the 1840s cannot be called physiological, his inspiration draws on the same models used by the volume's writers, including earlier physiological sketches and Sue's popular novel. However, Dostoevsky's works conflate the journalistic feuilleton with both Gogol's Hoffmann-esque tales and George Sand's more tempered, socially conscious romantic tendencies. Gothic fiction, which Dostoevsky had read since childhood, also served as a major influence.[21] Those works Dostoevsky set in Petersburg from this period create a cityscape, at times fantastic and at times realistic, that underscores the psychological state of his protagonists. An examination of Dostoevsky's 1845–9 Petersburg texts reveals the interplay between the concept of city as ideological symbol and fantastic dreamscape.

Poor Folk (*Bednye liudi*, 1846), Dostoevsky's earliest novel, is set in the Petersburg slums and depicts daily existence in language that implies concealed mysteries and horrors. The most overtly gothic scene maps to a rural landscape, not an urban one. Varvara writes to Devushkin on 3 September, describing her daydream:

> At that time of year everything grows gloomier, the yellow leaves strew the paths along the edges of the bare woods, which turn dark blue, almost black – especially at evening, when a damp mist descends and the trees loom out of it like giants, like terrible, monstrous apparitions. I might

delay in returning while out on a walk, fall behind the others, walk alone,
quickening my step – it was sinister! I myself would be trembling like one
of those leaves, there, I would think, at any moment some fearsome being
will look out of that tree-hollow; and all the while the wind would be
rushing through the woods, whistling, moaning and howling so dolefully,
tearing the clusters of leaves from the withered twigs, whirling them in
the air; and, in a long, wide, noisy flock, the birds hurtling after them with
wild, penetrating cries, turning the sky black as they covered it across.
I would grow afraid, and then I would seem to hear someone's voice whispering: "Run, run, child, don't delay; terrible things will happen here in a
moment, run, child!" A sense of horror would grip my heart, and I would
run and run until my breath gave out. I would reach home, panting; there
it was noisy and cheerful.[22]

Varvara's daydream emphasizes both the experience of terror and the
pleasure that can come from fear in retrospect, when one feels safe. In
Dostoevsky's St Petersburg, however, safe havens are altogether absent.
The city's gothic descriptions in *Poor Folk* are subtle but serve to create
a disturbing subtext of fear and anxiety. Cramped rooms are compared
to coffins. Gorshkov, Devushkin's neighbour, lives with his family in an
overcrowded room, and the sound of weeping comes from behind his
door. Degradation and deprivation seem quite literally to be killing his
family, beginning with his young son and then moving on to Gorshkov
himself. The anxiety Devushkin feels as he walks along, as well as his
fear of public life, sketch for the reader a cityscape characterized by
facades that hide secrets and horrors.[23] The epigraph of *Poor Folk* – from
Vladimir Odoevsky's gothic tale "The Living Corpse" (1844) – suggests
that one of Dostoevsky's underlying premises was that the city's poor
were trapped by both circumstance and the city itself.[24]

As we follow Dostoevsky's series of urban texts chronologically, the
city takes on a different form. It becomes almost a character in its own
right in these novellas, transforming the reader's perception of the city.
One early example of this phenomenon occurs in *The Double* (*Dvoinik*,
1846).[25] Here Golyadkin, the hero, while waiting outside a house party,
perceives that guests are staring at him through the windows. Instead
of blaming the party guests, he begins to blame the windows for his
discomfort, eventually asserting that the building itself is staring at
him. A projected manifestation of his anxiety, Golyadkin's uncanny
Petersburg becomes a living, anthropomorphized city.

In *The Landlady* (*Khoziaika*, 1847) Dostoevsky combines suggestions of physical horror in urban descriptions with hyperbole in the
depiction of the situations and characters. Here, though, rather than

serving as canvas for the story's events, Petersburg assumes an active role. The hero, Ordynov, finds himself drawn by unknown forces to a particular area of the city – the mysterious tenement – and takes lodging there. This building simultaneously conceals and points towards the transgressions and sins that lend the work its air of mystery. As Randi Gaustad has observed, the setting bears some overt similarities to Ann Radcliffe's castles or Matthew Lewis's monasteries.[26] While Gaustad's analysis focuses on the collection of gothic themes present in *The Landlady*, I mention the work briefly here as another example of Dostoevsky's evocation of a St Petersburg come to life. In this novella, Dostoevsky explicitly utilizes gothic tropes to give the impression of a living city, a city acting to propel an anxious hero along his narrative arc. This use of the gothic successfully associates St Petersburg with a sinister, fateful villain, more clearly delineating the "individual vs authority" theme in Dostoevsky's social fiction.

As Dostoevsky's Petersburg prose develops, the city's depiction becomes increasingly bound with the hero's psychological state and emotional experience. Dostoevsky's narratives begin to focus more on his heroes' internal reveries, drawing on both sentimental romantic fantasies and the Kantian sublime, one of the driving narrative forces of the gothic as it manifested in a "sublime anxiety."[27] In several works from this period, Dostoevsky takes as his hero a character type called the "dreamer." In the fourth and final feuilleton of his "Petersburg Chronicle" (dated 15 June 1847), for example, Dostoevsky writes of such types, describing their basic tendencies as they relate to the Petersburg topography:

> Then in characters eager for activity, eager for spontaneous life, eager for reality – but weak, effeminate, gentle – there arises little by little what is called reverie, and a man becomes at length not a man but some strange creature of an intermediate sort – a *dreamer*. Do you know what a *dreamer* is, gentlemen? It is a Petersburg nightmare. It is sin personified, it is a tragedy, mute, mysterious, gloomy, savage, with all the furious horrors, with all the catastrophes, peripeties, plots and denouements – and we say this by no means in jest.[28]

This character becomes both a symptom and a cause of Petersburg's peculiar atmosphere. Outside circumstances, both emotional and physical, compel the "dreamer" to the peak of inspiration. His experience channels the Kantian sublime: terror and awe of the incomprehensible overwhelm him, but this feeling leads him to new understanding of the world around him.

In "A Weak Heart" ("Slaboe serdtse," 1848), the hero's sublime moment occurs as a sort of epilogue to the text's events. The story relates the experiences of two dear friends, Vasya and Arkady, clerks living together in Petersburg. When Vasya announces his engagement, the friends and Vasya's fiancée plan to live happily together after the wedding. Shortly afterwards, Vasya takes some copying home with him. Although Vasya is a good worker and takes great pride in his calligraphy skills, he begins to feel anxious and a fearful dread descends upon him that he will not finish in time. Vasya suddenly goes mad and is sent to an asylum. Arkady goes to visit Vasya's distraught fiancée. Returning from this visit, he has a vision while crossing the Neva River and the piece ends. We are left wondering: what happened?

While "A Weak Heart" leaves this question – and many others – unanswered, the sublime "Vision on the Neva" scene that concludes the work provides some clues.[29] A favourite gothic technique, sublime anxiety compels characters to open door after door, exploring their prisons despite the horrors they anticipate. In the "Vision on the Neva," Dostoevsky uses the underlying anxiety that propels the narrative, the same anxiety that drives Vasya mad, to build the sublime experience that Arkady seemingly seemingly cannot comprehend.

From the passage's first sentence, we are struck with the unusually violent landscape description: "As [Arkady] approached the Neva he stopped for a moment and cast a penetrating glance along the river into the smoky, frost-deadened distance, which had suddenly flared with the last purple of a blood-red sunset that was burning itself out on the smudgy horizon."[30] The vivid image of the blood-coloured sunset in the smoky, dark distance transforms the cityscape into a fantastic canvas for Arkady's transcendent vision.

The episode continues: "Night was descending over the city, and the whole immense clearing of the Neva, which had swollen with frozen snow, was being showered, in the sun's last reflection, with infinite myriads of sparks thrown down by the hoar-frost." The natural elements of the passage here contribute to, or perhaps emanate from, Arkady's dreamlike state. The frozen river echoes the static passage of time, which seems to stand still during Arkady's vision. At the same time, the river shines and sparkles, suggesting the other-worldly. "It was minus twenty degrees. Frozen steam fell heavily from horses which had been driven to death, from the people hurrying by." Although the people are rushing along, busy with their day-to-day life, Arkady observes this as an afterthought. Just as the smoky air and river have frozen, the steam clouds over the city have also frozen. The description of horses "driven to death" gives rise to a morbid mood, already suggested by the "bloody" sunset in the first line.

This transformed world leads to the vision of the next few lines: "The taut air shivered at the slightest sound and, like giants, from all the roofs of both embankments columns of smoke rose into the cold sky and floated aloft, twining and untwining on their way." Suddenly the frozen atmosphere itself comes alive, quivering at the slightest sound. Smoke columns become like giants in the sky, rising ever upwards, away from the city, twining and untwining. These mythological creatures of epic proportions, although not quite real, usher in the brave new world of Arkady's idealistic vision: "It seem[ed] as though new buildings were rising above the old ones, as though a new city were being formed in the air." As Arkady catches a glimpse of the shining idealized city arising out of the smoky and gloomy old one, with its unaware, uncaring rushing people and its nearly dead, frozen, or static features, he begins to feel hope.

"Finally," he says, as though he has been waiting for this new city to emerge: "It was as if, at last, this entire world, with all its inhabitants, weak and strong, and all their habitations, the shelters of the poor or the gilded palaces for the delight of the powerful of this world, resembled a fantastic, magical vision, a dream that would in its turn vanish in a trice and evanesce towards the dark-blue heavens." The city with its problems, its vast discrepancies in wealth, its powerful and its downtrodden, disappears. It seems as though in this moment, Arkady has frozen with the city in his reverie, distanced himself from the rushing people, and thus become aware of a broader perspective. In this moment of distancing, a gothic-inspired experience of the sublime enters the vision.

Arkady experiences the effects of the sublime: "A strange thought visited the forlorn companion of poor Vasya. He quivered, and his heart seemed in that instant to fill with a hot jet of blood which had suddenly boiled up from the influx of some mighty sensation hitherto unknown to him." His heart is overwhelmed, both physically by the powerful rush of warm blood but also emotionally, as he remembers his dear friend Vasya's fate. Although we, the readers, do not gain new understanding, we learn that Arkady begins to understand why Vasya went mad: "Only now did he seem to understand all the anxiety there had been and to realize why his poor Vasya had gone mad, unable to endure his happiness. His lips began to tremble, his eyes flared with light, and at that moment his eyes seemed to open on something new." Beauty traditionally inspires sublime reveries, but here, as in *The Landlady*, Dostoevsky makes use of terror's ability to do so. Distraught over his dear friend's seemingly incomprehensible descent into madness, Arkady begins to see the city in a new, terrifying way.

Reflected through the hero's experience, the city does not stand on its own terms but begins to reflect a gothic mindset. Arkady's mental state colours the sunset "bloody" and the city murky, gloomy, and smoky. Through Arkady's eyes, Petersburg becomes a frozen wasteland filled with uncaring people and connoting death. Arkady's terror is evident in his widened eyes, trembling lips, and paling face. However, this same terror prompts the sublime moment and his imagined realization of a new, better city that is airy and intangible. Although Arkady initially cannot comprehend his friend Vasya's earlier anxiety and dread, his own anxieties propel him onwards, through the sublime vision, which is both beautiful – shining, glimmering, idealized – and terrible – static, frozen, dark – to revelation. While Vasya's madness seemed inexplicable, Arkady's vision supplies a bleak, sinister cause: daily life in the city itself.

As Dostoevsky's brand of the Petersburg Text evolves through this period, his later descriptions of the city absorb and build on these earlier textual cityscapes. Accordingly, in *Netochka Nezvanova* (1849), Dostoevsky's unfinished, last work from this period, the heroine's early life story contains all the previous elements of a gothic Petersburg Text. Netochka grows up in a labyrinthine tenement, trapped in a life of poverty as she witnesses her mother's abuse and exploitation at the hands of her stepfather, a drunk and failed musician with hints of madness about him. Netochka herself has a tendency towards obsession and daydreaming and frequently enters into lengthy reveries, just like Dostoevsky's other "dreamer" characters. This fragmentary novel relies heavily upon the Petersburg setting to convey Netochka's emotional experiences.

As Netochka falls into a deep obsession with her stepfather, she projects her feelings onto descriptions of a house that she associates with him. Returning home, Netochka sees her stepfather waiting outside this residence. After this incident she becomes fixated on the house:

> I remember that the pain in my arm grew worse and worse, making me feverish, and yet I was particularly happy because it had all turned out so well. I dreamed of the house with the red curtains throughout the night. When I woke up the following day my first thought and concern was for the house with the red curtains. As soon as mother had gone outside I clambered up to the little window and gazed out at the house. For a long time it had fascinated my childish curiosity. I particularly liked looking at it in the evening when the street was lit up and the crimson-red curtains behind the plate-glass windows gleamed with a peculiar blood-red glow.[31]

When her stepfather tells Netochka that he will be "born again" upon her mother's death, she begins to draw associations between her mother's death, her stepfather's rise in fortunes, and her own move into this abode. The house with curtained windows with a blood-coloured glow represents her idyll, but also has a darker side, tied to her mother's death.

As the fragment progresses, Netochka begins to differentiate between her internal and external lives.[32] Her internal life provides an escape for her in the first part of the fragment, allowing her to transcend the drudgery and poverty that characterize life with her mother and stepfather. When the tension within the apartment becomes overwhelming and she needs physical escape, she retreats to liminal spaces: her apartment's corner, her tenement stairwell, her building courtyard. Like the apartment building in *The Landlady*, Netochka's tenement resembles a dark castle in a gothic novel. It harbours locations like the stairwell, an exploratory space from which Netochka overhears truths, as well as the apartment itself, a chamber characterized by hidden horrors such as, at first, the disintegration of her parents' relationship, and then her mother's stiffening corpse.

Her mother's death destroys Netochka's idyll and signals the beginning of the girl's isolated life with her stepfather. The nightmare she describes having while her mother lies dying becomes real, projected onto the city streets. Initially, walking through the city at night under a light snowfall with her stepfather, Netochka feels happy that their dream is coming true, but switching her focus to the cityscape – the ice-covered canals, the dark, looming houses, and the isolation of city streets at night – she realizes that her stepfather is now fully mad and will abandon her. The scene quickly turns into the nightmare tableau: Netochka chasing her stepfather, always out of reach, down St Petersburg alleys in blind terror, afraid of returning to her mother's corpse but equally afraid of being left without any guardian or protector. Her frantic chase ends without resolution.

The fragment lacks the detailed descriptions of St Petersburg that other texts set in the city during this period incorporate, but the cityscape nonetheless comes to characterize Netochka's earlier life. Netochka's early life revolves around three key gothic moments: her fatal obsession with the red-curtained house, the hidden secrets of her tenement building, and the chase through streets of St Petersburg, her quarry always just out of reach. First, as she grows to love her stepfather, she associates him with the house with red curtains. Then, as her stepfather's life spins out of control, she hides, fearful, on her tenement stairs, waiting for him. The dark tenement staircase, with its shadows and hidden spaces, seems to reflect her fear. Finally, when her life changes following her mother's death, the transition occurs against the city backdrop. These three scenes all contribute to a depiction of life among lower classes in St Petersburg as fraught with fear and anxiety.

Physiological Petersburg, Gothic Petersburg

By the late 1840s, generic gothic markers and cues that evoked claustrophobia and terror for readers were already incorporated into the meta-narrative of the Petersburg Text. The gothic had grown so familiar in early realism that the mere mention of a dark and cramped tenement staircase or an icy canal sufficiently conjured readers' expectations. This gothic dwelling on psychological states caused by anxiety or dread evokes the earlier romantic-fantastic Petersburg texts of Pushkin and Gogol, while providing a frame for more physiological depictions. The Petersburg of Pushkin's nervous "Queen of Spades" or Gogol's frenetic tales represents the anxious psychological state that pervaded society at this time. By framing their texts thus, Petersburg writers of this transitional period emphasized anxiety, fear, and dread without using the uncanny methods of Pushkin and Gogol, staying true to the new realist mode of writing, which eschewed the fantastic.

As a tool used to describe the city's interiors and exteriors, the gothic mode enhanced the realist agenda by using pathos to appeal to readers' consciences. The genre's immediate associations with transgression and moral wrong made it an ideal backdrop to influence the dramatic scenes unfolding on its Petersburg canvas. For writers depicting Petersburg, the gothic's use was twofold: its signifiers underscored social injustices and moral wrongs, but as a mode of writing, it also allowed romantic depictions of Petersburg to carry over into realist texts. In accommodating the hyperbolic language and extreme moods of the gothic in their writing, these authors changed the basic setting and array of conventions, effectively translating the genre not only deeper into the Russian literary language but, more importantly, into the realist project. In appropriating the genre for this purpose, the early realist writers evoke the sense of the gothic – its psychologies, modes, and themes – without relying upon its trappings – its settings, character types, or master plots. Instead, they use their own setting: the Russian capital. This newly exposed, gritty, gothic Petersburg signified an important shift in Russian literary history and set the stage for the discussions of social change to come.

Chapter Six

Gothic Subjectivity
and the Woman Question

"I am no bird; and no net ensnares me:
I am a free human being with an independent will."

Charlotte Brontë, *Jane Eyre*

"All my hope rests now on gaining the only blessing still accessible to me –
independence, and, consequently, together with it, peace."

Evgeniya Tur, *Antonina*

In these epigraphs, two nineteenth-century heroines assert their independence. Jane Eyre's statement, a favourite feminist quote, comes as Rochester, in a prelude to his proposal, teases her into thinking he is marrying another. However, Jane's statement could be taken as an articulation of the goal she is working towards throughout the novel as she moves from one scenario in which she is metaphorically fettered to another. Antonina's wish for independence, and, through it, peace, echoes Jane's. Female captivity – not just in a literal sense but also as an extended metaphor for structures of power that inequitably work against women, rendering them vulnerable and weak – is a common theme in eighteenth- and nineteenth-century novels that engage with the gothic, such as Charlotte Brontë's *Jane Eyre* (1847) and Evgeniya Tur's *Antonina* (1851). In the Russian tradition, other examples range from Nikolai Karamzin's gothic tale "Bornholm Island" ("Ostrov Borngol'm," 1794) to Nikolai Chernyshevsky's socialist utopian novel *What Is to Be Done? (Chto delat'?,* 1863).[1] In "Bornholm Island," a melancholy traveller discovers a woman literally imprisoned in a cave under a castle for (we assume) committing incest, while in *What Is to Be Done?,* the heroine, Vera Pavlovna, dreams multiple times about her own entrapment in a cellar and sees the socialist future – with its emphasis on equality – as a means of escape. Such recurring images of entrapment engage with contemporaneous discourse about women's abilities and roles in society, a discourse that became known as "the woman question" in the mid-to-late nineteenth century.

In early gothic narratives of entrapment, female subjectivity – that is, the experience of female characters of existing in their own consciousness – provides the characters with a sort of escape. In the gothic tradition, Ann Radcliffe's writing most famously uses this trope. In *A Sicilian Romance* (1790), *The Romance of the Forest* (1791), *The Mysteries of Udolpho* (1794), and *The Italian* (1797), Radcliffe's heroines find themselves imprisoned, but they are able to transcend physical captivity through mental flights that take them to sublime heights. Mark Pettus connects Radcliffe's model with a spatial trajectory: the heroine, moving within her imprisoning structure, repeatedly shifts from the cell to the "consolatory turret," that is, a tower from which she takes in a panoramic view.[2] This movement invariably takes place within the prison but still affords the heroine a feeling of freedom prompted by the sublime vista. In *The Italian*, for example, Ellena finds a means to mentally escape her imprisonment through the discovery of a tower room with a view. When she sees this view, the reader learns that its

> grandeur awakened all her heart. The consciousness of her prison was lost, while her eyes ranged over the wide and freely sublime scene without [...] To Ellena, whose mind was capable of being highly elevated, or sweetly soothed, by scenes of nature, the discovery of this little turret was an important circumstance. Hither she could come, and her soul, refreshed by the views it afforded, would acquire strength to bear her with equanimity through the persecutions that might await her.[3]

This experience sets a boundary between outer and inner life: Ellena's physical imprisonment and her mental freedom. Her freedom of mind, however, is tightly connected to a sense of rejuvenation that prepares her for future travails. In this sense, the turret is "consolatory."

In some Russian texts of the 1840s and 1850s, the barrier between women's subjective experience and outer lives becomes more pronounced. In Alexander Veltman's novel *Heart and Mind* (*Serdtse i dumka*, 1838), for example, the heroine's heart and mind literally separate from her body and travel around Russia. And in Karolina Pavlova's lyrical novel *A Double Life* (*Dvoinaia zhizn'*, 1852), the heroine retreats from the whirl of society life each evening to the quiet of her private bedroom, where she removes her "mental corset" (умственный корсет) and engages in poetic creation prompted by a visiting spirit.[4] In other works, the practice of reading enables subjective freedom. In Radcliffe's *A Sicilian Romance*, for example, heroine Julia's turret retreat includes a fine view and a collection of books; her subjective sense of spiritual rejuvenation comes as much from the experience of reading as from the view. Similarly, Nadezhda Khvoshchinskaya's heroine Lelenka in *The Boarding-School Girl* (*Pansionerka*, 1860) describes reading as a means to escape her daily life: "I take up a book and often simply don't sense where I am. You can go to another world entirely."[5] Female subjectivity as an escapist mode with connections to elements of both freedom and the gothic is a frequent trope in literary depictions of women's inner lives.

Gothic subjectivity – in which subjective experience becomes a conduit for the uncanny, the terrifying, and the transgressive – is one way of asserting women's agency in narrative. Diane Long Hoeveler suggests a gendered definition of the term. In her formulation, gothic subjectivity refers both to the location of the masculine self in the decaying, corruptible human body, and to "the majority of Female Gothic texts [in which there is] a railing against the physical body and endorsement instead of the life of the mind, reason, spirit, and the intellect."[6] In an essay arguing that Elena Gan (1814–42) is an example of a Russian writer of female gothic fiction, Carolyn Jursa Ayers articulates one of Gan's key methods of engaging with the gothic in terms of the subject: "The boundaries of the self are fluid, the integrity of the self is questioned [...] The Gothic tonality serves to express an anxiety about the position of the self in the world."[7] Ayers does not use the phrase "female gothic subjectivity," but her approach aligns with Hoeveler's later explanation of that concept. In its preoccupation with fear, anxiety, and transgression, the gothic enables a narrative exploration of the subject that breaks out of the limits imposed by the confines of the physical body and the integrity of the self. By extension, the gothic subject might also be breaking free of limits imposed by hierarchies predicated on social identity, tradition, and the law. In this sense, gothic subjectivity carries not only a kind of freedom but also the possibility of imagining alternative social models in which women have more rights and opportunities.

This chapter examines the way female subjectivity in nineteenth-century Russian realist prose is articulated using gothic imagery, focusing at length on Tur's *Antonina*[8] and its intertextual relationships with Brontë's *Jane Eyre* and Ivan Turgenev's *Diary of a Superfluous Man* (*Dnevnik lishnego cheloveka*, 1850). Women's critical discourse appeared most frequently within the medium of literary fiction,[9] and the gothic mode allowed for a way of representing and thinking about women's experience within narrative that critical discourse did not.[10] Analysing gothic narrative elements in these works reveals a framework for understanding links between uncanny or gothic depictions of women and greater social anxieties surrounding the woman question. As I will argue, gothic subjectivity in this context creates spaces in which women's agency and independence is possible.

Women's Experience and Female Gothic

The rise of gothic writing in England and France was linked to debates about the rights of women in the late eighteenth century. This was not the case for the genre's transmission to the Russian literary scene. Yet in both Western European and Russian cultural contexts, the gothic genre was characterized by women's writing and women's reading.[11] A significant number of the notable early gothic novelists who established the genre's conventions through their writing and whose works were imported into Russia were women: Clara Reeve, Sophia Lee, Charlotte Dacre, and, of course, Radcliffe, to name a few. Mary Wollstonecraft wrote her feminist treatise *A Vindication of the Rights of Woman* (1792) just a year after Radcliffe had published *The Romance of the Forest* and two years before *The Mysteries of Udolpho*. Wollstonecraft also wrote novels of her own – *Mary, a Fiction* (1788) and *The Wrongs of Woman, or Maria* (1798), both of which begin within the realm of the sentimental and quickly veer into the gothic. As Hoeveler has observed, "Female gothic ideology originated in the hyperbolic gestures and the frenzied poses of victimage that tip these novels over the edge from sentimentality into gothicism [...] Wollstonecraft exposed the tyranny of sentimental literary formulae for women."[12] The exploration of victimhood and the power structures and injustices it reveals is central to scholarship of the female gothic. Furthermore, as a genre associated with women's practices of writing and reading, the gothic functions particularly well as a conduit for discussions of women's situation in society and, by extension, women's education. After all, a significant strand of gothic fiction is predicated on the dangers that an uneducated or too-sheltered woman faces in the world. In the Russian context, while these themes emerge in gothic fiction by Karamzin, Mariya Izvekova, Nadezhda Durova,[13] and others who drew direct inspiration from the English genre, the connection between gothic writing and women's agency has not emerged as part of critical scholarship around the genre.

"Female gothic" is a term originally coined by Ellen Moers as a way of classifying gothic texts by women that particularly dwell on feelings of anxiety and entrapment in relation to traditional women's roles such as wife and mother.[14] In her influential interpretation of Mary Shelley's *Frankenstein* (1818) as a gothic birth myth, the female gothic becomes a mode encompassing the "fear and guilt, depression and anxiety" that accompany the birth of a baby.[15] For Moers, female gothic is a means of expression limited to women writers, but others have expanded the term to include the anxieties attendant upon a broader spectrum of gothic literature, especially those that subvert traditional domestic ideology. As Judith Wilt puts it, the female gothic offers "deep revelations about gender, ego and power."[16] Susan Wolstenhome's feminist reading of the gothic tradition goes one further, arguing that the very structure, form, and allusions inherent in gothic works have "special potential to deal with the issues of writing and reading as a woman […] [they] participate in establishing 'woman' as a textual position […] a pattern that becomes a recognizable symbolic code."[17]

In this vein, identifying gothic narrative as part of the female gothic tradition provides a critical framework through which the latent feminist voice of the author can come to the fore. Kate Ferguson Ellis's work ably demonstrates the power of such a reading in the English context. In her study of gothic fiction and the subversion of domestic ideology, Ellis argues that "the Gothic novel […] [creates] a resistence [*sic*] to an ideology that imprisons [women] even as it posits a sphere of safety for them,"[18] and in doing so, focuses on feminine gothic and reads masculine gothic as a reaction to it. In a feminist reading of Radcliffe's *Mysteries of Udolpho*, for example, the plot acts as a vehicle for Emily St Aubert to expose Montoni's subversion of the safe space of the home, represented by his castle, which becomes her prison; in the end, she reclaims the space from him. A feminist reading of Matthew Lewis's *The Monk* (1796) reveals the novel's engagement with the feminine gothic, as established by Radcliffe. Ellis reads Lewis's novel as "an attack on the 'cloistered virtue' of monks, but also of women brought up in circumstances created to protect them from contact with evil."[19]

Read in this way, eighteenth- and nineteenth-century gothic novels can be understood as texts that enabled women's intellectual freedom but also exposed their vulnerability through traumatic experiences. Brontë's *Jane Eyre* is a prime example. The novel focuses on Jane, an orphan with a vivid inner life whose life experiences do not align with her imagined world, drawn from books, music, and art. She is tormented as a child, abused and neglected at boarding school, and constantly finds herself torn suddenly from any comfortable situation. When she makes a single close friend at school, that friend dies tragically of consumption. When she finds happiness in the love of her employer, Rochester, their wedding is interrupted by the revelation that the groom's first wife is still alive and locked in the attic. When Jane flees and happens upon a cottage where cousins, previously unknown to her, are living, they offer a warm home life, honest employment, and kindred intellects, but after she receives a proposal from one of her cousins, she realizes she cannot stay. Finally, returning to Thornfield, she discovers the house a burned-out ruin, Rochester blinded and wounded, and his wife dead in the blaze. At this point, Jane is able to gain what she has sought throughout the novel: a stable and loving family life. The novel ends on a happy domestic scene, and while Jane's inner reveries and external life finally seem to have united by the final chapter, her vulnerability throughout the narrative has demonstrated women's precarity and Brontë's own anxiety in relation to it. *Jane Eyre* and the Brontë sisters' other works were particularly timely in this regard, as they appeared just as the discussion of the woman question across Europe was revived in the 1830s and 1840s.[20]

When *Jane Eyre* and *Antonina* appeared in print, the woman question had not yet risen to prominence in Russia; it would only do so in the mid-1850s. In the 1830s and 1840s, however, critical discussions about the role of women in Russian society were taking place. Barbara Alpern Engel traces these discussions to male reformers' and radicals' self-reflection in the wake of the 1825 Decembrist revolt and to their ensuing recognition of "the connection between the autocratic political order, which they opposed, and the patriarchal family that subordinated women and children to men."[21] As they worked to reconcile this inconsistency in their program through democratization of the family, they first "exalted women" and then later "tried to create equality between the sexes" through debate. These discussions were concerned particularly with the role of women within the family, and the potential of a shift in women's roles for revitalizing Russian society more broadly. However, while the debates about women's roles took place in literary salons and *publitsistika*, the average upper-class Russian woman was not touched by them.

This process of shifting women's roles has historically been couched in terms of a shift in consciousness. As Arja Rosenholm phrases it, "the 'awakening' of the sleeping girl [is] a 'progressive' step on her way to emancipation."[22] Rosenholm rightly identifies the problem in this paradigm, namely that it locates women's experiences on the side of "non-reason and non-culture."[23] This kind of phrasing frequently appears in, for example, Richard Stites's history of the women's liberation movement in Russia: "The gentry woman of pre-reform Russia, though often possessed of great will and strong character, was not yet ready to give voice to her feelings in terms of the terrible question which heralds the beginning of woman's consciousness: Is there nothing more to life?"[24] Such characterizations of women's experience assume that "pre-liberation" women have no consciousness of their situation.[25] Tur's *Antonina* is striking in that it demonstrates the range and capacity of women's emotional freedom during this time. In its depiction of its heroine's inner life, it examines women's consciousness, while its use of gothic subjectivity reveals the latent anxiety surrounding women's experiences in 1840s and 1850s Russia.

Evgeniya Tur: Creating a Russian Jane Eyre

Jane Eyre caused a stir when it was published in Russia in 1849–50. Brontë's novel appeared in three different versions in short succession: a summary with translated excerpts in *Library for Reading* in April 1849[26]; a full translation in *Fatherland Notes* beginning in May 1849[27]; and a second summary with translated excerpts in *The Contemporary* in 1850.[28] The anonymous author of the literary narrative account of the novel in *Library for Reading* emphasizes the centrality of inner life and emotion that characterizes Brontë's works and speculates about the work's authorship, musing:

> Who wrote these impassioned and fluent pages? [...] The subject and details of this book compel us to believe readily that *Jane Eyre* is the product of a woman's pen; but no matter who the author, no matter which merits earned him renown and success with a first publication, only one thing strikes the reader: the high literary [высокий] and energetic local character of the novel.[29]

This account highlights emotion in the characterization of both the novel and its author, who is assumed to be a woman. In the preface to the translation in *Fatherland Notes*, translator I.I. Vvedensky contrasts the pseudonymous author of *Jane Eyre* with William Makepeace Thackeray, author of *Vanity Fair*, and notes that the two works approach the same theme and plot but from such radically different perspectives that *Jane Eyre* must be the work of a woman.[30]

This characterization of women's style and topics in prose writing is by no means surprising in mid-nineteenth-century Russian *belles lettres*. In the first decade of the century, as the Russian literary language was developing, Karamzin wrote extensively about the reductive connection between women's speech and so-called refined culture. In his view, women are the ideal general reader because of their feminine sensibility, which in turn results in an elevation of literary language.[31]

In Daria Khitrova's summation, this is a reciprocal relationship: "poets must learn compassion and charity from their female readers," and in turn, "poets must create a language refined and flexible enough to capture the richness and sensibility of women's emotional worlds."[32] Barbara Heldt, distilling the essence of male-female relations in nineteenth-century Russian fiction, summarizes this bluntly: "The female culture is based on feelings; the male culture is based on ideas."[33] Heldt's formulation is based on fictional characters, but her observation echoes the paradigms established in critical writing from the early nineteenth century. As Olga Glagoleva observes, "the female soul, in contrast to the male, was [seen as] gentle and sensitive by nature."[34] It was in this cultural context that Evgeniya Tur appeared on the Russian literary scene.

Tur (the pseudonym of Countess Elizaveta Vasilyevna Salias De Tournemire, née Sukhovo-Kobylina) was hailed as a major new literary talent when her first novel, *The Mistake* (*Oshibka*), was published in *The Contemporary* in 1849, the same year *Jane Eyre* was first published in Russia. Her follow-up novel, *The Niece* (*Plemiannitsa*), appeared in 1851. While *The Niece* received mixed reviews, part 3, which Tur published as a stand-alone novella called *Antonina* in the journal *The Comet* (*Kometa*), also in 1851, was universally lauded by critics. Turgenev famously wrote of it, "These pages [...] will remain in Russian literature." He praised the novella's ability to arouse "deep sympathy" as well as the "simple feeling" and "aspiring, sincere passion" of its form.[35] The nearly simultaneous publication of Tur's and Brontë's works in Russia invited critical comparison, particularly as both writers were noted for their depiction of emotion. Like *Jane Eyre*, *Antonina* relates the first-person history of its heroine's neglected childhood, her experiences working as a governess, the travails of separation from her true love, Michel, and her later marriage to a businessman. Evidently, the novel takes *Jane Eyre* as a significant point of inspiration, not just in the experiences of Antonina but also in its details. While Jane is orphaned and raised first by relatives who despise her and then sent to a boarding school, Antonina's orphanhood leaves her under the guardianship of not one but two villainous step-parents. Antonina's abusive English stepfather is called Millcote (Милькот), a reference to the village near Thornfield Hall, also called Millcote. *Jane Eyre* and *Antonina* are works about young women growing up and finding family but in both, education is of primary importance. Both relate the histories of a governess for whom education enables a means of forging a life independent of a family. While the experience of education in each is a trial – Jane's experience at Lowood is harsh and deprived, while Antonina's education with her step-parents is characterized by abuse – both heroines are grateful that education allows them to become self-sufficient.

While *Antonina* and *Jane Eyre* are intertextually linked, the differences between Tur's novella and Brontë's novel are significant. The majority of Jane's time spent at Thornfield exposes her to the gothic mysteries that are central to Brontë's novel, such as the brooding Edward Rochester and the famous madwoman in the attic.[36] Jane's escape onto the Yorkshire moors brings her to family life with her cousins, but a mysterious voice calls her back to Rochester. This gothic framework plays a significant role in *Jane Eyre*'s structure and plot, but seems to be largely absent from Tur's realist novella. The majority of Antonina's time in her step-parents' care is spent planning her escape, first into service as a governess at a neighbouring estate, then into marriage with Michel. However, when her marriage plans are thwarted by Michel's weakness and inability to oppose his aunt's wishes, Antonina goes back into service. Eventually she attracts the passionate love of Albert Bertini, an Italian businessman, but cannot return his love. She marries him, but his jealous passion for her destroys their marriage. However, in the end, both Jane and Antonina find happiness in their children and in creating the kind of family structure that neither had growing up. *Jane Eyre* draws on the supernatural aspects of the gothic tradition, while *Antonina* is more grounded in realism, but as I will demonstrate, Tur's engagement with gothic narrative devices constitutes another link with Brontë's novel.

In an early scene, which also makes explicit the work's connection to *Jane Eyre*, Antonina has a transformative reading experience with gothic overtones.

> I see myself in a large, cold, towering room; it's dark all around me; a bright fireplace stands along one side; a dim candle burns in the corner. The glow of the fire, red and flickering, flares up and dies down, at times brightly illuminating objects in the room, casting their long, pale shadows on the lacquered parquet. Ancient portraits on the walls stare sternly from their darkened, once-gilded frames; in the clear reflection of the flames, they exert a powerful grip on my childish sensibility and frighten me. I sit cowering in one corner of the room, completely alone – I'm cold and afraid. My shoulders and hands are exposed; the fireplace draws me invitingly and irresistibly [...] I sit down on a little bench that has been left next to the fire and sink into a reverie – far off, like an echo, I hear loud shouting and children running in the next room; my stepmother [...] can't leave them alone, so I'm completely safe. Then I surrender entirely to the pleasure of physical well-being; a book lies on my lap, my hands folded on it, but my

eyes are fixed on the fire and follow the flickering flames, their bending and curling. Suddenly, a harsh, robust voice resounds behind me.[37]

The gothically tinged scene conflates two episodes in Brontë's novel. Solitary reading with the sounds of the household in the background evokes the scene where Jane is illicitly reading beind a curtain, grateful to have a few moments alone with her book until she is interrupted and reprimanded. The red glow of the fire and fear of ancestors' grim glares recalls the gothic scene in which Jane – locked in the red room where her uncle died – becomes so overwrought and frightened that she faints.[38] Crucially, for both Jane and Antonina, gothic exaggeration marks subjective experience, an emotional space that centres the young heroines in their stories as much as the first-person narration does. The gothic description of the flickering fire's shadows and Antonina's fear echo Jane's terrified hallucination of her dead uncle. Whereas in *Jane Eyre*, aborted reading leads to Jane's imprisonment in the red room,[39] in *Antonina*, the terror of the red room is dispelled through the pleasure of reading. Antonina's escapist reading forges a safe space for her in the household where she can indulge in her rich inner life. *Antonina*'s intertext with *Jane Eyre* is predicated on these moments of subjective liberation, often tied to the appearance of gothic narrative cues within the text. Whereas Bronte's *Jane Eyre* inspired *Antonina*, as seen in the gothic intertextual nodes linking the two texts, Tur's work also responds to Turgenev's novella *Diary of a Superfluous Man*.[40]

Jane and the Superfluous Man

Tur, then an established hostess of a famous literary salon, first met Turgenev in November 1850 when he attended her salon. Tur had already published two well-received novels, *The Mistake* and *The Debt* (*Dolg*, 1850), and was widely regarded as "Russia's leading female author."[41] *Diary of a Superfluous Man* impressed Tur, so much so that she wrote Turgenev and suggested that they write together:

> Do me a favor, write a novella with me. It is sure to turn out well, and I would so enjoy writing with you. We could create a really good work, as authors we would supplement each other [пополняя один другого] – although, of course, I place you much higher than myself.[42]

Turgenev's response has been lost and the two never shared authorship, but Tur's suggestion demonstrates both the high esteem in which she held Turgenev's writing and her openness and desire to engage with the ideas raised in his novella.

Diary of a Superfluous Man is a narrative told from its young dying hero's perspective. Chulkaturin recounts several incidents from his life in a series of diary entries that describe his inability to feel connected with others, and in particular, his unrequited love for Liza. Chulkaturin despairs in the face of Liza's obvious distaste for him, and her visible love for Prince N. further alienates him. In the formulaic context of the superfluous man's narrative domain, as in *Rudin* (1855) or *Oblomov*, women play active roles, but most often their narrative function is to provide a contrast with the hero's passivity and inability to fulfil his intentions.[43] In Jehanne Gheith's analysis, Tur's "supplementation" of Turgenev's novella in *Antonina* attacks two fundamental aspects of the superfluous man narrative: his alienation, and the dependency of the heroine's story. Gheith argues that by centring the experience of the heroine in *Antonina*, Tur recalibrates the superfluous man's story and ascribes agency to the heroine.[44] Gheith's juxtaposition of the two texts reveals how Tur's authorial choices undermine the superfluous man narrative.

Examining the gothic intertextual nodes shared by the two texts, however, adds an additional layer of meaning: they reveal Turgenev's hero's feelings towards his own inner life as not just ambivalent but actively destructive. By contrast, Tur uses gothic subjectivity to differentiate between dangerous and safe spaces for her heroine and to craft a protective inner world that can withstand external pressures and structures bent on destruction. In this way, Tur – using gothic subjectivity – revises Turgenev's superfluous man narrative model to centre women's experiences and to generate a model (based on the superfluity chosen by Chulkaturin) wherein her heroine can choose either superfluity or connectivity on her own terms.

Turgenev's novella can be read as depicting a struggle to contain emotion, from the ironic asides about the proper behaviour expected of the dying to the animated characterization of Chulkaturin's dead mother: "Looking at her, it seemed to me that her face expressed subdued astonishment; with half-open lips, sunken cheeks, and meekly fixed eyes, it was as if it breathed the words, 'How good not to stir!'"[45] Chulkaturin's first physical description of a woman in *Diary of a Superfluous Man* is the memory of his mother's corpse in its coffin. He notes that in life she had been "crushed beneath the burden of her own virtues, and tormented all, beginning with herself."[46] He compares her endless busyness to that of an ant and grounds it in animal instinct.[47] Whereas Chulkaturin's superfluity is characterized by an inability to act, his mother acts to excess, to the point that he imagines that her corpse's movement continues and that she must restrain herself. He describes her as "perfectly peaceful" in death, precisely because she is finally able to rest.[48] This scene serves two purposes in the novella. First, it provides distance from the terror of the fatal diagnosis that haunts Chulkaturin, introduced in the first paragraph. Second, it establishes the relationship between the hero and women in the novella: women are animated solely through their importance for him. In this case, Chulkaturin's mother continues to be animated after death through his narration and its projection of suppressed motion onto her.

In *Diary of a Superfluous Man*, gothic subjectivity enters the narrative when the protagonist is overwhelmed with emotion. In one passage, jealousy turns into a beast that "gnaws" at Chulkaturin's organs, and he in turn projects destruction outwards: "I devoured him with my eyes."[49] In another, rage changes the protagonist into a Spanish bandit hidden in the shadows, waiting for his victim.[50] Each time, the brief imagined flame of transformation is quickly doused with prosaic detail, which signals Chulkaturin's inability to act on his emotions. In the first scene, Chulkaturin interrupts his use of bestial imagery to observe that "the prince really was an agreeable young man" (действительно весьма любезный молодой человек).[51] In the second, the landscape he imagines and the dangerous persona he adopts are immediately refuted by the intrusion of everyday life and the inflexibility of the realist narrative.

> I swore to myself, wrapping my cloak about me like a Spaniard, to emerge from some corner and stab my happy rival, and imagined Liza's despair with brutal joy [...] But, first, in the town of O—— such corners were few; and, second – with the timber fence, the street lamp, and the policeman on duty in the distance [...] No! in such a corner it's somehow much more decent to sell buns than to shed human blood.[52]

The shift from gothic narrative to the mundane happens in nearly the same breath as his imagined fancy. It is part of the same sentence, connected with meaning-laden ellipses and a conjunction. Each time that the gothic signals a fissure in the narrative fabric and allows a glimpse into deeper emotion, the text's realism resists these intrusions. Finally, even when, on the point of death, everyday objects interrupt the vision of abstract terror, he speaks of his terror: "I'm terrified [мне жутко]. Yes, I'm terrified. Half hanging over the silent, gaping abyss, I shudder, turn away, with eager attention inspect everything about me. Every object is twice as dear to me. I don't look at my poor, dull room, saying farewell to every speck on my walls."[53] In each of these instances,

Chulkaturin uses gothic narrative – just as he uses other genres, including the romance – in his diary to manipulate his readers. Nonetheless, these glimpses into the depths of his emotion seem believable. One could argue that Chulkaturin's wry use of gothic narrative devices serves to distance himself from the reality of his impending death, creating a situation in which internal life cannot be sustained from the constant distractions of daily life. He is rendered superfluous to his own subjective self.

By contrast, *Antonina* explores gothic emotion in a more balanced way. Tur's novella contains two contrasting types of affective engagement with gothic subjectivity. The first, a sense of oppression characterized by fear, is evident in the fear Antonina feels when the portraits in the red room, representative of those who alienate her – the rightful denizens of the house – seem to gaze down at her in the library. In scenes in this vein, the oppressor takes on the guise of gothic villain. The portraits in the library stare sternly down, and in their "powerful grip" she feels fear. She feels horror and disgust towards those who oppress her: first and foremost, her stepfather, Millcote, but also Michel's overbearing aunt, and finally her husband, Bertini. At the root of these feelings, however, is what Tur describes as "instinctual fear" (инстинктивный испуг)[54] or "instinctively" felt fear (я невольно испугалась).[55] For example, when her stepmother first introduces Millcote as her new stepfather, Antonina observes, "'How can I express what I experienced at that moment? I felt dread and bitterness; I was filled with indescribable horror mixed with disgust and anger."[56] Similarly, encountering Michel's aunt, Antonina feels "instinctual fear," but first she likens her to Lady Macbeth, remarking that she "has neither soul nor heart."[57] Michel's aunt in this scene holds sway over Antonina's future; it is she who withholds her blessing from her nephew's engagement to Antonina. "Instinctual fear" throughout the novella refers to a prescient feeling of fear, a fear of an anticipated future trauma. This gothic representation of oppression exists in parallel to a gothic representation of inner life.

A second affective manifestation of gothic subjectivity carries a more positive connotation. Just as Antonina's fears in the library give way to an escapist reverie, so too are emotions she cherishes, like love, couched in gothic imagery throughout the novella. Antonina's gothic inner life is populated by ghosts: first and foremost, the "still vital" memory of her father, which functions the same way as music or reading to open a gateway to her inner world. Her father appears in her memories as a "pale, poetic figure" with a "melancholy face and wonderful eyes," which "seemed to follow [her] everywhere."[58] Antonina imagines an aesthetically gothic portrait of her father, but in his case, the uncanny gaze of the dead does not provoke her fear, only "love [...] [and] nour-ishment."[59] When Antonina falls in love with Michel at first sight, her love is awakened by his voice, which "reminded [her] of the remote, unfamiliar resonance of [her] ... father's voice, still vital, perpetually pleasant, stored deep within [her] soul."[60] In this way, both Michel and her father become indelibly associated with her safe inner life.

While Antonina's inner life is a safe space, fear emerges when her inner life spills out into her external life. This is apparent, for example, when Antonina and Michel set in motion their first plan to spend time together at his grandmother's house party. The following conversation takes place just as Michel meets Antonina after an absence of three weeks; the abrupt question of Michel's aunt (also Antonina's employer) emphasizes the intrusion of reality onto their dreamy reunion.

> Then he said that his grandmother was organizing a gathering of all her neighbors for Shrovetide; there would be carriage rides and masquerades. She was eager to amuse him before his departure.
> "Are you going somewhere?" asked [Michel's aunt].
> I felt a deathly chill run down my spine; I sat still, as if I'd turned to stone.[61]

Antonina's reaction seems unprovoked by the discussion of a house party that precedes it. The feeling of fear could be attributed to a pre-monition related to Michel's imminent departure, but Antonina and Michel have just planned for their reunification and this conversation precisely follows that plan. So what is the source of the fear? Antonina feels this fear each time her inner world and external life seem to come together, as if only by keeping them entirely separate can she retain the safe freedom of her internal reverie.

In another incident when Antonina's inner and external life clash, terror intrudes on her inner world and destroys it. On the eve of her planned elopement with Michel, Antonina dreams of her father:

> I saw my father: he appeared pale and sad, just as on the night before his death. Twice he said my name, calling me. I struggled between a desire to follow him and a desire to remain behind for Michel, whom I was expec-ting. My father summoned me several times and finally disappeared, moving down a winding road. I rushed after him and suddenly found myself amid a desert and quicksand. I was completely alone and feeling very tired, but I advanced indomitably under the burning sun and stifling heat. I looked everywhere for my father but couldn't find him. My energy

exhausted, I tried to return home, but couldn't find the way out. I awoke exhausted and sighed deeply as I escaped this painful nightmare.[62]

This dream is a peculiar one for Antonina, since elsewhere, her dreams and reveries always represent her safe space. Her father's desertion of her inner world in the face of Antonina's indecisiveness leaves her isolated. Solitude is typically a positive experience for Antonina, one that allows her free rein over her inner life. However, when her inner world becomes isolating, solitary reverie is destroyed as a safe space and becomes instead just another space that requires escape. After this dream, Michel no longer inhabits her safe space and his connection with her father's memory seems severed. Years later, after the failed elopement and her marriage to Bertini, Antonina encounters Michel by chance in Italy and is surprised that she feels "trembling, horror, and agitation," feelings she associates most readily with her oppressors, Millcote and her husband.[63] Antonina's "horror" at meeting him viscerally demonstrates the change that has taken place within her. Horror, a key gothic affect, manifests here because she encounters Michel, formerly tightly connected to her inner life, in the external world as another being and therefore uncanny: familiar and yet alien.

This peculiar dream parallels a gothic scene in *Diary of a Superfluous Man*. Chulkaturin sees Liza in church several weeks after she has apparently been jilted by Prince N. He describes her as corpse-like: "that pale face, that extinguished glance [погасший взор], those sunken [впалые] cheeks."[64] These three features echo the description of his mother's corpse from the beginning of the novella: "with half-open lips, sunken [опавшие] cheeks, and meekly fixed eyes."[65] The phrasing invites comparison between the mother's corpse and Liza as living corpse. Where the mother's eyes are "meek" (кротко), Liza's are extinguished (погасший), as if the prince's abandonment has metaphorically killed her. For Chulkaturin, both images signal the final moments for the women within his consciousness. His mother is buried and, after seeing Liza, he deems her "lost." Afterwards, Chulkaturin observes that she is nothing like the girl he knew. Being tricked and exploited forces Liza to grow up, but there is no space for her suffering or emotion in Chulkaturin's diary. The gothic moments only serve to alienate women or enact metaphorical violence upon them, and her real trauma remains unexplored and, as a result, unresolved. *Diary of a Superfluous Man* uses gothic to create spaces that are unsafe for women, whose inner lives are of little concern.

In the novella *The Unhappy Woman* (*Neschastnaia*, 1868), Turgenev directly responds to *Antonina* using specifically gothic signals. Jane

Costlow has analysed the narrative structure of the work, observing that "the narrator of 'Neschastnaia' takes a woman's story and frames it: In the ambivalence and anxiety of this literary appropriation lies Turgenev's most revealing confession of unacknowledged relationship," namely his literary debt to Tur.[66] The intertextual dialogue between the two works effectively "silences the feminine."[67] Turgenev's novella describes, through the male narrator's frame, the travails of Susanna, the illegitimate daughter of a nobleman who grows up in her father's house but is never acknowledged. After her mother's death, she is left in the care of her cruel stepfather. Susanna falls in love with Michel, in parallel with Tur's Antonina, but in *The Unhappy Woman*, Michel is Susanna's first cousin and their union would be incestuous. Turgenev's pair are separated by the family and Michel later dies. Susanna is sent to Moscow to live with her stepfather's family, who tolerate her for her annuity but mistreat her. She dies after she perceives that she has been abandoned by another love interest. There is a suggestion that her death may have been suicide, or that it may have been murder at the hands of her unscrupulous guardian.

Intriguingly, the imagery of the living corpse deployed in *Diary of a Superfluous Man* appears again in *The Unhappy Woman*. The narrator first describes Susanna as having, among other corpse-like features, "sunken, also black and dull, but beautiful eyes" (впалые, тоже черные и тусклые, но прекрасные глаза) and a "greenish-paleness of smooth skin" (зеленоватая бледность гладкой кожи).[68] Her coldness and paleness are reiterated, again and again. At one point, after she perceives she has been jilted, the narrator observes Susanna standing pale, by the window, and is struck by "a feeling of horror, longing, and pity."[69] Arguably, the narrator's sense of horror here comes from seeing her framed in the window, a living corpse. Scholars have analysed this moment as the moment of her death,[70] but for the narrator, Susanna has always been associated with death. Later, the narrator returns repeatedly to the image of Susanna's corpse in the coffin.[71] Each time he sees her in terms of her animation: she was "on the point of shrieking";[72] she "wanted to say" something;[73] and, finally, he fancies that "her dead lips were whispering."[74] However, Susanna remains dead, and although her emotional life is the focus of the manuscript that describes her story, it is mediated by the male narrator. In the end, it is the narrator who has the last word, "instinctively" whispering, "Unhappy woman, unhappy woman."[75] In *The Unhappy Woman*, as in *Diary of a Superfluous Man*, there is no narrative space for women's emotional lives.

Gothic affective moments in *Antonina* revise the model put forward in *Diary of a Superfluous Man*, generating a framework that clearly demarcates oppressive and safe environments and centring the emotional experience of woman on her own terms. In *Antonina*, although gothic narrative markers identify both types of environments, feelings of horror, disgust, and, above all, fear characterize the external world, while reverent memories of the heroine's dead father colour her inner life. In the end, it is her gothic inner life that enables Antonina to persevere through her unhappy marriage, her stepfather's machinations, and her family's bankruptcy, and even to forge the space that enables her to correct her own tortured upbringing through maternal love for her daughters. As Monica Cristina Soare argues, "The Gothic is especially potent as a conduit to an ideal world to which the ideology of normative femininity stands opposed."[76] Unlike Jane Eyre – who seizes her own happiness, thereby throwing off the gothic shadows that have oppressed her – Antonina embraces her gothic inner life as a source of strength and resilience. Inner life creates a space of true belonging.

The Value of Feeling

The echo of Jane Eyre's domestic bliss at the end of *Antonina* may strike an odd chord with readers familiar with Tur's review of Elizabeth Gaskell's *Life of Charlotte Brontë* (1857). In "Miss Brontë, Her Life and Works" ("Miss Bronte, ee zhizn' i sochineniia," 1858), Tur speaks scathingly of marriage: "Mrs Brontë [Charlotte's mother] was not only submissive, but also timid, and we know that she never tried to fight or complain in her role and carried out all her husband's orders precisely, without departing from them a single step. Women of weak character, overrun and crushed by the mighty will of the man, not only do not recognize their slavery, but also love it, and if they call it dependence, it is not just necessary, but also absolutely natural and ordinary."[77] However, at the end of *Antonina*, the importance of gothic subjectivity comes to the fore. It has created a safe space where the heroine can assert her will and thus avoid falling into the kind of role Tur suggests Brontë's mother held, one of subjugation and dependence. For Tur, the ability to create such a narrative space was a mark of talent and also validated women's writing.

Tur's review of Gaskell's biography was a direct response to Turgenev, whose review of Tur's *The Niece* had made some strong gender-driven points around the dichotomy between feeling and objective truth (объективность). Turgenev's review of *The Niece* may have lauded *Antonina* as "pages [that] will remain in Russian literature." Nevertheless, his praise of the work's ability to arouse strong feelings fed into a paradigm that juxtaposed women's writing, characterized as laden with emotion, with men's writing, characterized as more objective.[78] This distinction emerged from the same culturally embedded line of reasoning that caused the author of the first Russian narrative summary and translation of *Jane Eyre* to assume that the novel was written by a woman: namely, the association of emotion and feeling with women's literary voices.

In this review essay, Turgenev identifies women writers – exemplified by Tur as well as Gan and George Sand – as having an undeveloped, unprofessional talent. Women are not afraid to "fill dozens of pages with either unnecessary reasoning, or narratives that are irrelevant, or even just blathering – she is not afraid to make a mistake"; women write "greedily, quickly, with some kind of involuntary respect for writing generally, but without literary routines or planning."[79] Turgenev asserts that such writing holds value but is not literary, remarking:

> We are very happy Mrs Tur is what she is, and the reason for that is simple: Mrs Tur is a woman, a Russian woman, and, no matter how great our respect for this much-vaunted "objectivity," the thoughts, heart, and voice of a Russian woman, all this is dear and close to us.[80] [...] [Don't] think that we demand of the woman writer some kind of unconscious, instinctive creativity. A thought, with all its suffering and joy, life, with all its visible and invisible secrets – these are available to her as much as to a man. We only claim that in female talents (and we do not exclude the highest of them – George Sand) there is something wrong [неправильное], non-literary [нелитературное], running straight from the heart, not thought out in the end – in a word, something without which they would not attempt much, including, among other things, a four-volume novel.[81]

Turgenev's review of *The Niece* critiques the novel's length, word choice, characters, and plot; he complains that it should have been significantly reduced before publication. The elements of the novel that Turgenev praises are largely its nuanced depiction of feeling: "the novel is written from the heart and speaks to the heart."[82]

This appraisal of Tur's work seems to echo Turgenev's original impression of her upon their first meeting, as he reported in a letter to Pauline Viardot. He described Tur as "a delightful [прелестная] woman with a great intellect and talent" and wryly noted that "although she is a writer, she is not a bluestocking."[83] In his next letter to Viardot, he again praised Tur: "She is witty, good, and genuine; in her manners there is something that reminds me of you. We are great friends [Мы с ней большие друзья] [...] She is not young, not good-looking, but is so likeable that you immediately feel at ease with her. As you know, this is a very good sign; and, besides, she indeed has a real talent [у нее и вправду настоящий талант]."[84] The main aspects of Tur that seem to have made an impression on Turgenev are her talent and her emotional intelligence, which go hand in hand. He concludes his review of *The Niece* with a similar evocation of talent, calling Tur's a "true talent" (истинный талант).[85] Turgenev's review is perhaps not meant to be dismissive. However, in categorizing women's writing as emotional and focused on the subjective – and juxtaposing this category with a talent that exists independently of subjective experience and is connected with professional authorship – he ranks writers according to gender stereotypes and places women writers second in this hierarchy.

The disagreement between Turgenev and Tur that emerges from between the lines of these reviews aligns with the broader discourse related to women's roles in society taking place during the 1830s and 1840s. During this time, discussions related to women's places focused on those few women who had risen to public prominence: for example, salon hostesses and women writers. Tur was both. Russian salons were the predominant location of early nineteenth-century intellectual and cultural life, and women played a prominent role in them, both as hostesses and as active participants.[86] As a space where men and women could interact both socially and intellectually as equals, the salon provided women a means to be recognized for intellectual activity and even gain social status by excelling in it.

The obverse of this role was that of the woman writer. While salon hostesses were celebrated, early nineteenth-century women writers fell into a more ambiguous cultural position. Joe Andrew reads the career of Anna Bunina (1774–1829), the first female professional writer in Russia, as a measure of what women writers experienced during the early nineteenth century more broadly. At first, Bunina was lauded, her works seen as a "civilizing influence to literature." But by the 1820s, she mainly received criticism, as Andrew observes, "both because of the general reaction to women's greater involvement and therefore threat to male supremacy, but also because it was felt that Bunina herself had overstepped her allotted role."[87] In an 1839 letter, a decade after Bunina's death, Gan, writing about her experiences as an woman writer, complained, "But here people look at me just like at a crocodile in flannel or a dancing monkey. People look at me as if I were a fairground fright."[88] While women were indelibly bound up in Russian cultural life of the early nineteenth century, the woman writer's experience was one that Evgeniia Stroganova, writing about Gan, has described as "emotional trauma."[89]

Turgenev's review of *The Niece* demonstrates a complete lack of understanding of Tur's position and the challenges she faced in publishing.[90] Tur turned to professional writing as a means of supporting herself and her children after her husband's expulsion from Russia. By the time she was reviewing Gaskell's biography of Brontë, she was not only established as a novelist but also employed as the head of the fiction section for Mikhail Katkov's thick journal *The Russian Messenger*. Tur's comments on Brontë's career as a popular woman writer who was respected for her talents carry an additional message, a rebuttal to Turgenev's review of her own Brontë-inspired work, *The Niece*. She writes:

> For women, whose lives are broken, the writer's career opens a new horizon, gives them a new life; if reality refused them anything, or, even worse, if it ruthlessly tore the best treasure of their soul and heart from them, they will recreate their own reality, fulfil their dreams in the fictional characters of the novel. In this way, reliving again the lost joys and sorrows, they will destroy or at least soften and mitigate their personal suffering. Writing offers more than satisfaction, it is a kind of reward, the rebirth of the whole being.[91]

Here Tur, perhaps drawing from personal experience, connects the writer's craft with selfhood. The writer – and specifically, the writer who is able to engage with the world of emotions – has the possibility for self-transformation. Tur's review seems to agree with Turgenev's valorization of women's ability to write feelings and to write from personal experience, but the subtext of her discussion of Brontë's craft is that the value of women's writing is equal to that of men's. Tur concludes her review with warm praise for Brontë's ability both to engage readers on an emotional level and to effect social change as a result:

> How many hearts throughout Europe responded to her complaints, doubts, suffering indignation! Charlotte's heart beats and trembles on every page of her work and attracts the hearts of all readers. Whatever you say, the so-called subjective talents are especially attractive in this capacity; they speak more to the heart than to the mind [...] Touch a person's heart and he draws closer to correction and change; touch the heart of people, and be certain that you're doing good work and that your voice is not lost in the wasteland.[92]

For Tur, deploying gothic subjectivity in her prose provides a framework that has the potential to generate social change well beyond the boundaries of the text.

Tur and the Woman Question

As we have seen, Tur's *Antonina* valorizes women having choices beyond the domestic sphere and creates an explicit unfettered imagined space for those choices to manifest. However, as observed in "Miss Bronte, Her Life and Works" and in Tur's 1856 essay on George Sand's *A History of My Life* (*Histoire de ma vie*, 1854–5), Tur's views on the woman question emerge more explicitly in her critical writing. In Russia, the woman question became a major theme in intellectual discourse beginning in the mid-1850s, and Tur's first forays into criticism coincide with the publication of Nikolai Pirogov's "Questions of Life" ("Voprosy zhizni," 1856), an essay that catalyzed the debate. Drawing on his experiences directing a women's nursing corps in the Crimean War, Pirogov discussed the social effects of "artificially" limiting women's education. Pirogov asserted the value of more educational opportunities for women but relegated them to assistant roles, leaving men the dominant sex in society. Another major critical step in the debate was the publication of Mikhail Mikhailov's article "Women, Their Education and Meaning within the Family and Society" ("Zhenshchiny, ikh vospitanie i znachenie v sem'e i obshchestve," 1860), which argued that improvements in women's education would be the first step towards a more equal social status. In Mikhailov's view, educated women would eventually no longer be deemed the weaker sex or subservient to men, although their traditional role in the family would continue.[93]

In 1860, Turgenev published *On the Eve* (*Nakanune*), which tells the story of heroine Elena Stakhova's dull life on her family estate and her escape. Stakhova meets Insarov, a Bulgarian freedom fighter, decides to follow him when he plans to return to Bulgaria to fight the Turks, marries him against her parents' wishes, and leaves for Bulgaria. Even after Insarov dies on the journey, Elena continues and goes on to become a nurse on the front. The critical discussion surrounding the work was not just about the merits of Turgenev's writing but about larger social issues: the capability of Russians to effect social change and action, and the role of women in society. When one of the first critics praised Stakhova as "the best Russian woman in Russian literature since Pushkin's Tatyana," the tone for the debate was set.[94]

Tur wrote a series of polemical responses to Turgenev's novel and to other critics' views on it that specifically addressed the woman question. In these, she asserted that in Russia, Russian women did not yet exist although their potential did; instead of Russian women, there were uneducated women who "vegetate under their fathers' roofs [...] and stagnate under the coarse despotism of domestic slavery," and women who "have been educated as foreigners and are almost alien to our way of life."[95] Tur blamed Russian society for its lack of viable options for women's development. Although written and published before these debates began in Russia, *Antonina*, by engaging with gothic subjectivity and articulating the need for alternative social models, puts forward a similar view. For Tur, the woman question was not a question of whether women should be educated but a question of how Russian society had to change to accommodate women's agency in its social fabric.

Chapter Seven

Political Terror and the School of Horror

The revolutionary is a doomed man.
Sergei Nechaev, "Catechism of a Revolutionary"

Mysteries, secrets!
Where did so many mysteries and secrets suddenly appear from!
Fyodor Dostoevsky, *Demons*

In March 1881, Tsar Alexander II was assassinated by members of the revolutionary terrorist group the People's Will (Narodnaia volia). The tsar was travelling in a carriage when a member of the group, Nikolai Rysakov, threw the first bomb. It landed under the horses' hooves and exploded, damaging the carriage, wounding the driver, and killing one of the attending Cossack guards and a boy passing by. The carriage stopped and Alexander got out to inspect the damage. Another People's Will member, Ignacy Hryniewiecki, threw a second bomb, which landed right at the tsar's feet and exploded. Adrian Dvorzhitsky, a police chief colonel and member of the tsar's retinue, experienced the attack and recalled its aftermath:

His Majesty was half-lying, half-sitting, leaning on his right arm. Thinking he was merely wounded heavily, I tried to lift him, but the czar's legs were shattered, and the blood poured out of them. Twenty people with wounds of varying degree lay on the sidewalk or on the street. Some managed to stand, others to crawl, still others tried to get out from the bodies that had fallen on top of them. Through the snow, debris, and the blood you could see fragments of clothing, epaulets, sabers, and the bloody chunks of human flesh.[1]

Dvorzhitsky's account is marked by the grisliness of the scene: bloody snow, chunks of flesh strewn on the ground, mutilated bodies. The assassination took place in central St Petersburg and was witnessed by a crowd of onlookers. The tsar's violent murder publicly exposed the divinely appointed imperial body as a mortal body, which could suffer wounds and pain just as any other. This moment in history served as both the culmination of the People's Will plots to kill the tsar and an initial act of terror in a series of spectacular political assassinations that continued through the last decades of the nineteenth century and up to the October Revolution of 1917. In its act of regicide, its physical bloodiness, and its mandate to destroy governmental function one appointed official at a time, Russian revolutionary terrorism recalled the French Reign of Terror. In both, the divinely appointed royal body's weakness was exposed in a gruesome way: in the bloody chunks of Alexander II's flesh staining the snow of the St Petersburg streets red, and in the severed head of Louis XVI being held up for the cheering Paris crowd, blood dripping from its open neck arteries onto the scaffold below.

Members of the nineteenth- and early twentieth-century Russian radical intelligentsia had been fascinated by the mythology of the French Revolution long before Tsar Alexander's assassination. After the failed Decembrist uprising in 1825, a period of relative calm occurred, but new interest in the "Jacobin phenomenon" took hold, with attendant anxiety from the reactionary Nicolaevan government.[2] Alexander von Benckendorff, founder and first executive director of the Third Section of the Imperial Chancellery – that is, Nicholas I's secret police – wrote the following on the revolutionary trend:

> The youths, i.e., noblemen from seventeen to twenty-five years old, make up the mass of the most gangrenous part of the Empire. Among these madmen, we see the embryo of Jacobinism, the revolutionary and reformatory spirit, emerging in various forms and most often hiding behind the mask of Russian patriotism. The exalted youths [...] dream of the possibility of the Russian constitution, the destruction of the Table of Ranks, [...] of freedom.[3]

Benckendorff's report was written in 1827, just two years after the Decembrist revolt and within a year of the Third Section's establishment, and his statement is striking for its anxious, even paranoid tone.

The notion of secret Jacobins whose radical and destructive political beliefs are disguised as Russian patriotism speaks to a central aspect of the Russian imperial machinery from Nicholas I onwards, what Daniel Beer has called "the imputation of design to disorder and conspiracy to chaos."[4] Arguably, the conception of the Russian radical terrorist in the early nineteenth century emerged from this widespread tendency to see conspiracy and plots, and from the conflation of democratic calls for a constitution and a loosening of society's ranks with Jacobinism. The Jacobins were the most radical and violent political group during the French Revolution; it was the Jacobins who instituted the Reign of Terror in 1793–4, during which more than 16,500 people were sentenced to death and public executions by guillotine were a daily sight.

These bloody events also inspired increased gothic literary fervour in both France and England.[5] Contemporaneous critical commentaries on these events by writers such as Edmund Burke, Thomas Paine, and Mary Wollstonecraft used gothic imagery as a rhetorical device, while Matthew Lewis's novel *The Monk* (1796) launched a new "school" of gothic fiction, the so-called school of horror.[6] Nineteenth-century Russian political radicalism obviously developed along a different path from the French revolutionary fervour of the 1790s, yet just as gothic imagery expressed political anxiety and revolution-related trauma in school of horror works of the late eighteenth and early nineteenth centuries, so too did the gothic appear in nineteenth-century Russian literary works related to revolutionary terrorism. Intriguingly, the gothic predominantly appears in these later works in relation to the question of morality and revolutionary conscience that Maximilien Robespierre articulated, rather than simply to herald the violent aesthetic of terrorist action.

This chapter explores the function of school of horror-style gothic tropes and imagery in works that imagine the revolutionary underground, examining Fyodor Dostoevsky's *Demons* (*Besy*, 1872) and, more briefly, Boris Savinkov's novel-memoir *A Pale Horse* (*Kon' blednyi*, 1909). Where *Demons* warns against the dangers of terrorism, *A Pale Horse* valorizes political extremists. The chapter argues that Dostoevsky uses gothic elements to illustrate the dangers of acting against a moral system, whereas Savinkov's inclusion of gothic functions to delineate a new moral absolutism, one more in line with Robespierre's. In both works, however, gothic imagery centres on the figure of the terrorist-revolutionary.

From Terror to Terrorism: A Gothic Literary Genealogy

Gothic fiction and the French Revolution are indelibly linked. As Joseph Crawford has recently argued, "the [French] Revolution *created* gothic, transforming a marginal form of historical fiction chiefly concerned with aristocratic legitimacy into a major cultural discourse devoted to the exploration of violence and fear."[7] In 1797, "A Jacobin Novelist" anonymously wrote to an English journal editor, explicitly and parodically discussing the connection between the new gothic novels and the French Revolution:

> Alas! so prone are we to imitation, that we have exactly and faithfully copied the SYSTEM OF TERROR, if not in our streets, and in our fields, at least in our circulating libraries, and in our closets. Need I say that I am adverting to the wonderful revolution that has taken place in the art of novel-writing, in which the only exercise for the fancy is now upon the most frightful subjects, and in which we reverse the petition in the litany, and riot upon "battle, murder, and sudden death."[8]

The anonymous author connects the new trend in gothic fiction with the French Revolution, somewhat cynically, and goes on to assert that the "description of human life and manners" that characterized many contemporaneous novels could be tiresome, whereas the revolution had introduced a new topic: "It was high time, therefore, to contrive some other way of interesting these numerous readers, […] and just at the time when we were threatened with a stagnation of fancy, arose Robespierre, with his system of terror, and taught our novelists that *fear* is the only passion they ought to cultivate, that to frighten and instruct were one and the same thing."[9] Such views were common in Western European critical discourse of the time, but the most famous formulation of them appeared in the Marquis de Sade's essay "Reflections on the Novel" ("Idée sur les romans," 1800). In the essay, Sade observed that gothic fiction was the "inevitable outcome" of the 1790s revolutions across Europe, and that in order to create works that distracted from or rivalled the horrors of revolution, writers had to "call upon the aid of hell itself."[10]

Lewis's gruesome and scandalous novel *The Monk* recounts the story of Ambrosio, a celebrated monk who enters into a sexual relationship with Matilda, a demon in disguise. Over the course of three volumes, Ambrosio is spurred on to carry out increasingly evil acts, first by Matilda, then by his own uncontrollable sensuality, in particular his lust for the virtuous Antonia. These acts include selling his soul to the devil, murder, poison, rape, and, in a shocking twist, incest. Several subplots and tangents embellish the narrative with additional lurid details: an accidental elopement with the ghost of the Bleeding Nun, an exorcism aided by the Wandering Jew, an evil Prioress who imprisons young ladies in a dungeon and then is severely beaten by an angry mob, bandit attacks, and other such adventures. In its accounts of mob violence, the trials of the Spanish Inquisition, imprisonment, and the tensions between rebels and tyrants, *The Monk* engages indirectly with the French Revolution.[11] One additional link between Lewis's novel and the revolution was its graphic descriptions of injury, torture, and death, as in the following passage, which describes part of Ambrosio's death throes:

> Headlong fell the Monk through the airy waste; The sharp point of a rock received him; and He rolled from precipice to precipice, till bruised and mangled He rested on the river's banks. Life still existed in his miserable frame: He attempted in vain to raise himself; His broken and dislocated limbs refused to perform their office, nor was He able to quit the spot where He had first fallen [...] Myriads of insects [...] drank the blood which trickled from Ambrosio's wounds; He had no power to drive them from him, and they fastened upon his sores, darted their stings into his body, covered him with their multitudes, and inflicted on him tortures the most exquisite and insupportable. The Eagles of the rock tore his flesh piecemeal, and dug out his eyeballs with their crooked beaks.[12]

The physicality of Ambrosio's injuries described here is a hallmark of Lewis's novel, which tends towards gruesome detail. In the passage, Ambrosio's limbs are not just broken but also dislocated. Insects do not just drink his blood but fasten upon his open sores and sting him. Eagles do not just consume him but explicitly tear his flesh and dig out his eyeballs. The resulting effect, at least from the passage I include here, is predominantly disgust.

The German *Schauerroman* tradition was another influence on the school of horror; it influenced this school in part because its theme of political plotting resonated with anxieties about the French Revolution. *Schauerromane*, or "shudder" novels, are a subset of gothic novels that developed in the 1780s in the German kingdoms. One example is Friedrich Schiller's *The Ghost-Seer* (*Der Geisterseher*, 1787–9). The novel relates a series of horrifying, uncanny, and sometimes supernatural events surrounding a prince's ascension to the throne in his home kingdom. In the end, the narrator reveals that the disturbing events are part of a campaign conducted by a secret Jesuit society, which has been engaged in trying to convert the prince to Catholicism and then establish him on the throne through nefarious means as their puppet. *The Ghost-Seer*, while fragmentary and unfinished, was Schiller's most popular novel during his lifetime.

Even though many of Schiller's novel's episodes are horrifying and its graphic descriptions disgust readers, its primary source of terror is the mysterious society, which accomplishes its goals from the shadows, working according to a secret plan to effect significant political change. This element of the *Schauerroman* is not confined to Schiller's novel. The notion of secret political societies working behind the scenes spoke to the real anxiety about the perceived secret revolutionary societies that precipitated the Reign of Terror, and therefore was one of the primary reasons that the *Schauerroman* was adopted into the English and French gothic models.[13] Two elements of the school of horror are thus tied to the French Revolution: the trauma of graphic violence, and the expression of anxiety related to secret political plotting.

Within the gothic genre, the school of horror is opposed to the school of terror, which is often associated with the novels by Ann Radcliffe and others in that vein. In "On the Supernatural in Poetry" (1826), Radcliffe defines the two schools by the main function of their namesake emotions, horror and terror. "Terror and horror are so far opposite, that the first expands the soul, and awakens the faculties to a high degree of life; the other contracts, freezes, and nearly annihilates them."[14] In Radcliffe's view, terror is predicated on the unknown and the imagined; it is this quality that allows space to access the sublime. Schiller, writing on the sublime ("Vom Erhabenen," 1793), observes that "The indefinite [das Unbestimmte] is an ingredient of the terrible, and for no other reason than it gives the imagination freedom to paint the image according to its own discretion."[15] Terror's central emotion is fear, which is a product of the imagination and is future looking. Fear centres on the unknown but imagined, whether that is the pain of torture and death, the world beyond the grave, or the machinations of a secret society bent on destroying the status quo.

Horror, on the other hand, is visible and visceral; it shocks with its extreme graphic imagery and its directness. Horror also utilizes fear, but a central emotion in its formula is disgust, an immediate reaction to a determined stimulus that is thus connected to the present and past. As I argued in chapter 4, *The Idiot* uses both master plots – horror and terror – to forge a new gothic realist novel. In this chapter, I am interested in the way realist writers engage with the themes and tendencies of the school of horror to depict a culturally constructed, imagined revolutionary figure.

The Jacobin leader Robespierre saw terror – by which he meant the violent system of revolutionary justice associated with the Reign of Terror – as the only way to sweep away the old regime, antiquated ideas, and past inequalities to make way for an ideal future republic. In this formulation, terror is bound up with the emotion of fear, but in its incarnation, the concept aligns more closely with Radcliffe's definition of horror. For Robespierre, terror was a reaction to the September Massacres of 1793: a swift method to transform society and thus avoid similar widespread unplanned violence. He explained in a 1794 speech, referring to the government-led program of repression and execution, that "terror is nothing more than speedy, severe, and inflexible justice; it is thus an emanation of virtue."[16] The equation of political terror, and by extension the visible horrors of the revolution, with conscience forged a new morality in which mass murder was acceptable and even virtuous for the sake of a just future society.

Robespierre's moral absolutism made its way into nineteenth-century Russian intellectual discourse. In the early 1840s, for example, the literary critic Vissarion Belinsky became fascinated by Robespierre and his program. He penned a series of letters extolling the virtues of the French revolutionary leader. In an 1842 letter, he declared, "The thousand-year Kingdom of God will be established on earth, not by the saccharine and enthusiastic phrases of the naive Girondists, but by terrorists, by the double-edged sword of Robespierre's and Saint-Just's words and deeds."[17] In this formulation, Belinsky is discussing politics; he refers to socialism when he mentions the Kingdom of God.[18]

The moral question of what level of sacrifice is worthwhile for the good of the whole played a central role in Dostoevsky's polemic with Nikolai Chernyshevsky in the early 1860s. Vera Pavlovna – the main character in Chernyshevsky's *What Is to Be Done?* (*Chto delat'?*, 1863) – dreams of a utopian future based in rational egoism, in which everyone acts according to their own interests, which are rationally also in the collective best interest. This dream raised Dostoevsky's concerns, expressed in *Notes from Underground* (*Zapiski iz podpol'ia*, 1864). Such a society, he suggested, does not consider that irrational behaviour is inseparable from human individualism and free will. Dostoevsky considered what is a worthwhile sacrifice for a collective good in *Crime and Punishment* (*Prestuplenie i nakazanie*, 1866) – in which Raskolnikov justifies murder by plotting to kill the old pawnbroker for the greater good of society – and ultimately suggested that this kind of logic is fatally flawed.

Sergei Nechaev's "Catechism of a Revolutionary" ("Katekhizis revoliutsionera," 1869), a programmatic manifesto for secret revolutionary society members, illuminated the psychology and morality of the terrorist. As Nechaev explained, "For [the revolutionary], morality is everything that contributes to the triumph of the revolution"; which is to say, echoing Robespierre's justification of the Terror, that everything leading to successful revolutionary action is permitted and moral.[19] *Demons*, Dostoevsky's next novel, questions this morality in broader relief, within the context of a revolutionary terrorist cell.

Signalling Danger: The Gothic Body in *Demons*

"The muzhiks are coming with axes in hand, something most dreadful will happen." These lines from an anonymous poem published in Herzen's *Polar Star* suggest political revolution, peasant rising up against landowner. In part 1, chapter 1 of Dostoevsky's novel *Demons*, Stepan Trofimovich falls into the habit of muttering these lines to himself. Out of context, the lines "The muzhiks are coming with axes in hand, something most dreadful will happen" evoke gothic anxieties of future cataclysm. Stepan Trofimovich's repetition of such a statement, as if in a trance, verges on the uncanny: it could conflate a suggestion of supernatural sight into the future with a kind of ritual chanting. However, the narrator undermines these lines with humour, noting that they are "rather forced-sounding" and must have been written by "some liberal landowner of old." The more practically minded Varvara Petrovna reacts to Stepan Trofimovich's new habit on one occasion by exclaiming "Rubbish!" and angrily leaving the room. However, Liputin – a dedicated member of the revolutionary cell – adds a new frisson of terror, giving readers a moment of doubtful pause when he observes, "It would be a pity if their former serfs do celebrate by doing something really unpleasant to their lords and masters," while miming a cut throat with his finger.[20]

This minor episode demonstrates how narration functions within *Demons*. The novel – called by some critics Dostoevsky's most terrifying – is tempered by humour, much of it arising from the narrator's contextualization of events. The dramatic out-of-context lines coming from Stepan Trofimovich's mouth are coupled with Varvara Petrovna's scornful ridicule, and the narrator's commentary exposes these lines as ridiculous. Liputin's gesture, then, is ambiguous: it could be seen as an additional comedic note, or as a threat. Ambiguous moments like these allow the narration to shift easily between the social humour and buffoonery that characterize the novel's earlier society scenes and the disturbing scenes of fire, murder, and other violence in the end of part 3. Much of the novel's terror sits just below the surface, just out of sight – but creates, nevertheless, an atmosphere of dread. Such an atmosphere is appropriate for a work about a shadowy organization and allows gothic suspense to take hold.

Demons abounds in gothic motifs: family secrets, the seduction of innocents, a despotic patriarch, descriptions of apparitions, corpses, threats, a murder. Scholars have also observed a sense of uneasiness, anxiety, or even fear based in the novel's structure and spatiality. Lyudmila Saraskina has examined the curious way that characters suddenly appear in the text, without warning.[21] Anne Lounsbery has argued that the novel's lack of resolution – despite the finality of the destruction and death that accompany it – is symbolized by the railroad system, "a network linking everything but going nowhere, a grid you cannot escape [...] that lingers in our minds, the reflection of an endgame that never resolves itself in an ending."[22] Barry P. Scherr argues that the novel's setting "epitomizes [...] a 'landscape of fear'" because "the city seems both spread out and suddenly filled with the other."[23] He notes the sense of claustrophobia, entrapment, and the "sense of fear and, ultimately, terror" that the novel's spatial construction carries.[24] Lewis Bagby argues that the novel "contains a frightening level of gravitas, suffused as it is with disaster, lies, manipulation, stupidity, madness, murder, suicide, and horror, as well as moments of tenderness, honesty, soulful reflection, and spiritual recovery, not to mention scenes of carnival laughter, painful exposure, outright farce, buffoonery, comic twists, and sudden reversals."[25] As Bagby's list highlights, there is a tension between the serious and the humorous written into the novel's structure. For Kate Holland, these contrasting narrative elements are symptomatic of the novel's representation of "the sense of disintegration and atomization that is fundamental to the experience of modernity," and in turn indicate Dostoevsky's search for a form that could convey this experience.[26]

Gothic poetics was one such form. Mary Pilkington's 1798 novel *The Subterranean Cavern; or, Memoirs of Antoinette de Monflorance* is an example of political gothic that engages directly, not metaphorically, with the French Revolution. Many gothic novels evoke anxious terror but are set centuries earlier. Pilkington's heroine, however, is contemporaneous. She becomes involved with revolutionary ideas in 1790s France and eventually must investigate this revolutionary violence. In *The Subterranean Cavern*, the mystery is the revolutionary cell. Dostoevsky's novel similarly finds its inspiration in revolutionary terrorism and dwells, at first, on anxieties below the surface of society. In *Demons*, he places the onus on the reader to unwind his characters' ideologies and follow them to their eventual ends. In *The Subterranean Cavern* and works like it, revolutionary activity supplies the work's central gothic mystery, much as a family secret or haunted monastery may have provided this plot device in other works of the genre. The terrorist cell has a similar gothic function in *Demons*.

In *Demons*, the revolutionary activities are increasingly gothic, but their ambiguity destabilizes any authoritative reading. Through graphic horror, they force the reader to question both the status quo and extreme ideological positions, drawing the reader emotionally into the novel's inherent critique of ideologies such as nihilism, socialism, and anarchism. In the novel, narration is often couched in a register that conflates humour and terror, as in Stepan Trofimovich's repeated mutterings about the muzhiks with axes. However, as the corpses pile up throughout part 3, humour gives way to terror, and gothic description informs scenes featuring dead bodies. In this way, as the novel explores different political extremes and their possible outcomes, gothic language directs reader attention to the potential horror of these eventualities, helping to separate and qualify points of view in a polyphonic novel where many voices appear.

The first corpses to be discovered are those of Marya and Captain Lebyadkin. Leading into this scene is a scandalous social event, where gothic language functions as it has elsewhere in the novel; it is parodied and deflated, used to describe banal events or to exaggerate social faux pas. The conflagration that fails to burn the corpses of Marya and Lebyadkin also marks a transitional point. After the fire, as the revolutionary activities become more visible, violent, and harmful, the gothic language grows less ambiguous. At this point, the terror of revolutionary activity takes over the novel's narrative. Discovering the fire, the provincial Governor von Lembke yells, "It's all arson! This is nihilism! If anything is burning, it's nihilism!"[27] The narrator and others react with horror, and for the first time, the narrator is horrified. He also maintains the sense of horror in the ensuing narration rather than undermining or deflating it. As von Lembke observes, "The fire is in people's minds and not on the roofs of the houses."[28] That being said, the description of Marya Timofeevna's and the Captain's murder scene is graphic and unnerving:

> The captain had been found with his throat cut, on a bench, fully dressed, and that he had probably been murdered while dead drunk, so that he had heard nothing, and that the blood had gushed out of him "like from a bull"; [...] his sister, Marya Timofeyevna, had been "stabbed all over" with a knife, and was lying on the floor in the doorway, so that she probably had been awake and had struggled and fought back with her killer. The servant, who had also probably woken up, had had her skull completely smashed.[29]

With the horrible details related matter-of-factly, the reader learns that Lebyadkin bled like a slaughtered animal. Gothic description is not needed to render the scene horrifying. The narrative description of the corpses provides speculation about how they died and suggests the details of their suffering, pain, and fear, which the reader's imagination then embellishes with horror.

The narrator reflects on the nature of sensational events, remarking on the crowd's experience. A great fire at night is exciting if it is staged, like fireworks, but a real conflagration, with its danger and lack of control, "is another matter: here the horror and a certain sense of personal danger, coupled with the exhilarating impression created by a nighttime fire, produces in the onlooker [...] a certain concussion of the brain, and a challenge, as it were, to his own destructive instincts, which – alas! – lurk in every heart [...] This gloomy feeling is almost always intoxicating."[30] So too the reader is drawn to the gothic descriptions that follow: terrified by Shatov's premonition of his own death, uneasy as Shatov's body is furtively hidden in the dark woods after his murder, anxiously listening for the shot that will signal Kirillov's suicide while waiting behind the door with Pyotr Verkhovensky. Gothic scenes are terrifying but thrilling, and the pleasurable and suspenseful anticipation of horrors attracts precisely because of this destructive instinct. As a result, as the bodies pile up in part 3, the reader is thrilled yet horrified. Disgusted, yet tantalized. This reaction supports Dostoevsky's critique of violence, which is not only fearsome and dangerous but also morally transgressive, and of the perverse pleasure humans take in watching the gruesome spectacle.

Death, Horror, and Gothic Narrative Force

Elsewhere, Dostoevsky embeds gothic narrative force in key scenes: Marie's childbirth scene, Shatov's murder, and, finally, Kirillov's death. The childbirth scene is marked with gothic language, heightening anticipation that something vile will happen. The contrast of language that is coded with sentimental or ecstatic emotions during the scene and gothic language denoting fear and loathing taps into the same narrative vacillations between humour and horror elsewhere in the novel. At the end of the scene, for example, Shatov accepts his wife's illegitimate son as his own. Very moved by witnessing the birth of Marie's child, he exclaims, "The old ravings, the shame and the decay are all over and done with! Let's work hard and set out on a new path, the three of us, yes, yes!"[31] This hopeful moment of birth and a new beginning is then destroyed by Shatov's murder, which precipitates Marie's deranged wandering with her newborn and their subsequent illnesses and deaths. Even on his way down to meet Erkel, who will guide him to the planned murder site, Shatov exclaims, "But this is now absolutely the last step! And then a new path, and we shall never ever again think of the old horror!"[32] This narrative vacillation between ecstasy and gloom increases tension for the reader, who is dreadfully aware of what awaits

Shatov. Even moments of domestic tranquility, such as when Marie holds Shatov's hand as they sleep, take on a gothic tinge because of Shatov's planned murder.

The reader's knowledge of what will happen builds up gothic tension in the childbirth scene, but a second source of that tension is the instinctive, prescient knowledge of events that some characters – in particular Shatov – seem to demonstrate. When Erkel comes the first time to deliver the message to him about the meeting, Shatov does not know that the revolutionaries are planning his murder, but he does have a premonition:

> [Marie] didn't answer, and closed her eyes in exhaustion. Her pale face became like a dead woman's […] [Shatov] again looked at her face uneasily, clasped his hands tightly in front of him and went out of the room into the entryway on tiptoe. At the top of the stairway he pressed his face into a corner and remained standing there like that for about ten minutes, without speaking or moving. He would have stood even longer, but suddenly quiet, cautious steps were heard below. Someone was walking up the stairs […]
>
> "Who's there?" he asked in a whisper.
>
> The unknown visitor kept walking up the stairs without hurrying and without replying. Once he reached the top, he stopped. It was impossible to see him in the darkness. Suddenly a cautious question was heard:
>
> "Ivan Shatov?"
>
> Shatov identified himself, and immediately held out his hand in order to stop him; but the stranger grabbed his hand and Shatov gave a start, as if he had touched some horrible reptile.[33]

Marie's dead-looking face and the appearance of the silent stranger from the darkness in the shadowed staircase together evoke the gothic, but Shatov's uneasiness is present before Erkel's appearance. Shatov's shudder upon touching the stranger and his feeling of revulsion, as if he has touched a reptile, evince disgust. This combination of fearful uneasiness and disgust suggest Shatov's awareness of his doom, even without knowing the specifics of the plot.

Shatov's death scene is replete with gothic imagery, particularly the repeated word "gloomy" (мрачно). The park is "a very gloomy place" (очень мрачное место) where "huge ancient pine trees [stand] as gloomy [мрачные] and vague shapes in the gloom [во мраке]."[34] This seems clichéd, particularly because of the repetition, but the gothic setting contrasts with the task at hand, Shatov's murder. The murder is carried out swiftly and with little struggle – a single shot to the head – but in its wake, the members of the group are transformed. The narrator denotes this transformation in terms of its abrupt unexpectedness: "Suddenly something strange happened, completely unexpected, and surprising to almost everyone."[35] The strange thing that happens is a fit of conscience, perhaps, which spreads quickly through the group. First Virginsky begins screaming that "it isn't right" (это не то).[36] Then Lyamshin completely loses control, squeezes Virginsky from behind, and begins to "shriek in an inhuman way."[37] Virginsky, Lyamshin, and Erkel begin to struggle, Lyamshin screaming all the time. The narrator interjects, "There are powerful moments of fear, for instance, when a person suddenly begins to scream in an unnatural voice, one that you could never before have imagined to be his, and that's sometimes even a terrifying thing."[38] Despite the others' fear-ridden responses, Pyotr Verkhovensky remains unmoved.

By contrast, when Kirillov commits suicide and Verkhovensky goes to inspect his body, terror infects him. The corpse is first described using gothic narrative markers. The body is ambiguously positioned: it is standing, not lying, as expected. Verkhovensky has the distinct sensation that it is hiding, and then that it is looking at him. This uncanny experience fills him with horror.

> What struck him most of all was that the figure, despite his shouts and his furious attack, hadn't even stirred, hadn't moved a single limb, as though it were made of stone or wax. The pallor of the face was unnatural, the black eyes were completely fixed and were staring at some point in space. Pyotr Stepanovich [...] suddenly noticed that although Kirillov was looking somewhere in front of him, he could see him out of the corner of his eye and perhaps was even watching him [...] Suddenly he imagined that Kirillov's chin had moved and that a mocking smile had passed across his lips – as if Kirillov had guessed what he was thinking.[39]

This episode evokes the scene in Alexander Pushkin's "Queen of Spades" (1833) in which Hermann discovers the Countess's corpse and imagines a conversation with her. Kirillov's mocking smile evokes the Countess's mocking wink, which drives Hermann insane. As the scene continues, Verkhovensky, too, loses touch with reality. He feels haunted as he imagines that Kirillov bites him and then shouts after him as he flees. When Verkhovensky returns with a lit match, the narrator describes Kirillov's corpse clinically: "The shot had been fired at the right temple and the bullet had exited at the top of the left side, shattering the skull. Splashes of blood and brains could be seen."[40] There is no haunting and no reaction of disgust to the corpse in this description, just the cold facts. Verkhovensky's first reaction to Kirillov's corpse is not caused by the abject horror of encountering a corpse – he has already encountered a number of them by this point and has remained calm – but is a gothic manifestation of moral conscience, which appears and quickly dissipates.

Only one body provokes Kristevan reactions in the novel: the dying Stepan Trofimovich's. Early signs of his illness include nightmares, a dream of gaping jaws full of teeth. His face is described as "wasted," "sunken," and has "pale quivering lips," and his liminal state also provokes a reaction in his visitors. Varvara Petrovna shakes "with terror" and has "pale cheeks" as she realizes his death is nigh.[41] Fear of death and an abject description of a dying body are not unique to *Demons*, but what strikes one here is that this death scene is deliberately drawn out and uses marked gothic language, as the characters reflect on the meaning of life and death.

Shortly before his demise, Stepan Trofimovich invokes the novel's metaphysics when he raves, "The eternal, immeasurable idea! Every man, whoever he is, needs to bow down before the Great Idea [Мысль]!"[42] Here he refers to a natural law. These sentiments echo those of Golyadkin and Underground Man about the "sublime and beautiful," but as in *Notes from Underground*, the concept is undermined because the ideal emerges from the mouth of a buffoon. Kirillov, surprisingly, discussing his vision of eternal harmony and his decision to commit suicide espouses similar ideas, holding love and joy up as ideals. In *The Idiot*, Ippolit's "Essential Explanation" or Myshkin's speeches before his seizure in part 4 contain nearly the same sentiments, coupled with the same enlightened state that the nearness of death or the pre-epileptic stage brings. Yet here, these words given to Stepan Trofimovich or Kirillov cast their meaning into doubt, critiquing not just revolutionary ideologies but all single-minded radical ideologies, as well as the act of submitting wholly to an idea without balance or tempering.

This idea of complete surrender to an ideology is articulated in Dostoevsky's essay *Winter Notes on Summer Impressions* (*Zimnie zametki o letnikh vpechatleniiakh*, 1863) in the context of the gothic. In *Winter Notes*, Dostoevsky uses his memory of reading gothic novels as a child as a segue into his desire to visit Europe. The rest of the work, then, outlines a critique of the West that elaborates on a major idea that would inform his mature works: "the conflict between the one and the many, between the human being and the inhuman state, between the single individual and the encompassing society."[43] Dostoevsky favours a unifying brotherhood, but in *Winter Notes*, this concept is threatened by bourgeois egocentrism. The bourgeois promotes individual gain, which results in a dangerous universal monologism. The oppressed individual fears to voice dissent. Communication breaks down, and individuals compete to have the last self-serving word rather than seeking engagement.

Radcliffe's gothic serves as an appropriate referent for this argument, as one of her novels' key themes is the breakdown of authority. She introduces readers to a world where traditional authority is suspect and asks them to consider how they should understand characters, events, or, indeed, novels themselves from this perspective. In *Demons*, as in Radcliffe's novels, there is no trustworthy authority in the end. Even the narrator is suspect. The revolutionary cell turns out to be an ouroboros, but instead of renewing itself, the idea consumes and destroys, endlessly and pointlessly. Working on behalf of a Great Idea can be dangerous, as the increasingly violent actions of the revolutionary cell demonstrate.

Ideologies are likened to demons: perverse, untrustworthy, capable of great destruction, all-consuming. Demons, as well, are supernatural, going beyond human comprehension of the Euclidean world (even if they appear in humble guise, as Ivan's devil in *Brothers Karamazov* [*Brat'ia Karamazovy*, 1880] does). Stepan Trofimovich relates the parable that gives the novel its name, in which Jesus exorcises demons from a man and they leap into pigs, who rush into water and are drowned. The demons function as an illness: "all the sores, all the contagions, all the uncleanness, all the demons, large and small, who have accumulated in our great and beloved sick man, our Russia."[44] However, while the parable of the swine is direct – they, after all, are possessed by demons, directly resulting in their demise – the man who is no longer possessed, too, is a source of fear for those observing him.

The Gothic Anti-Hero in the Revolutionary Imaginary

Up to this point, my discussion has not touched on the character at the centre of the novel, Nikolai Stavrogin. Although all the characters are infected to some degree by gothic narrative, Stavrogin is the catalyst for gothic destruction. His appearance in the town incites Pyotr Verkhovensky and sets the events of the novel in motion. As soon as he appears, rumours begin to circulate, which hint at his past: "All our ladies were besotted with the new visitor. They divided sharply into two camps: one adored him, while the other hated him with a vengeance [...] some were especially intrigued by the possibility that a fateful secret lay hidden in his soul; others positively liked the fact that he was a murderer."[45] Stavrogin inspires strong opinions and yet remains undetermined. In his appearance, also, positive qualities and features are rendered ambiguous and even uncanny:

> I was also struck by his face: his hair was somehow almost too black, his bright eyes were somehow too calm and clear, his complexion was somehow too delicate and white, the colour of his cheeks was somehow too bright and clear, his teeth were like pearls, his lips like coral – you might say that he was a picture of beauty, but at the same time there was also something repellent about him. They said that his face resembled a mask; but they talked a great deal, by the way, about his extraordinary physical strength.[46]

Here the uncanniness of the features is a result of their extremity. Every feature is extended several degrees beyond the superlative. He is not just handsome, but too handsome. In the description of his physical features – eyes too calm, complexion too white, hair too black – there is something that produces a sense of unease, that repels. He is conventionally good-looking, and yet at the same time disgusting. The statement that his face "resembled a mask" provides an additional note of ambiguity but also signals deception. While this line is part of the townspeople's gossip about him and does not mean he wears a mask, it does imply that everyone – not just the narrator – feels the same sense of unease around him, as if his true self is hidden like the other mysteries that swirl around him. Emotionally, Stavrogin has "the kind of constitution that [knows] no fear"[47] and possesses a "cold, calm, and [...] *rational* rage [...] the most repellent and most dreadful kind there can be."[48] These aspects of Stavrogin's characterization – his uncanniness, isolation, and emotional control – align with the traits of the gothic anti-hero. Furthermore, his deeds are consistently amoral. He secretly marries Marya Timofeevna Lebyadkina and then becomes complicit in her murder; that is, he is aware of the plot and does nothing to intervene. He is also the father of Shatov's estranged wife Marie's child and is similarly complicit through inaction in all of their deaths: Shatov's, Marie's, and the child's. In the censored chapter, "At Tikhon's," an additional, hidden transgression comes to light in Stavrogin's confession: the rape of a young girl, whom he then drives to suicide. This history haunts the novel. "At Tikhon's" informed the development of Stavrogin's character but was cut from the text by the editor Katkov.

While being consumed by the Great Idea may be dangerous, the true terror is the absence, the emptiness at the heart of the novel, which for Dostoevsky may exist in humanity as well. In *Brothers Karamazov*, Dmitry says that "beauty is mysterious as well as terrible. God and the devil are fighting there, and the battlefield is the heart of man."[49] For Dmitry, filled with the Karamazov life force, there is an importance in action, in opinion. For Stavrogin, on the other hand, inner life is characterized by gothic landscape. In his final letter, he describes his house in Switzerland: "The mountains restrain one's sight and thought. It's a gloomy place."[50] This claustrophobic, confining landscape seems the complete opposite of Myshkin's Switzerland, which is filled with sublime vistas and enables contemplation and enlightenment. While Myshkin and Dmitry Karamazov both desire to do good and are motivated by their own life force, Stavrogin's desire for an ideal or for goodness diminishes the more involved he becomes in revolutionary activity. In *Demons*, Liza Tushina's accusation prompts emotion and a confession, but Liza's vision of life with a reformed Stavrogin is strange and gothic: "It always seemed to me that you would carry me off to some place where a huge evil spider as big as a man lives, and we would spend our entire lives looking at him and being afraid of him. That's how our mutual love would pass," she relates.[51] While in other Dostoevsky novels, love is capable of transforming individuals and is the foundation of the universal brotherhood, in *Demons*, it too represents an empty idea. Stavrogin is tormented by the thought of the murders and crimes, but in the end, he is unmoved.

In his confession, Stavrogin writes, "I am still [...] capable of wanting to do a good deed and I take pleasure in this; at the same time I want evil as well, and I also feel pleasure. But both feelings are too shallow, as always before, and they are never enough. My desires are too weak; they can't guide me."[52] While Stavrogin has left destruction in his wake, a gothic anti-hero would wreak havoc for a purpose. For example, Ambrosio in Lewis's *The Monk* wreaks havoc to satisfy his overwhelming lust; the mysterious Armenian stranger in Schiller's *The Ghost-Seer* does so to gain political power. A gothic anti-hero would revel in his vice, just as Fyodor Karamazov revels in his own vileness. Stavrogin, however, cannot own either good or evil deeds. His life is devoid of meaning, like the empty centre of the revolutionary cell that has formed around him but that he has never come to lead. One lady calls him a vampire, but a romantic vampire is tormented; Stavrogin, on the other hand, is "neither hot nor cold."[53]

In a gothic novel, the discovery of a corpse results in sensationalistic drama. In *Demons*, Stavrogin's corpse is anticlimactic and the final autopsy gives a last ambiguous message to the reader. The doctors completely reject Stavrogin's insanity, but the last lingering word of the novel is still "insanity." Similarly, the discovery of murders is proof that "there really was a secret society of murderers, revolutionaries, arsonists and rebels,"[54] but what does its existence mean? It is an entity that causes terror but to no purpose. This absence at the centre of revolutionary ideology, which reflects the egocentrism Dostoevsky critiques in his earlier works such as *Crime and Punishment*, is the greatest source of horror of all. Dostoevsky's imagined revolutionary is, in the end, not a revolutionary but a source of gothic horror, a locus for anxiety in the face of a growing radical movement.

Gothic Morality and the Revolutionary Novel

Dostoevsky's *Demons* preceded the period known as the Age of Assassinations in Russia, while Savinkov's loosely autobiographical novel *A Pale Horse* appeared near its end, in 1909.[55] Published under the pseudonym V. Ropshin, the novel caused a stir because it included thinly veiled details of Grand Duke Sergei Alexandrovich's notorious assassination in February 1905. Set during the 1905 revolution, the novel takes the form of diary entries from a terrorist leader called George (Жорж) and focuses on a small cell that is planning to assassinate a government official. In addition to terrorist activity, George engages in an affair with Elena, a married noblewoman, and deflects the romantic overtures of his fellow terrorist Erna, a chemist and bombmaker.

In *A Pale Horse*, graphic and violent death, such as in a bomb construction accident or the assassination, is described matter-of-factly, while scenes related to the affair with Elena are described gothically. Gothic imagery appears but is used to different ends than in *Demons*. Particularly striking is the sense of remorse George feels after he kills Elena's husband in a duel, a feeling couched in gothic language in the text. His remorse after this killing seems at odds with his absence of feelings related to the assassination. In general, gothic narrative in *A Pale Horse* underscores the anxiety about actions George finds morally questionable, while the absence of gothic denotes a corresponding lack of moral quandary.

The scene of George's duel with Elena's husband, for example, includes a shift in tone to a gothic mode of narration:

> A milk-white fog crept in and melted in waves of darkness. I walked on without any goal or thought, like a ship on the waves without a rudder. Suddenly a dark spot thickened in the fog, and an indeterminate shadow flickered. An officer walked directly towards me. I recognized him: Elena's husband.[56]

Here the gothic description connotes indeterminacy, ambiguity, and the terror that accompanies them. The contrasting light and dark shades that appear here and elsewhere in the novel always describe an aspect of (or situation related to) George's affair with Elena. Whereas Elena's husband appears as a dark shadow approaching in white fog, Elena often appears as a white-gowned figure retreating into darkness. The milk-white fog (молочный туман) that creeps in to set the atmosphere for the duel scene also appears when George considers the bond that he and Elena share, as well as multiple times after her husband's death. In contrast to the death of Elena's husband, which is couched in metaphor and gothic gloom, the deaths of George's associates, martyred for the revolutionary cause, are described graphically and explicitly.

A Pale Horse is a novel about death, and its focus is on two killings: the governor's assassination and Elena's husband's murder. George associates the governor's death with duty and the revolutionary cause, while Elena's husband's death is more ambiguous. The milky fog that enters the novel most heavily in the duel scene seems to obscure George's ability to understand his motivations in the death of his lover's husband. The fog is contrasted with another image that occurs often in the novel, that of the red sun. Its red rays appear in the room as George embraces Elena and feels "no remorse."[57] Similarly, it carries associations with childhood, with love, and with certainty. The dilution or distortion of the clear red sun with the gothic milky fog suggests the addition of doubt. As George becomes increasingly beset by moral doubts, he loses his ability to feel clarity and truth in the red sun's rays. In the final scene, he describes a "melancholy sun extinguished in the sea," and the novel ends with the allusion to his likely suicide.[58]

The use of gothic description to delineate moral questioning echoes Savinkov's own questioning, as recounted by Dmitry Merezhkovsky and Zinaida Gippius in 1907–8. Savinkov turned to Merezhkovsky for advice about his growing moral concerns related to his terrorist lifestyle. As Gippius recalled later, "The main burden was that Savinkov himself seemed to feel killed by killing. He said the blood of the dead crushes him with its weight."[59] Savinkov engages with the moral quandary posed by the question: Is the sacrifice of one justifiable for the good of all? Dostoevsky had previously grappled with this question, and his writing on it influenced both Savinkov and Merezhkovsky, who formulated a new imagined terrorist type in this vein, the Christian terrorist.[60] This is a terrorist who both believes in the justness of the cause and feels remorse for the violent actions undertaken on its behalf. In moments where Savinkov engages with the question as to what, if anything, is a worthy sacrifice for the good of all, gothic infects his text, adding notes of indeterminacy that map to his own moral uncertainty. This new literary incarnation of the terrorist was rejected by Savinkov's contemporaries in the Socialist Revolutionary Party as being farcical, but it helped forge a new image of the terrorist – one with a conscience.

Political Terror and the Gothic Imaginary

In 1869, the nihilist Sergei Nechaev wrote "Catechism of a Revolutionary." The text gives a list of the qualities, duties, and relationships of a generalized figure Nechaev terms "the revolutionary," under headings including "the duties of a revolutionary towards himself," "the relations of a revolutionary towards his comrades," "the relations of a revolutionary towards society," and, finally, "the attitude of the society towards the people."[61] In its characterization of the ideal revolutionary, the "Catechism" describes many of the traits of the gothic anti-hero from the school of horror. From the text's opening statements, a picture emerges of an individual whose existence is characterized by isolation, single-mindedness, and emotion directed towards a specific goal:

1. The revolutionary is a doomed man. He has no personal interests, no business affairs, no emotions, no attachments, no property, and no name. Everything in him is wholly absorbed in the single thought and the single passion for revolution.
2. The revolutionary knows that in the very depths of his being, not only in words but also in deeds, he has broken all the bonds that tie him to the social order and the civilized world with all its laws, moralities, and customs, and with all its generally accepted conventions. He is their implacable enemy, and if he continues to live with them it is only in order to destroy them more speedily.[62]

The sense of doom, isolation, and fervent single-mindedness focused on destruction aligns well with the gothic anti-hero's characterization. Social isolation enables the creation of a new morality: in Nechaev's case, one based only in the success of the revolutionary cause and predicated on mass destruction. Nechaev argues that all emotion – including sentimentality, exuberance, or even hatred and revenge – must be eradicated. This lack of emotion seems, on the surface, to go against the type of the school of horror anti-hero, who is usually ruled by uncontrolled passions, but Nechaev's revolutionary is also consumed by overwhelming feeling. In place of emotion is "revolutionary passion," which Nechaev states must be "practised every moment of the day until it becomes a habit" and which "is to be employed with cold calculation." Both the gothic anti-hero and Nechaev's ideal revolutionary are set on a path to "merciless destruction." The difference between the two is that the gothic anti-hero is unaware that his plot is inevitably doomed, whereas Nechaev's revolutionary must steel himself for self-destruction in the name of the revolutionary cause.

Nechaev was not a revolutionary when he wrote the "Catechism" in the late spring and summer of 1869, at least in terms of taking revolutionary action. In 1868–9, he was teaching in a parish school in St Petersburg and auditing classes at St Petersburg State University. Inspired by the attempted assassination of the tsar by Dmitry Karakozov in 1866, Nechaev became involved in radical reading circles and student activism. As his radical activity expanded, so too did his desire for a revolutionary lifestyle. Some have attested that he even went so far as to imitate Chernyshevsky's fictional revolutionary character, Rakhmetov, who consumes only black bread and sleeps on a bed of nails.[63] Nechaev's revolutionary fervour originated in literary texts, initially took the form of words in pamphlets like the "Catechism," and only then moved on to deeds.[64] In November 1869, he carried out a terrorist act: the murder of a student, Ivan Ivanov.

The summer before the murder, Nechaev had been in Switzerland visiting Mikhail Bakunin, the radical Russian émigré writer. When Nechaev returned to Russia in the fall of 1869, he brought with him a fake identity. Bakunin had given him papers that identified him as a secret Russian representative of the World Revolutionary Alliance, a fictional organization established by Bakunin himself. When Nechaev arrived in Russia, he began building his own revolutionary group, which he used these credentials to support. He named it the People's Violence (Narodnaia rasprava). Ivanov the student was a member of the People's Violence, and, in November 1869, he began to challenge Nechaev's authority. Nechaev and his supporter Pyotr Uspensky convinced the other group members that Ivanov was dangerous, a threat to the cause, and a core group of People's Violence members lured Ivanov to a remote location, strangled him, and then shot him in the head. Nechaev took the lead and, following the murder, fled Russia. The event sounds like the murder of Shatov because Dostoevsky used the particulars of Ivanov's murder in *Demons*.[65]

Ivanov's murder does not seem like a significant event in the greater scheme of events transpiring in Russia in the 1860s. Karakozov's failed assassination attempt targeted the tsar, whereas Ivanov was just a student. But on Russia's path from literary terror to revolutionary terrorism, Ivanov's murder was a watershed moment because of Nechaev's performance during his trial. Nechaev insisted that the only motivation for the crime was political and, furthermore, that he embodied the revolutionary described in the "Catechism": cold, calculating, single-minded,

and willing to sacrifice for the cause. The government saw the danger
of this. A report of 19 January 1872 to the Third Section warns,

> Nechaev's agitational activity warrants extremely serious attention and
> it is necessary to end it, since it is capable of inspiring fantasies in young
> people, and it is impossible to remain confident that from among these
> fantasy-ridden youths another Karakozov will not come forth.[66]

While the report mentioned the possibility of Nechaev plotting against
the tsar, his "agitational activity" was the key concern. The danger was
Nechaev's performance of revolutionary behaviour and its potential
for indoctrinating others through the power of imagination. Writing
about the relationship between terrorism and the literary imagination
of the 1860s, Daniel Brower observes that "it is surprising how quickly
the urge to take blood manifested itself in radical literature, and how
soon afterwards words led to deeds."[67] As the image of the revolutionary terrorist evolved, literary text influenced revolutionary act, which
in turn led to literary inspiration. In this sense, Nechaev's performance,
while occurring in life as a part of courtroom record, could be viewed
as another radical text, an embodiment of the hero of his "Catechism,"
the ideal revolutionary.

In 1869, Russian revolutionary terrorism existed primarily in the literary text. As Lynn Ellen Patyk has argued, "Russians wrote their terrorism into being in every available genre – travelogue, pamphlet, lyrical
poem, novel, prose poem, profile, sketch, and memoir – in addition to
writing it in blood."[68] The development of Russian literary terrorism
has an intriguing parallel in depictions of the French Revolution in cultural production. The gothic wave of the 1790s and 1800s was a direct
reaction to the Reign of Terror, and many of the popular assumptions
about the violence, chaos, and brutality of the Jacobins' time in power
are based not in historical reality but in the literary – and more specifically the gothic – imagination. Similarly, the Russian terrorist did not
exist per se when Dostoevsky wrote *Demons*, but the 1872 novel helped
enshrine an idea of what a terrorist was like in the Russian cultural
imagination, an idea that went on to inform later incarnations of the
type. For Dostoevsky, the creation of the literary terrorist emerged from
fear of potential terrorism, a fear underscored in the novel by engagement with the school of horror.

Chapter Eight

The Fall of the House
on the Russian Estate

But evil things, in robes of sorrow, / Assailed the monarch's high estate
(Ah, let us mourn, for never morrow / Shall dawn upon him, desolate!);
And, round about his home, the glory / That blushed and bloomed
Is but a dim-remembered story / Of the old time entombed.
> Edgar Allan Poe, "The Fall of the House of Usher"

When an old society is dying, its corpse cannot
be nailed into a coffin and put into a grave.
It decomposes in our midst; the corpse rots and infects us.
> Vladimir Lenin, speech

"There are families over whom an inescapable fatalism seems to weigh heavily," observes Mikhail Saltykov-Shchedrin towards the end of *The Golovlyov Family* (*Gospoda Golovlevy*, 1875–80). He continues:

> The petty, insignificant gentry, who, having nothing to do, without any connection with life in general and without an administrative importance, at first found themselves sheltered beneath the shield of serfdom, scattered across the face of the Russian land, but nowadays living out their final days defenselessly in their crumbling estates.[1]

Saltykov-Shchedrin's novel focuses on one doomed family, but the unhappy family is hardly a unique theme in Russian literature. Across the long nineteenth century, we see such families in works ranging from Denis Fonvizin's play *The Minor* (*Nedorosl'*, 1782) to Anton Chekhov's last drama, *The Cherry Orchard* (*Vishnevyi sad*, 1904), from Nikolai Gogol's *Dead Souls* (1842), with its declining and decaying estates, to Lev Tolstoy's *Anna Karenina* (1877), with its famous meditation on unhappy families. Serfdom's abolition in 1861 led to a shift in the role of Russia's landed gentry class, but as Saltykov-Shchedrin suggests, the family was in a declining state even before Alexander II's reforms. As the century progressed, family decline narratives became increasingly prevalent in Russian realism, and writers employed gothic elements in them to emphasize familial and social breakdown.

The decline of a family is not a uniquely gothic plot,[2] but it is closely associated with the genre, as the gothic has a long history of "fall of the house" narratives. The narrative convention derives its name from Edgar Allan Poe's 1839 story "The Fall of the House of Usher," although the plotline within the gothic canon predates Poe's tale considerably.[3] In the gothic variant, the family is cursed in some mysterious and yet palpable way. Transgressions that occurred in the family's history drive its current circumstances. Gothic tropes such as live burials, imprisoned innocents, villainous guardians or patriarchs, suggestions of the supernatural, and a fascination with fear, terror, and dread abound. Unsurprisingly, in the end, the cursed family is doomed or destroyed outright.

The gothic motifs that appear in nineteenth-century Russian family novels are symptomatic of a heightened sense of anxiety related to decline and degeneration. Describing the cultural climate at the turn of the century, Mark Steinberg observes that "'falling' and 'ruin' were common terms in what was often a melodramatic account of modern sickness," and he describes an obsession with "excess, sickness, and decline."[4] While Steinberg discusses the experience of the individual in the city, the anxiety he identifies permeated Russian life – both urban and rural, as many scholars note.[5] The gothic genre enabled writers to access an array of tropes and conventions that combine melodrama, enhanced fear, and a backdrop of social breakdown to portray feelings of overwhelming anxiety. In this way, the gothic mode enables a way of describing the world that relies not only on a fascination with the gloomy or macabre but also on the anxiety that emerges from encounters with these elements and the related psychologies of dread and fear.

This chapter looks at three Russian literary narratives of family decline – Sergei Aksakov's *Family Chronicle* (*Semeinaia khronika*, 1856), Saltykov-Shchedrin's *Golovlyov Family*, and Ivan Bunin's *Dry Valley* (*Sukhodol*, 1912) – and the way gothic elements in each effect the "fall of the house." The works, which encompass early and late realism, each describe a family in a different stage of its life cycle, oppressed in some sense by the "inescapable fatalism" identified by Saltykov-Shchedrin. Aksakov's work chronicles the foundation of a new dynasty and its first three generations; gothic episodes hint at the family's secrets, which become hidden traumas that are passed down from generation to generation. Saltykov-Shchedrin's novel uses gothic tropes to show a family in a process of decline across multiple generations. The Golovlyovs' traumas are not secret but openly acknowledged, creating a legacy of destruction that hastens the family's ruination. Bunin's novella rounds out the trilogy, describing a house that has already fallen, drawing on the gothic mode to create an atmosphere of gloomy nostalgia. As Bunin's narrator reflects back on his family and childhood, he seeks resolution but is unable to find answers.

The gothic mode and especially the "fall of the house" plot resonate with the anxieties about decline, degeneration, and destruction that were widespread in Russia as a result of the post–Reform era social upheavals. While some recent studies have demonstrated specific connections between gothic writing and fin-de-siècle culture,[6] this chapter aims to show that Russian writers used the gothic tradition to express the same sensibility and concerns across different historical contexts. Indeed, episodes from the histories of Aksakov's Bagrovs, Saltykov-Shchedrin's Golovlyovs, and Bunin's Khrushchevs demonstrate that themes associated with the fin de siècle – gloom, destruction, and fatalistic thinking – had seeped into Russian realism in gothic guise. The prevalence of these themes in the nineteenth-century Russian family novel points to the "inescapable fatalism" hanging over Russian society, exposing latent anxieties about family legacy and decline, the estate system, and Russia's backwardness in the face of a rapidly modernizing Western Europe.

Blight: The Fall of the House of Bagrov

Urged by Gogol to create a new literature based on life, Aksakov began writing the sketches that became *The Family Chronicle* in the early 1840s.[7] Gogol's *Dead Souls* evocatively depicts a conniving civil servant visiting a series of estates featuring "perverted or distorted forms of domesticity."[8] As described in chapter 2 of this book, the narrator uses gothic poetics to describe Plyushkin's "dismal," "woebegone" home, the last stop on the antihero Chichikov's journey in part 1.[9] Whereas Gogol's novel seems at times preoccupied with decay and corruption, Aksakov's work appears to take a more positive line. *The Family Chronicle* tells the story of the Bagrov family across multiple generations, beginning with the establishment of Novoe Bagrovo, the family's estate. The family's patriarch, Stepan Mikhailych, is portrayed as a legendary creator figure, and the work's early parts describe Novoe Bagrovo in nearly mythical terms. Life there becomes an ideal for the work's narrator, Stepan Mikhailych's grandson and heir to the estate. The *Chronicle* ends on a hopeful note with the narrator's birth, seen as both a continuation of the family's legacy and an affirmation of its blessing.

Yet while the novel's structure and narrative voice seem affirmative, the dysfunctional marriage of Stepan Mikhailych's ward Praskovya Ivanovna in part 2 sharply contrasts with the Russian pastoral idyll established in part 1. The narrative takes a Gogolian turn as it describes improbable extremes such as imprisonment and starvation; it even suggests devil worship. Since the family eventually rallies and revives, *The Family Chronicle* is not a true "fall of the house" narrative, but part 2's preoccupation with disharmony and decline undermines Aksakov's idyll. The gothic motifs of part 2 highlight underlying anxieties, which centre on notions of heredity and legacy, a theme that constantly emerges in "fall of the house" gothic writing.[10] While in *The Golovlyov Family* and *Dry Valley*, as I will show, family houses decline and fall, *The Family Chronicle* presents a strong family but uses gothic motifs to illustrate the anxiety surrounding the potential "fall of the house," with ramifications for our understanding of the work as a whole.

In part 2, the fortune hunter Mikhail Kurolesov tricks the fifteen-year-old heiress Praskovya Ivanovna into marrying him. Despite Stepan Mikhailych's displeasure, the young couple is happy at first. Kurolesov takes Praskovya Ivanovna's neglected estates in hand, making them prosperous again, and is admired in the district for his good management. However, as time passes, Kurolesov's tendencies towards violence and alcoholism become habit, and horrors escalate:

> Strange rumours meanwhile arose, which grew and spread in all directions: it was whispered that the Major was not merely severe, […] but he had begun to treat his retainers with cruelty: that he went so frequently to Ufa in order that he might give himself up to unrestrained drunkenness and vice of every possible description: that he had gathered together an unholy company who practised abominations under his directions: that the worst thing about him was the unutterable cruelties that he inflicted on his serfs when he was intoxicated; and that already two men had died under torture.[11]

Later, Kurolesov's behaviour intensifies:

> His innate cruelty developed into a mad lust for torture and bloodshed. Encouraged by the terror and submissiveness of all around him, he rapidly lost all sense of humanity, and reveled in unrestrained acts of violence and brigandage.[12]

Kurolesov's decline from respected landowner to cruel tyrant stems from his misplaced desire for material wealth and amusement, as well as from his tendency towards alcoholism. Aksakov's narrator notes that hard work distracts Kurolesov, but growing bored, he spins more wildly out of control.

Conversely, Stepan Mikhailych runs Bagrovo well and prospers, precisely because of his obsessive interest in continuing the family line. He chooses a wife because of her bloodlines, not her fortune, and he puts the estate and well-being of his family above all. Although Stepan Mikhailych's relatives and retainers fear his temper, his honourable character sharply contrasts with Kurolesov's villainy. However, Kurolesov's striking similarities to Stepan Mikhailych – his authority, temper, and potential for cruelty – reveal the thin line between noble patriarch and destructive wastrel.[13] In this light, the gothic horror that colours Kurolesov's story emphasizes latent anxiety about the family's potential decline just as significantly as the infant deaths of the second generation's children. If, even one generation removed from the strong founder figure, destruction of estate and legacy is possible on such a scale, the family is undermined.

As the gothic episode continues, Praskovya Ivanovna eventually discovers her husband's activities and sets out to deprive him of authority over her estates.[14] Kurolesov beats her and locks her in the cellar to starve until she signs her property over to him. Stepan Mikhailych comes to rescue his former ward:

> One may well imagine the state of Stepan Mikhailovitsch's mind when he heard of the happenings at Paraschino [...] Praskovia cruelly used by her ruthless husband, Praskovia starving in a damp dungeon – perhaps already dead – the awful picture stood so clearly before his eyes that the old man sprang to his feet almost beside himself with agony.[15]

The gothic vision in this episode emphasizes the striking difference between Stepan Mikhailych's and Kurolesov's understanding of and loyalty to family. It takes an unnatural death to resolve the situation: ultimately, Kurolesov is poisoned with a mixture of arsenic and kvass, thus freeing Praskovya Ivanovna and returning her lands to the Bagrov family's holdings.

In the character of Stepan Mikhailych, Aksakov puts forward a Slavophile agenda, calling for a return to moral and religious law, ancestral tradition, and the primacy of the right and just over the state's written laws. Although Stepan Mikhailych represents order and wisdom, maintaining his estates justly and prosperously, the episode detailed in part 2 emphasizes his limitations, another source of anxiety. Praskovya Ivanovna has inherited his sense of duty and justice, as well as his honour and courage, but she is unable to act, oppressed by both her husband and the legal system that gives him power over her. Stepan Mikhailych's desire to continue his line depends not only on his will but also to some extent on chance, on the influx of others into the family by marriage, and on the personalities of his descendants; ultimately, he is unable to control all aspects of his legacy.

These gothic plot elements, although sequestered in the second sketch, carry an ominous shadow. They appear out of place amidst the affirmative foundation narrative and pastoral idyll described in the first section of the *Chronicle*. Although the situation ends happily for Praskovya Ivanovna, who is rid of her husband and returns to Novoe Bagrovo, and for the Bagrov family patrimony, which regains her estates, the episode carries a hint of potential decline and degeneration. In this sense, the gothic mode in Aksakov's *Family Chronicle* can be read as an early indicator of the fin-de-siècle motifs that became pervasive in later Russian realism. While the novel's conclusion valorizes the family, the work as a whole seems to reject the grim present, characterized by marital discord, in favour of an idealized mythical past and bright future. However, the gothic anxiety that emerges in relation to marriage and legacy in Praskovya Ivanovna's sketch problematizes notions of family continuity and stability and undermines the work's affirmative ending. While *The Family Chronicle* ends on an optimistic note, Aksakov's gothic interlude echoes intellectual rumblings against the family coming from Western Europe and informs Saltykov-Shchedrin's *Golovlyov Family*,[16] a strong indictment against the contemporary family packaged neatly in a "fall of the house" narrative frame.

Curse: The Fall of the House of Golovlyov

The prevalence of family novels throughout the nineteenth century points to the broader discourse about the family underway in Russia and Western Europe at this time. As the century progressed, the rise of industry led to a separation between home and workplace and, consequently, a shift in family values. Champions of the traditional family such as G.W.F. Hegel put forward its economic strength and its moral stability as a societal unit. Leftists such as Karl Marx and Friedrich Engels spoke out against the traditional family as an institution. For them, the family not only stood for inequality because of the uneven division of labour between the sexes but also represented an unsustainable economic unit. In *The Communist Manifesto* (1848), they called for the abolition of the bourgeois family, writing, "The bourgeois family will vanish as a matter of course [...] with the vanishing of capital."[17] Upheaval in the family unit was a particular cause for concern in Russia, as the traditional family provided the backbone of the estate system.[18]

The Golovlyov Family stands as a biting satire on the family problem and an examination of the social ramifications of degeneration theory.[19] Thematically and structurally linked with Aksakov's novel, *The Golovlyov Family* presents a family chronicle across three generations. Where Aksakov's story ends on an optimistic note, however, Saltykov-Shchedrin's novel narrates the Golovlyovs' decline and degeneration, ending with their doom. Despite this bleak subject matter, Saltykov-Shchedrin's scathing satirical pen imbues the novel with dark humour. The work significantly undermines the traditional family novels that Saltykov-Shchedrin despised. He equates these "false" family novels and their insincere portrayal of society with the Russian countryside's stagnation. The gothic elements in *The Golovlyov Family* serve a dual function. On the one hand, gothic exaggeration strikes a humorous note, parodying the sincerity of the traditional family-oriented novel and adding to the work's overall satiric quality. On the other hand, the novel exploits the gothic conventions of the "fall of the house" plot to offer an ideologically charged indictment of Russian society and an implied call for change.

Saltykov-Shchedrin's Golovlyovs are doomed from the start, "cursed" in the gothic literary tradition. While the narrator never gives specific details about this curse, the matriarch, Arina Petrovna, and her son, Porfiry, also known as Little Judas (Иудушка), seem preoccupied with it. We learn that Arina Petrovna can put a curse on Little Judas and others in the family, and she takes this power seriously.[20] Radiating from interactions with Arina Petrovna, the fear of an unknown power permeates the novel, informing the family members' relationships with each other. Thus *The Golovlyov Family* lends itself especially well to the gothic sensibility, even beyond its "fall of the house" narrative structure.[21]

As relationships are perverted, the gothic mode signals their degeneration. For example, Pavel first describes his brother as a monster, a basilisk: "He knew that little Judas' eyes oozed an enchanting poison, that his voice, serpent-like, would creep into your soul and paralyze a person's will."[22] Fear and dread characterize the brothers' relationship and ultimately underscore the trajectory of the family's disintegration as this fear appears in gothic-tinged passages recounting other Golovlyovs' degeneration or deaths. As some family members spiral into death, they become fixated on the idea that the Golovlyov estate itself represents a tomb. Anninka, Arina Petrovna's granddaughter, perceives the estate itself as a harbinger of death:

> Golovlyovo – that is death itself, malicious, spiritually empty; that is death eternally lying in wait for a new victim. Two uncles died here. Here the two brothers, her cousins, received "particularly serious" wounds, of which death was the consequence. Finally, Lyubinka as well … Although it seemed as though she had died somewhere in Krechetov "on her own," nonetheless the beginning of the "particularly serious" wounds doubtlessly lay here in Golovlyovo. All the deaths, all the poisons, all the sores – everything originated from here.[23]

Golovlyovo not only foreshadows deaths but also causes them; returning to the family estate figures in the death of nearly every family member. It is a monster waiting to devour its victims, even from afar. The estate consequently becomes a catalyst for growing anxiety among the family members.

Although they all live together in the same house, each member of the Golovlyov family lives in isolation. First Stepan, then Pavel, then Little Judas become wrapped up in their own affairs and lock themselves away. A tendency to forgetfulness allows this isolation to grow. Stepan becomes an alcoholic and drinks himself to death in the estate office; no one checks on him until it is too late. Similarly, Pavel wastes away with his fatal disease alone, until the family members recall that they must arrange his affairs. Little Judas becomes so embroiled in petty busywork that he has little awareness of the outside world, even as his sons die one by one. He seems to give little thought to his legacy's disintegration or to the descendants who should be his heirs. Whereas in *The Family Chronicle*, Stepan Mikhailych is concerned to the point of obsession with preserving his family legacy for future generations, the second-generation Golovlyovs not only appear to view their legacy with apathy but actively neglect it, ignoring the third generation or driving it away.

As the passage quoted above shows, this isolation appears as both a characteristic of Golovlyov family life and another manifestation of the family home's destructive and anxiety-inducing properties. In a similar vein, earlier in the novel, the narrator describes a deathly silence that follows the family members:

> The dining room emptied as everyone dispersed to his room. The house gradually grew quiet and a deathly silence crept from room to room and

finally reached the last refuge where the ritual life persisted longer than in other secluded corners, that is, the study of the master of Golovlyovo.[24]

This "deathly silence" persists, mentioned again and again as the novel draws to a close. Similarly, the narrator constantly describes the house as plunged in darkness or playing host to an "impenetrable gloom." The silence, here a symbol of the family curse, pervades the house, enveloping the various Golovlyovs one by one and Little Judas last of all. The passage underscores a phenomenon widely reported in in the early twentieth century as a symptom of modernity and the fin-de-siècle atmosphere: an "emptiness of solitude," to use Grigory Gordon's 1909 phrasing.[25]

Not surprisingly, given both the "fall of the house" trajectory and fin-de-siècle anxiety, eventually the house of Golovlyov is extinguished. Unlike Aksakov's *Chronicle*, which hints at decline in its central gothic episodes, this "fall of the house" narrative has an absolute end:

> From every direction, from every corner of this hateful house, the dead victims seemed to come creeping out. Wherever one turned, wherever one went, the gray specters were rustling. There was papa, Vladimir Mikhailych, in a white bed cap, sticking his tongue out at everyone and quoting from Barkov. There was brother Styopka-the-Dunce and beside him brother Paska-the-Silent and there was Lyubinka, and there was the final offspring of the Golovlyov family, Volodka and Petka … All of this drunkenness, lechery, torment, oozed blood … And over all of these specters hovered a living specter, and this living specter was none other than Porfiry Vladimirich Golovlyov himself, the final representative of this family which had forfeited itself.[26]

The scene is reminiscent of the House of Usher's spectacular collapse in Poe's story. That narrative revolves around the siblings Roderick and Madeline, the last descendants of the Usher family. The family's final moment is anticipated by various escalating events: Roderick buries Madeline alive, Madeline escapes and attacks Roderick, and the two collapse into a deadly embrace. The narrator, a passing traveller, flees but looks back to see the house collapse and sink into the ground, dark water covering its last traces. In Poe's tale, family and house are destroyed together, the one precipitating the other. However, when Golovlyovo falls, instead of physical destruction the house undergoes a metaphysical collapse, crumbling under a pile of family ghosts.

In the end, the lost Golovlyovs, victims of the family curse, haunt Little Judas. Here Saltykov-Shchedrin uses the hybrid gothic-satire genre to lighten the terrible scene with humour. The narrator lists the early curse victims almost gaily, as though they spend their time flitting about the estate without a care. While earlier in the novel, these transgressions merely accumulated without consequences for their perpetrators, in this last scene, the victims return to haunt the living. As the list grows, the tone becomes more sombre, and finally, the image of blood oozing from the family's transgressions lends an atmosphere of true horror and tragedy to the tableau. Little Judas's role as a "living ghost" (живой призрак), too, becomes humourless and bleak when we consider him as the doomed family's final representative. In this scene, he is prompted by his tormented conscience to the reconciliatory behaviour that leads to his demise: he begs his victims' forgiveness and begins a journey to his mother's grave, freezing to death on the way. And so Little Judas, the "living ghost," follows those other Golovlyovs in fear and anxiety and, eventually, death.

Because he was a rationalist and materialist, Saltykov-Shchedrin's use of the gothic seems odd; he did not believe in the metaphysical. In his gothic realism, terror has a concrete cause, and the spiritual hierarchy relied upon by gothic writers such as Ann Radcliffe or Matthew Lewis is absent. This materialism brings Saltykov-Shchedrin closer to the spiritual emptiness and ennui that characterize decadence, explored by fin-de-siècle writers such as Oscar Wilde, Aubrey Beardsley, or Joris-Karl Huysmans.[27] The phantoms that haunt, for example, Wilde's Dorian Gray or Huysmans's Jean des Esseintes are more in the line of psychological or existential torments than supernatural spectres. Similarly, as Ilya Vinitsky observes, "Shchedrin's phantoms come from within, rather than outside, historical reality: the supernatural here has social, economic, psychological, and biological causes."[28] As an example of the "fall of the house" narrative, *The Golovlyov Family* evinces the gothic's role in the theme but simultaneously showcases its fin-de-siècle preoccupations avant la lettre, exposing their presence in the ideological realist novel.

Spectre: The Fall of the House of Khrushchev

Building on Saltykov-Shchedrin's novel, thematically linked "fall of the house" works appear with increasing frequency in the Russian cultural context as the nineteenth century draws to a close. Milton Ehre names a few: "*The Golovlyovs* stands with Goncharov's *Oblomov*, Bunin's *Dry Valley*, Chekhov's *Cherry Orchard* as one of the great Russian literary epitaphs on a dying social order."[29] Ehre's identification of the works as "epitaphs" plays on the idea of memorialization, a theme we see expressed in the particular nostalgic tone used throughout *Dry*

Valley. This tone sets Bunin's work apart from Aksakov's or Saltykov-Shchedrin's family novels. Aksakov's novel rejects the present for the legendary past and the promise of an unknown but idealized future, paying homage to the family's past greatness while acknowledging its future potential. In Saltykov-Shchedrin's novel, neither the past nor present merits accolades, and the future seems bleak. In Bunin's *Dry Valley*, however, the narrative's emphasis shifts: it mourns the demise of a way of life, even as the gothic motifs describing it emphasize its inevitable decline.[30]

Dry Valley tells the story of the Khrushchev family and its ancestral estate, Sukhodol, through the eyes of its last descendants. In the beginning, the narrators are children, but they grow up as the novella continues. Accordingly, their initially naive descriptions and retellings of Sukhodol's legends and history become increasingly tinged with awareness. At first, the narrators engage nostalgically with the image of Sukhodol's past glory: "Our passionate dreams of Sukhodol were understandable: for us it was a poetic image of the past."[31] The Khrushchev family chronicle, related by Natalya, a peasant on the estate, enthralls the house's young descendants, who clamour to hear more stories from "olden times." Characterized by violence, transgression, greed, and betrayal, these bygone days seem exciting to the children. The young Khrushchevs take pride in their legacy, boasting of their father's status as the sole true heir to Sukhodol and extolling their family's importance:

> My sister and I lived for a long time in the steady tow of Sukhodol, lived under the spell of its antiquity [...] But it was always our ancestors, of course, who ruled that family, and we felt this through the ages. The history of family, kin and clan, is always subterranean, convoluted, mysterious, often terrifying. But it's that long past, those dark depths and legends, that often give a family strength.[32]

Pride in family for them includes pride in family secrets, transgressions, and fears; these trappings of legend become a source of strength, a way of binding a family together.

Hints of the supernatural attend the estate, contributing to the family legend. When the Khrushchev children first travel to Sukhodol, they meet Aunt Tonya, who appears suddenly, mystically out of darkness, terrifying the children. Although she later becomes a beloved folk feature of the estate experience, the fear they feel is palpable in the moment. Their account of Tonya's appearance represents the first indication that Sukhodol's reality may contradict the stories told to the children. Likewise, other events tied to folklore carry a connotation of fear. A local sorcerer called in to cure the ailing mistress uses folkloric magic to provoke terror. Later the devil seems to haunt the house. Finally, the constant discussion of thunderstorms reveals that several family members have died under mysterious circumstances during storms. In these instances, the family's legend seems to combine with some unnatural, destructive, and terrifying force.

The family's place in local society preoccupies the children as they repeat the peasant Natalya's tales, and, through their naive assumptions, a picture of hierarchy and hegemony emerges. Natalya tells the children that Khrushchev, in the early days of the estate, carried a whip, a symbol of his authority. The children look forward to one day also carrying whips, thus continuing the family legacy, although they seem to have little understanding of the whip's meaning. Natalya's story further reinforces this point. The affectionate children at first see the peasant as a pseudo-family member and enjoy her jolly Sukhodol stories, but in adulthood they feel sadness and guilt when they hear Natalya recount her "broken" life spent at Sukhodol. For the children, the family and estate is legendary, but the adult narrators realize that they have played an oppressive role in the lives of the peasants they admired as children. This awareness adds to the anxious undercurrent that accompanies the story's gothic narrative.

As Joost van Baak observes in his study of the house in Russian literature, "The disappearance of a way of life is accompanied by the inevitable dissolution of the spaces that supported it. Empty or derelict houses are 'read' by the reminiscing narrator as metonymic material images of the former inhabitants, often his direct ancestors, and the ways in which they lived."[33] For van Baak, it is the decaying and crumbling house and estate themselves that symbolize the transience of time and the dissolution of the way of life they supported. As in Poe's "Fall of the House of Usher," the destruction of the decaying Sukhodol estate and the demise of the Khrushchev family are linked. However, the "fall of the house" of Khrushchev is not spectacular as it is in Poe's story or Saltykov-Shchedrin's *Golovlyov Family*:

And now the Sukhodol estate is completely empty. All those mentioned here have died, as have their neighbors and their peers. And sometimes you think: Is it true? Did they really live on this earth? It's only at the graveyard that you feel they really did exist – feel, in fact, a frightening proximity to them. But even for that you must make an effort; you must sit and think beside a family headstone – if you can find one. It is shameful to say, but impossible to hide: we don't even know where the graves […] lie.[34]

The peasants who worked the estate are entirely forgotten, and the Khrushchev graveyard is so overgrown and decayed as to suggest that the family lives on only in the stories told by the novella's narrators. From the story's beginning, the estate has been in a state of decay. The air smells of it, and the narrators describe the house's physical dilapidation, its rotting gardens and sagging balconies. But it is only in this moment in the graveyard that we understand that the family, too, has died out. The narrators' nostalgic ruminations reinforce this point:

> No knight's descendant could ever say that in half a century an entire class of people vanished from the earth. He could never speak of such great numbers of people who deteriorated, who committed suicide and drank themselves to death, people who went mad, let go of everything, just disappeared. He could never admit, as I confess here, that the lives of not only our ancestors but even the lives of our great grandfathers are a complete and utter mystery to us now [...]![35]

Like its decaying estate, the Khrushchev family has become a sad husk that exists only in remembered stories, and those memories are growing dim. Here the narrators identify the true tragedy of a noble house's fall as its loss of identity and structure. They mention some causes of this malaise: suicide, alcoholism, madness. These, however, are the symptoms of a larger problem, caused by generations of decline. Unlike Aksakov's work (which is set in the present but idealizes the past and future) or Saltykov-Shchedrin's (which sees only darkness and decay in the past, present, and future), in Bunin's novella there is no future. The family's gothic past has built a legacy of nothing, its estate crumbling and its legends forgotten. In an expression of fin-de-siècle anxiety par excellence, the Khrushchevs' end has already come, and all that remain are emptiness, melancholy, and the unknown. Despite its nostalgic tone and lack of overt violence, *Dry Valley* is the most destructive and bleak of the three "fall of the house" narratives examined in this chapter.

The Fall of the House after the Revolution

Made rotten by stagnation and greed, the noble families of Russian literature collapse with increasing frequency as the twentieth century approaches. In chronicling the Golovlyov family's downfall, Saltykov-Shchedrin invents an extreme case study, emphasizing what he sees as the gentry's problems – or transgressions. Whereas Saltkyov-Shchedrin's *Golovlyov Family* stands as a model "fall of the house" narrative, Aksakov's *Family Chronicle* is more ambiguous, contrasting the notion of the idealized happy family with a model for an unhappy, disintegrating one. Eventually, when *Dry Valley* takes up the plot as a lens through which to reflect upon a vanishing way of life, the gothic – with its historical emphasis, links to destructive forces, and fascination with nostalgia, gloom, and death – seems a natural mode of expression.

Extending the "fall of the house" plot into the post-revolutionary period reveals its curious uses, each informed by the gothic "fall of the house" genealogy in Russian realism. Works such as Marina Tsvetaeva's *House at Old Pimen* (*Dom u starogo Pimena*, 1934) take up the theme as a lens through which to reflect upon a vanished way of life, the "fall" after the fact. Tsvetaeva's memoir-story chronicles the decline of her grandfather Ilovaisky's line. One by one, Ilovaisky's descendants die off. Their illnesses are mysterious, unexplained, and take them in youth's bloom. Some go willingly and knowingly. Others die in horror, unable to reconcile their youth with death. In describing her half-brother Andrei's death, Tsvetaeva names its source as "the hereditary illness of Old Pimen," indicating that the *house* itself causes these deaths and hinting at a family curse.[36]

Tsvetaeva describes her grandfather Ilovaisky's house as a gothic castle. It contains portraits of the dead, who stare down at trespassers from where they hang, inspiring horror: "And decades later I can't stave off a shudder from the accumulation of terror: 'living pictures' in a dead house, dead pictures made of living people."[37] Tsvetaeva always describes the house in terms of death, perhaps most evocatively in this passage:

> It was a house of death. Everything in that house died out except death. Except old age [...] except Ilovaisky. The stiff-necked, cruel-necked old man decided to live. "He's using up other people's lives ... he's buried all his children but he ... A twenty-year-old son is in the ground and a seventy-year-old is walking around up above ..." To the sound of this whispering and even murmuring, he went on living [...] Hundred-year-old men in some stoney [*sic*] desert lie in wait for and lure in young travelers and pump the blood out of them which they need to live on. [Ilovaisky] did not drink anyone's blood; no, in his own way he even loved his children, but the analogy is valid all the same: in such longevity, rare in itself, there is something monstrous.[38]

Like the Golovlyovs' "living ghost," Ilovaisky seems to haunt his own empty house. The juxtaposition of drinking blood and loving one's children points to the old man's perceived monstrosity, just as Tsvetaeva describes his only remaining legacy – his longevity – as monstrous.

Tsvetaeva later intimates that Ilovaisky has himself created the pestilence hanging over the house, although he remains oblivious of his own culpability to the end.

Old Pimen, and the Ilovaisky line with it, succumb to the rot and stagnation that plague the gentry, but the march of history causes the house's final death throes. While Ilovaisky manages to stand up to the authorities and preserve his pride when the Cheka summons him for questioning, the officers see him more as a curiosity. He becomes a quaint relic when he claims not to know political figures such as Lenin or Trotsky and maintains his loyalty as a monarchist. Following Ilovaisky's death, the house finally falls, its last surviving members scattered: "The House at Old Pimen came to an end in twice-shed blood."[39] The last sentence of *The House at Old Pimen* states that the Old Pimen church, sacred burial ground for the noble Ilovaisky family, currently houses a Komsomol youth club. This new, Soviet use of a formerly sacred family space shows that no place for this venerable house exists in the new society.

Shortly before describing Ilovaisky's death, Tsvetaeva comments on his role as historian, making a play on the house's name, Old Pimen, and that of the chronicling monk in Alexander Pushkin's *Boris Godunov* (1831). The chronicler Pimen, like the historian Ilovaisky, records events but does not seek to influence them. A passive observer of turbulent times, he writes obliviously onward as political regimes rise and fall. Furthermore, under the house at Old Pimen lie "Godunovian vaults" (годуновскими сводами), which shroud the house with an atmosphere of guilt and retribution. Tsvetaeva's association of the Ilovaisky house at Old Pimen with Boris Godunov's story adds an additional meaningful layer to the tale of an old family slipping into decline. Boris Godunov represents idealism and courage but also treachery, deceit, greed, violence, and guilt. These transgressions echo the implied guilt of late nineteenth-century Russian society.

The gothic-inspired "fall of the house" theme carries with it many significant meanings relevant to the political situation in Russia as the revolutionary years approached. The genre's implied transgressions hint at moral wrongs and pestilence in society. Lenin, tellingly, in a 1919 speech described tsarist society's ideological legacy as a rotting corpse: "When the revolution comes, it is not like when an individual dies and the corpse is simply removed. When an old society dies, its corpse cannot be nailed into a coffin and put into a grave. It decomposes in our midst; the corpse rots and infects us."[40] As we see in this quote, the gothic fascination with death and decay lends itself especially well to the depiction of a declining society. Marx also used this simile, but the particular brand of violence implied by Lenin's text makes for effective rhetoric. In the context of other works discussed in this chapter, this rhetorical device does not appear radical and new, but rather simply adds to the gothic "fall of the house" legacy in Russian writing.[41]

The "fall of the house" plot cannot avoid its ending, and its inevitable trajectory symbolizes destruction and doom. In this sense, the curse of the Golovlyovs and other families becomes the curse of late imperial Russia: the feeling of "inescapable fatalism" and approaching cataclysm, the mystery of moral transgressions committed but never confessed, stagnation and decline over generations. Reinforced by socio-economic and historical circumstances, these gothic elements promoted a cultural climate in Russia that manifested in degeneration, fin-de-siècle anxiety, and revolutionary violence, eventually leading to what could be described as a much larger "fall of the house."

Conclusion: Chekhov's Ghosts

Ghosts, as we all know, are a superstition,
the product of undeveloped intelligence,
but Vaksin, nonetheless, pulled the blanket over his head
and closed his eyes more tightly.

Anton Chekhov, "Nerves"

Anton Chekhov is not known for ghost stories. His one noted foray into the genre is "The Black Monk" ("Chernyi monakh," 1894), a story about a scholar, Andrei Kovrin, who is visited by a ghostly monk who convinces him he is a genius and destined for greatness. "The Black Monk" contains a plethora of canonical gothic tropes. Kovrin returns to the estate of his former guardian and teacher, Pesotsky, which is described as "gloomy and severe" (угрюмый и строгий).[1] The estate's gothic qualities are highlighted as the description continues, denoting the unsociable gleam of the pond. Introducing a hint of incest to the story, Kovrin is encouraged to and eventually decides to marry Pesotsky's daughter, Tanya, who had been like a sister to him in childhood. The most gothic element of the story is the ghost, a long-dead (or possibly never living) monk who visits the hero multiple times. The first scenes take place in a mysterious orchard at night (with curling tendrils of smoke from fires to dispel frost around the trees), and the appearance of the black monk further reinforces the suggestive atmosphere:

A monk in black robes, with gray hair and black brows, arms crossed over his breast, swept past … His bare feet did not touch the ground. Having raced ahead three fathoms [about twenty feet], he looked back at Kovrin, nodded his head, and smiled at him gently but at the same time slyly. But what a pale, frightfully pale, thin face! Starting to grow again, he flew across the river, collided with the clay bank and pines without a sound, and passing through them, disappeared like smoke.[2]

The descriptions of the ghost's appearance are recognizably gothic and sharply contrast with the narrative that surrounds them. These gothic interludes signal to readers to suspend their disbelief as they identify the ghost story's tropes and conceits. The absurdity and tragedy of the hero's lengthy philosophical chats with the black monk and the extent of the hero's dissociation from reality do not strike the reader until the gothic mode breaks, when Tanya, Kovrin's wife, reveals that Kovrin has been talking to himself. After this break, the atmospheric elements that signal the ghost's presence vanish.

In view of the preceding chapters, it may strike readers as odd that I conclude with "The Black Monk" and not a story more closely connected to the realist canon. My focus in this book has been the way that writers incorporated the gothic genre into their narrative practice and ultimately into literary realism. In the previous chapters, I have deliberately selected works that are not typically associated with the gothic for my analysis. Many of the writers examined in this study have written more recognizably gothic works – for example, Alexander Pushkin's "Queen of Spades" ("Pikovaia dama," 1833), Nikolai Gogol's "The Portrait" ("Portret," 1835), Fyodor Dostoevsky's "Bobok" (1873), and Ivan Turgenev's "Phantoms" ("Prizraki," 1864) and "Klara Milich" (1883). I have excluded analysis of them because my argument focuses on the presence of gothic narrative elements in realist texts; these works incorporate fantastic or supernatural structural elements and veer significantly away from literary realism. "The Black Monk" is different, however. The story includes gothic narrative force and elements of the supernatural, but within the bounds of everyday life. I conclude with "The Black Monk" because Chekhov's ghosts represent the apex of gothic realism – the moment in literary history when the supernatural gothic and literary realism exist harmoniously within the bounds of a coherent narrative.

Gothic Realism in "The Black Monk"

"The Black Monk" has generated a good deal of discussion as scholars have tried to make sense of the story within Chekhov's oeuvre. Chekhov's stories of the 1880s and 1890s demonstrate a marked tendency towards *byt*, "the category of the everyday."[3] Yet "The Black Monk" clearly resembles the earlier gothic works that informed it, such as E.T.A. Hoffmann's *The Golden Pot* (*Der goldne Topf*, 1814) and Vladimir

Odoevsky's "The Sylph" ("Sil'fida," 1836).[4] Lev Shestov read the story as an exploration of Chekhov's own doubts: "The author himself wonders where reality ends and phantasmagoria begins."[5] Reading "The Black Monk" through the lens of the fantastic, Claire Whitehead argues that the ghost represents the moment when irrationality and rationality merge: "Not only is the monk a *product* of mental illness, he is also the *catalyst* for more severe psychological disturbance."[6] Ann Komaromi connects Kovrin's illness to decadence and its psychological disturbances, noting that Chekhov would have come into contact with decadent malaises such as the "fixation of genius" (гениальная одержимость) or "divine sickness" (божественная болезнь) during his travels abroad in the early 1890s.[7] In all three readings, and many others, Chekhov's story represents a reaction to modernity.[8] Komaromi explicitly articulates the tension between the past and the modern: a "legendary" madness rooted in romantic tropes and a clinical "modern" psychological disturbance based in science.[9] Reading "The Black Monk" as a work of gothic realism, however, reveals that the story is by no means unique within Chekhov's corpus or, indeed, in late nineteenth-century Russian prose.

Fear and terror appear in the story, but not because of the ghost. The legend of the black monk does not involve haunting so much as the spectral reproduction of the ghost in various locations. Kovrin expresses his interest in the legend, and when the monk appears, he reacts first and foremost with curiosity. Talking with the monk becomes part of his regular routine, to the point that when the ghost appears at dinner, he directs the conversation to topics that would be of interest to the spectral visitor. Although the monk seems to signify Kovrin's extraordinary genius, its appearance quickly becomes part of the *byt* that surrounds him. For Tanya, however, fear and terror grow around Kovrin's apparent mental disturbance, especially when she catches him speaking to an empty armchair one night. Tanya is not afraid of the ghost (because it does not exist for her); rather, she fears the signs of Kovrin's illness. The mechanism of fear in the story is not directed at the reader. In earlier realist works that featured gothic narrative force, the gothic signalled an attempt to provoke fear in the reader. In "The Black Monk," the ghost's prosaic appearance deflates the gothic atmosphere and dispels its accompanying emotions. The only moments of terror in the story are experienced by its characters, not the reader.

Tanya's fear emphasizes the connection between Kovrin's fascination with the monk and her father Pesotsky's obsession with his garden. The garden is fantastic in its scale and variety: "what quirks, exquisite monstrosities [изусканные уродства], and mockeries of nature there were!"[10] It features every conceivable colour and type of flower as well as trees trained to grow in shapes like umbrellas, spheres, pyramids, candelabras, and even the number 1862, commemorating the year Pesotsky first began gardening. The garden has begun to take over their lives. At the point when Kovrin visits them, Pesotsky is waking up at three o'clock in the morning each day to tend the garden. Concerned about the garden's welfare after his death, Pesotsky worries that Tanya will marry and be distracted from the garden's care by a family. He even grows abusive towards Tanya when she suggests cutting back on garden staff. The parallel between Pesotsky's garden and Kovrin's monk is obvious. Both become all-consuming and result in Pesotsky and Kovrin, respectively, retreating from life. The monk tells Kovrin, "I exist in your imagination and your imagination is a part of nature, which means I exist in nature."[11] Similarly, while Pesotsky's garden exists in nature, it also exists in his imagination and eventually takes it over, not unlike Plyushkin's gothic garden in *Dead Souls*.

The garden and monk both represent reactions against the dullness and monotony of *byt*, but they both manifest as new forms of *byt*. Just as Kovrin's visits with the ghost become routine, Pesotsky's garden fantasy becomes daily labour. The gothic atmosphere and ghostly visitor in "The Black Monk" seem to set the story apart from the rest of Chekhov's prose. Yet the story's gothic realism – in which gothic poetics become inseparable from realist narrative – connects it indelibly with his other works.

Chekhov's Everyday Ghosts

While only one monk haunts Chekhov's stories, in its spectral turn and engagement with gothic tropes in a modern setting, "The Black Monk" fits into a surprising pattern of spectrality in Chekhov's prose fiction that taps into the broader culture of spiritualism in Russia in the late nineteenth century. "Nerves" ("Nervy," 1885), for example, describes a man who goes to a séance, communicates with his dead uncle, and becomes so frightened at the thought of ghosts that he cannot sleep in a room by himself. In the story, the protagonist recalls a conversation at the séance that incrementally shifts the story's emphasis from the spiritualist techniques so popular during this time to lurid gothic mystery: "The whole evening had passed in terrifying conversation. A young lady had started talking, for no reason, about thought-reading. From thought-reading they passed calmly on to spirits, and from spirits to ghosts, and from ghosts to people buried alive ... Some gentleman had read a horrible story of a corpse turning over in its coffin."[12] Having established the gothic mode through suggestion, the story progresses through an exploration of fear via the spectral. The tongue-in-cheek narrator explains:

> Ghosts, as we all know, are a superstition, the product of undeveloped intelligence, but Vaksin nonetheless pulled the blanket over his head and closed his eyes more tightly. Images of a corpse turned upside down in a coffin, his dead mother-in-law, and a colleague who had hanged himself, and a girl who had drowned herself, came into his imagination … Vaksin began to drive these gloomy thoughts from his head, but the more energetically he tried to drive them away, the more frightful and clear his thoughts became. He began to feel afraid.[13]

For Vaksin, ghosts link to an irrational terror. We do not know why Vaksin is afraid here, but we can see that strong emotion, psychological impulse, and spectral apparition are linked tightly together. Vaksin's original spectral encounter, the one that provokes this fearful moment, is the voice of his uncle, a dull presence who offers financial advice from beyond the grave. However, Vaksin's fears soon multiply as he begins to sees spectral visions of all sorts of dead relatives and acquaintances, leading to fresh terror.

In addition to "The Black Monk" and "Nerves," Chekhov's corpus includes quite a few other ghosts that flit in and out of his narratives. Many of these spectral visitors offer humorous reflections on Russia's enthusiasm for spiritualism. In "The Privy Councillor" ("Tainyi sovetnik," 1886), for example, a young man describes waiting for his uncle's visit as resembling "the strained suspense with which spiritualists wait from minute to minute the appearance of a ghost."[14] The séance, the favoured practice of modern spiritualism, doesn't just become a potential opening of a link between the material and spirit worlds; it also is a practice predicated on the existence of a spirit world, one which, as the black monk says, exists in imagination and therefore in nature. In "Gusev" (1890), one character asserts his otherworldly agency, declaring, "Kill me and I will haunt you with my shade [убей меня – буду являться тенью]."[15] Similarly, in "Ward No. 6" ("Palata no. 6," 1892), Ivan Dmitrievich concludes a diatribe about death with the comforting thought, "We'll have our holiday in that other world … From the other world I will appear here as a ghost and scare these reptiles. I'll turn their hair gray."[16] Each of these incidences is marked by emotional language, further underscoring the links between imagination, feeling, psychology, and a spirit world while also demonstrating the manifestation of these links within the prosaic. Ilya Vinitsky's study of spiritualism and realism in the nineteenth century identifies two approaches to their paradoxical relationship: one "considers spiritualism as the (comic) shadow of Russian culture in the Age of Realism, while the [other] goes 'inside' the realistic mind and text and presents realism as haunted by numerous spectres."[17] Chekhov's gothic realist ghosts represent both approaches. These humorous manifestations are a counterpoint to the investigations of psychological states in works such as "The Black Monk" and "Nerves." All place the spectral within the everyday.

Chekhov's ghosts represent a point between knowledge and the anxiety of the unknown that manifests within the bounds of daily life. For example, in "Neighbours" ("Sosedi," 1892), the protagonist experiences a "haunting." The story describes family relations following a scandal. Pyotr Mikhailovich's sister, Zina, runs off with a married man from a neighbouring estate. Pyotr Mikhailovich shows no symptoms of mental illness, but his sister's situation disturbs him. When he goes to visit Zina, he expects to take the moral high ground, confront his sister's "abductor," and bring her home. His visit, however, does not go as expected: he does not confront Zina's lover, instead observing that his sister seems happy and well-treated. Feeling guilty and ineffective, he rides away, thinking about his sister:

> Pyotr Mikhailovich [...] imagined his sister's despair, her pale, suffering face, and the dry eyes with which she would hide her humiliation from other people. He imagined her pregnancy, the death of their mother, her funeral, Zina's horror … Fearful pictures of the future were painted ahead of him on the dark, smooth water, and among pale female figures he saw himself, cowardly, weak, and with a guilty face.[18]

The apparitions of his mother and sister are called up out of Pyotr Mikhailovich's own misery, not from the domestic scene he has just observed. The imagined emotions Pyotr Mikhailovich projects onto his mother and sister are not theirs, but his. Despair at his inability to act, guilt for wishing his sister ill, and fear for his mother produce these ghostly figures in his mind's eye. Chekhov's ghosts are not spectral manifestations of the past, a common device in ghost stories. Rather, they are anxious reflections of the present. Here, too, the ghosts become a generative narrative device, conjuring more stories with their appearance.

Suddenly, Pyotr Mikhailovich sees another figure: "A hundred paces ahead on the right bank of the pond, something dark stood motionless: was it a man or a tall post?"[19] Although "Neighbours" was written before "The Black Monk," the imagery here – a tall, dark, column-like figure – resonates with the imagery surrounding the appearance of the monk in the later story. This trope signals the advent of the gothic. Gazing at the figure, Pyotr Mikhailovich begins to think of Olivier, a murdered French divinity student about whom Zina had told stories and who had been thrown in that very pond. His mind links the story's violence and transgression with his own inaction in his sister's case and its imagined repercussions – the haunting projection he has just seen. As he thinks more about this connection, he continues to stare at the figure, which "looked like a ghost."[20] Pyotr Mikhailovich's apparitions – the haunting by those he could not help, the appearance of the divinity student's "ghost" – point to mental disturbance and an underlying fear. We see the manifestation of this terror when Pyotr Mikhailovich finds the divinity student's spectre real enough that he goes to investigate it and discovers that it is only a post. Structurally and in its use of gothic tropes to misdirect the reader, "Neighbours" parallels "The Black Monk." In both cases, Chekhov's ghosts are a manifestation of uneasy psychologies brought about by modern life.

Chekhov's ghosts, even those that died unnatural deaths, are prosaic. In the case of "Nerves," they give sensible financial advice. In Kovrin's case, they converse politely. These are not ghosts burdened by the unacknowledged trauma of the past. One of literature's more famous ghosts, Hamlet's father, spurs Hamlet to avenge his death; the Danish prince, consumed with despair over past injustice, destroys his own future. Like Hamlet's father, Chekhov's ghosts are a refraction of the self. Chekhov articulates this relationship specifically in a jotted-down story idea from 1894: "A man obsessed with the idea that he is a ghost: he walks at night."[21] However, a key difference between Chekhov's ghosts and those in the vein of Shakespeare's can be observed in their function. In *Hamlet*, the dead king's ghost motivates the entire series of murders and violence, while in Chekhov's stories, the ghosts become normalized in the narratives where they appear. In Chekhov's work, ghosts are so much a part of *byt* that the reader does not see them.

In a notebook entry from 1894, Chekhov quips, "Why did Hamlet bother about ghosts after death, when life itself is haunted by ghosts so much more terrifying?"[22] This phrase echoes the discussion about the spectral, fear, narrative, and the unknown from Chekhov's story "Terror" ("Strakh," 1892), with which I began this book: "There's no doubt about it, apparitions are frightful, but life is also frightful."[23] Vadim Shneyder has aptly observed that Chekhov's readers are "adrift in a fragmented and incomprehensible world," and his characters "find themselves lost in confusion and indecisiveness."[24] Chekhov's stories are grounded in the tedium and hyperreal detail of *byt*, an unexpected location for ghosts. Within them the spectral serves as another mode that refracts and articulates this experience of confusion and indecisiveness.

From Gothic Realism to Modernist Gothic

Chekhov's works sit on the boundary between realist poetics of the everyday and modernist experimentation with representations of consciousness. As examples of gothic realism, Chekhov's ghosts demonstrate realist narrative's ability not only to accommodate the gothic but to assimilate it and use the genre for its own purposes, particularly in the portrayal of subjective reality. His ghosts also speak to one of the key functions of the gothic within realism: to articulate that which is impossible, unfathomable, or unspeakable. I conclude my study of gothic realism with Chekhov's ghosts because they demonstrate a perfect synthesis of gothic and realism. In earlier works I have discussed, the gothic is a mode that is inserted into realist narrative for some purpose, whether to highlight injustice, emphasize subjectivity, or underscore latent anxieties. Chekhov's ghosts are also purposeful, but in these stories, the spectral becomes another facet of *byt*.

The gothic genre carries with it a specific set of narrative devices for engaging readers on an affective level, and gothic realism demonstrates one way in which writers have exploited these devices outside of conventionally gothic texts. Gothic realism showcases the patchwork of influences and artifices writers use to construct literary realism. Gothic poetics are grounded in the exploration of psychologies like fear, dread, and anxiety, which build narrative suspense. Bringing gothic narrative into other generic modes, like realism, enables the import of its characteristic suspense. While realism is a poetics of the everyday, gothic narratives conceal transgressions, guilt, and anxieties, the aspects of human experience that are no less a part of daily life but which are usually hidden from view. The gothic genre provides a vocabulary built in narrative clichés to address or hint at these secrets.

Gothic realism forges a mode that addresses not only objective reality but also a subjective experience of reality. This quality of the gothic is what Mikhail Bakhtin had identified when he stated that he had "added a new page to the history of realism [...] enriched the history of realism" and that "the whole of the Gothic is the history of realism."[25] Bakhtin's championing of the gothic addressed a gap in what was necessary within realist poetics to represent all of life. As Bakhtin observed, realist poetics must include "the idea of the eternal unfinalisedness [...] of the human being in the world"[26] – a mode of universal representation that includes not only a means of depicting life with verisimilitude and lived experience but also the unexpressed, repressed, or concealed aspects of human nature.

This gothic side of realism inspired modernist writers and critics. The case studies in the "Gothic Realism" section of this book have included some texts that are more commonly associated with modernism, including works by Ivan Bunin, Boris Savinkov, and Marina Tsvetaeva. Arguably, these writers use gothic narrative devices and tropes in ways similar to Sergei Aksakov, Fyodor Dostoevsky, Mikhail Saltykov-Shchedrin, and others more commonly associated with the practice of literary realism. The gothic poetics present in these twentieth-century works and others demonstrate a clear continuation of the nineteenth-century novel's gothic realism. Beyond this thematic and formal lineage, however, reading Bunin's *Dry Valley* or Tsvetaeva's *House at Old Pimen* with a consideration of gothic poetics reveals a tightly structured "fall of the house" tale that builds on the same fears and anxieties that nineteenth-century realist works draw on through engagement with this gothic classic plot, namely those surrounding social decline and collapse. Similarly, incorporating gothic themes into *A Pale Horse* allows Savinkov to introduce a new framework for terror and sensation that contrasts with the prosaic, detailed descriptions of the terrorist plot. Although Dostoevsky and Savinkov differ significantly in their political views, motivations for writing, and aesthetic concerns, their shared use of gothic narrative elements to suggest affective responses to the reader is surprisingly similar. These works represent a few examples from a much larger body of modernist and later texts that incorporate gothic themes and tropes.[27]

While the so-called gothic wave of the early nineteenth century has been seen thus far as a curious footnote in Russian literary history, gothic fiction – both imported and written in Russia – has had a lasting influence that remains generative to the present. Often in Russian literature, the story has been that "as an explicit mode or world view, the Gothic rarely appeared in the Russian pre-revolutionary literary tradition before the Decadents of the Symbolist period."[28] Such a reading neglects the vibrant gothic fiction that existed in the nineteenth century, from the gothic wave of 1790–1810 that Vadim Vatsuro examined to the Russian and Ukrainian gothic texts of the 1830s and 1840s that Valeria Sobol and others have recently analysed.[29] This reading also belies the rich corpus of texts that rely on gothic poetics from romanticism to the present day. Vatsuro and Sobol have uncovered ways the gothic persists in the nineteenth century. The study I have presented here demonstrates the way that the gothic continues to inform Russian writing throughout realism. While some Russian writers are often associated with the gothic, like Dostoevsky, my study situates his body of work alongside the broader trend for gothic realism and also adds writers not usually associated with the gothic to the ranks of those who felt its influence.

The gothic came to Russia in the late eighteenth century, fostered a vibrant literary tradition, and influenced generations of both romantic and, as I show, realist writers. The age of the great realist novel passed, but the gothic persisted, taken up anew by modernist writers attracted to the genre's ability to transform itself and transfigure its host genre. In the reflexive Russian literary tradition, gothic's entrance into literary structures and forms created a paradigm that enabled its transfer into the realist mode of writing. In nineteenth-century Russia, industrialization, social shifts, and divisive political and philosophical debates led to an era of rapid change, destabilization, and questioning. In this fragmented and confusing world, gothic narrative enabled articulation of the inarticulable within a literary text: dread, horror, anxiety, and especially fear. Gothic realism is more subtle than gothic incarnations within romanticism or modernism, but as Chekhov's ghosts demonstrate, its influence is unmistakable. His ghosts are not a sudden modernist apparition. Rather, they are the legacy of Russian literature's century of gothic migration and assimilation.

Notes

Introduction

1   All citations from Checkhov's text to this point have been from Chekhov, "Strakh," in *Polnoe sobranie sochinenii i pisem*, vol. 8, 130–1. This and all other translations in the text are my own unless indicated otherwise.
2   Jakobson, "On Realism in Art," 38.
3   Watt, *The Rise of the Novel*, 32.
4   Belinskii, "Vzgliad na russkuiu literaturu 1846 godu," in *Polnoe sobranie sochinenii*, vol. 10, 16.
5   On the history of Russian realism and the stakes of its study, see Vaisman, Vdovin, Kliger, and Ospovat, "Vvedenie: 'Realizm' i russkaia literatura XIX veka," in *Russkii realizm XIX veka*, 5–63.
6   P. Brooks, *Realist Vision*, 12.
7   Wellek, *Concepts of Criticism*, 241.
8   Nabokov, "On a Book Entitled *Lolita*," 211.
9   James, "Preface to Vol. 7: The Tragic Muse," 1107.
10 Jakobson, "On Realism in Art," 38.
11 Paperno, *Chernyshevsky and the Age of Realism*, 4.
12 Ibid.
13 Brunson, *Russian Realisms*, 4.
14 Ibid., 25.
15 On the relationship between the gothic, realism, and the modern subject, see Armstrong, *How Novels Think*. Nancy Armstrong reads "the familiar terrain of realism as the other side of the gothic, as if the two existed in a mutually defining relationship" (3).
16 Botting, *Gothic*, 3–4.
17 M. Maguire, *Stalin's Ghosts*, 10.
18 See Bowers, "The Gothic Novel Reader Comes to Russia."
19 Anonymous, "Terrorist Novel Writing."
20 Castle, "Ann Radcliffe's *The Mysteries of Udolpho*," 56.

21 Botting, *Gothic*, 2–3.

22 Punter, *The Literature of Terror*, vol. 2, *The Modern Gothic*, 146.

23 M. Maguire, *Stalin's Ghosts*, 10.

24 This definition first appeared in Bowers, "The City through a Glass, Darkly," 1238.

25 Baldick, introduction to *Melmoth the Wanderer*, ix.

26 On the relationship and divergence of gothic and melodrama, for example, see P. Brooks, *The Melodramatic Imagination*, 17–20.

27 Ibid., 17.

28 Radcliffe, *The Mysteries of Udolpho*, 330.

29 Tolstoi, "Detstvo," in *Polnoe sobranie sochinenii*, vol. 1, 80–1.

30 See Kristeva, *Powers of Horror*, 3–4 and passim.

31 C. Miller, "Genre as Social Action."

32 Studies of gothic influence on nineteenth-century Russian writers include, for example, Cornwell, *The Gothic-Fantastic in Nineteenth-Century Russian Literature*; Poliakova and Tamarchenko, *Goticheskaia traditsiia v russkoi literature*; on *Anna Karenina* specifically, Shneyder, *Russia's Capitalist Realism*, 66–100; and Naiman, "'Husband and Wife': An Approach to the Gothic in *Anna Karenina*"; and others.

33 See, for example, Arndt, "Theodor Sturm's *Der Schimmelreiter*"; Backus, "Irish Gothic Realism and the Great War"; Elbert and Ryden, "American Gothic Realism and Naturalism"; Garrett, *Gothic Reflections*; Komaromi, "Unknown Force"; Mahawatte, *George Eliot and the Gothic Novel*; Schroder, "Voodoo and Conjure as Gothic Realism"; Tarr, *Gothic Stories within Stories*; and others.

34 Mahawatte, *George Eliot and the Gothic Novel*, 2.

35 Garrett, *Gothic Reflections*, 222.

36 See Pan'kov, "'Everything else depends,'" 46. Pan'kov's fascinating article relies on interviews he conducted with Bakhtin's dissertation examiners.

37 "Stenogramma zasedaniia Uchenogo soveta Instituta mirovoi literatury im. A.M. Gorkogo. Zashchita dissertatsii tov. Bakhtinym na temu 'Rable v istorii realizma.' 15 November 1946," *Dialog Karnaval Khronotop* 2–3 (1993), 58ff; this translation appears in Pan'kov, "'Everything else depends,'" 46.

38 Pan'kov, "'Everything else depends,'" 52. On the alignment of Bakhtin's conceptualization of the romantic grotesque with literary gothic, see Tarr, *Gothic Stories within Stories*, 1–2.

39 "Zashchita dissertatsii tov. Bakhtinym," 96; cited in Pan'kov, "'Everything else depends,'" 52–3.

40 Punter, *The Literature of Terror*, vol. 2, *The Modern Gothic*, 183–4.

41 Pan'kov, "'Everything else depends,'" 46.

42 Nancy Armstrong's evocation of "the necessary gothic" in her study of the development of the modern subject in the realist novel also

emphasizes this same point, although she comes to it from a different theoretical perspective. See Armstrong, *How Novels Think*, 137–53.

43 Dostoevskii, *Brat'ia Karamazovy*, in *Polnoe sobranie sochinenii*, vol. 15, 158.

44 Robin Feuer Miller has examined the novel's gothic themes in relation to Charles Maturin's *Melmoth the Wanderer* (1820). See Miller, *Dostoevsky's Unfinished Journey*.

1. A Russian Reader's Gothic Library

1   Pushkin, "Pikovaia dama," in *Polnoe sobranie sochinenii*, vol. 8, 232.

2   On the development of the gothic novel reader in Russia, see Bowers, "The Gothic Novel Reader Comes to Russia."

3   On the development of publishing, literacy, and readership in this period, see Marker, *Publishing, Printing and the Origins of the Intellectual Life in Russia*, especially 184–211.

4   On this trend, see Hoogenboom, "Sentimental Novels and Pushkin." Hoogenboom's analysis reveals that "until the 1860s, over 90% of the market for novels in Russia consisted of foreign literature in translation (the percentage would be higher could we account for foreign literature in the original)" (553).

5   Karamzin, "O knizhnoi torgovle i liubvi ko chteniiu v Rossii," in *Izbrannye sochineniia*, vol. 2, 178–9.

6   See Hoogenboom, "Sentimental Novels and Pushkin," 553.

7   Karamzin, "O knizhnoi torgovle liubvi ko chteniiu v Rossii," in *Izbrannye sochineniia*, vol. 2, 180.

8   See Matveeva, "Immigration and the Book." Gary S. Marker also discusses circulating libraries; see Marker, *Publishing, Printing and the Origins of the Intellectual Life in Russia*, 171–2.

9   See J. Brooks, *When Russia Learned to Read*.

10 Belinskii, "Literaturnye mechtaniia," in *Polnoe sobranie sochinenii*, vol. 1, 21. Belinsky repeats this point on pp. 86, 88, and 147 for emphasis, but it is not his original idea (or statement). See the note on p. 517.

11 George Gutsche imaginatively explores Smirdin's business empire through the interaction of guests at one of the publisher's famous dinner parties. See Gutsche, "Dinner at Smirdin's."

12 Todd, "Periodicals in Literary Life of the Early Nineteenth Century," 38.

13 *Biblioteka dlia chteniia*, no. 1 (1834), 1.

14 See Frazier, *Romantic Encounters*.

15 On the complicated and sometimes paradoxical relationship between Kant's philosophies and gothic fiction, see Brown, "A Philosophical View of the Gothic Novel."

16 Vatsuro, *Goticheskii roman v Rossii*, iii.

17 Somov, "Matushka i synok," 328; Somov, "Mommy and Sonny," trans. Mersereau, 213.

18 On the translation and reception of Lathom's *Midnight Bell*, see Vatsuro, *Goticheskii roman v Rossii*, 200–10.

19 Austen, *Northanger Abbey*, 38–9.

20 Brian James Baer has written on Austen's probable influence on another Kharkov writer, Liubov' Krichevskaia, in his introduction to *No Good without Reward*; see especially 28–30, 33–5. Baer suggests Krichevskaia (and other Russians) read Austen in French translation; Isabelle de Montolieu translated the English novelist's works into French in the 1810s and 1820s. Montolieu's translation of *Northanger Abbey* appeared in 1824, years after the other translations, because of perceived waning interest in gothic fiction in France. See Bour, "The Reception of Jane Austen's Novels in France and Switzerland."

21 Cited and translated in Tosi, *Waiting for Pushkin*, 84–5.

22 See Hutcheon, *A Theory of Parody*, 84–99.

23 Somov, "Matushka i synok," 337; "Mommy and Sonny," 220.

24 Scott, "Horace Walpole," 64.

25 The classic study of this phenomenon is Sage, *Horror Fiction in the Protestant Tradition*.

26 Sade, *The Gothic Tales*, 50.

27 *New Monthly Magazine*, 1826; quoted in Kilgour, *The Rise of the Gothic Novel*, 6–7.

28 Austen, *Northanger Abbey*, 38–9.

29 Dostoevskii, *Zimnie zametki o letnikh vpechetleniiakh*, in *Polnoe sobranie sochinenii* (*PSS*), vol. 5, 46; Dostoevsky, *Winter Notes on Summer Impressions*, trans. Patterson, 1–2.

30 On the reception of English gothic novelists in Russia, see Vatsuro, *Goticheskii roman v Rossii*, 7–168.

31 On the Radcliffe phenomenon in Russia, see Bowers, "Ghost Writing: Radcliffiana and the Russian Gothic Wave."

32 Tosi, *Waiting for Pushkin*, 327.

33 On gothic publishing in Western Europe, see Potter, *The History of Gothic Publishing*.

34 Scholars such as V.E. Vatsuro, Anthony Cross, Mark S. Simpson, Gitta Hammarberg, and Derek Offord have sketched out the particular nuances of British gothic influence on "Bornholm Island." See Vatsuro, *Goticheskii roman v Rossii*, 78–105; Cross, *N.M. Karamzin*, 113–16; Simpson, *The Russian Gothic Novel*, 31–2; Hammarberg, *From the Idyll to the Novel*, 196; Offord, "Karamzin's Gothic Tale," 40–6.

35 Quoted in Simpson, *The Russian Gothic Novel*, 17.

36 Pursglove, "Does Gothic Verse Exist?," especially 86–92.

37 See Tosi, *Waiting for Pushkin*, 346–64.

38 Vigel', *Zapiski*, 342.

39 The term "genre ecology" originated in communication theory, but the idea of networked genre components works well for the kind of conceptual "meta-reception" visualization I am carrying out. For the original context of this idea, see Erickson, "Making Sense of Computer-Mediated Communication."

40 I envision genre in this sense operating like Toporov's concept of the "Petersburg Text." See Toporov, *Peterburgskii tekst russkoi literatury*.

41 Tosi, *Waiting for Pushkin*, 346. On Schiller's influence on Narezhny and Gnedich, see Vatsuro, *Goticheskii roman v Rossii*, 312–19.

42 See "Primechaniia," in Lermontov, *Sobranie sochinenii*, vol. 3, 575.

43 On the reception of *The Robbers* in 1830s Russia, see Drews, *Die Rezeption deutscher Belletristik in Russland*, 142–3.

44 See Dostoevsky's letter to N.L. Ozmidov, in *Dostoevskii, PSS*, vol. 30, book 1, 212.

45 Barkhoff, "'The echo of the question as if it had merely resounded in a tomb,'" 44.

46 For the extension of this argument, see Andriopoulos, *Ghostly Apparitions*, 73–104.

47 Tat'iana Gubskaia attributes *The Ghost-Seer's* generic affinity with the conventions of the gothic for its continued popularity among readers from the early nineteenth century to the present. Gubskaia, "F. Shiller v russkoi literature XIX veka."

48 Byron, "Don Juan," in *Lord Byron: The Major Works*, 614.

49 See Diakonova and Vatsuro, "'No Great Mind and Generous Heart.'"

50 On the parallels between Byron's poem and Walpole's novel, see Cochran, introduction to *The Gothic Byron*, 14–17. On Byron's gothic hero, see Ceron, "*Manfred*, the Brontes, and the Byronic Gothic Hero."

51 Diakonova and Vatsuro, "'No Great Mind and Generous Heart,'" 341.

52 On Odoevsky's gothic-phantasmagoric tales, see Cornwell, *The Life, Times and Milieu of V.F. Odoyevsky*, 55–68.

53 On Hoffmann's early translation history in Russia, see Passage, *The Russian Hoffmannists*, 36–8.

54 Gogol', *Polnoe sobranie sochinenii (PSS)*, vol. 11, 245.

55 Gogol', "Nevskii Prospekt," in *PSS*, vol. 3, 37.

56 On Western influence on the Russian fantastic, see Izmailov, "Fantasticheskaia povest'." For the extension of this argument, see Whitehead, *The Fantastic in France and Russia*. For Whitehead's readings of "The Nose," see 122–33 and 139–51.

57 Bestuzhev-Marlinskii, *Sochinenii*, vol. 2, 563–4. Cited in Frazier, *Frames of the Imagination*, 119.

58 See Sobol', "Monakh v Madride."
59 On the "The Queen of Spades" in this context, see Golburt, *The First Epoch*, 205–38.
60 Frazier, *Frames of the Imagination*, 119.
61 See Whitehead, *The Fantastic in France and Russia*, 17–29 and 32–8.
62 On Dickens's debt to the gothic, see Garrett, *Gothic Reflections*, 141–67.
63 Dickens, *Oliver Twist*, 448.
64 On Dickens's reception in the nineteenth century, see Katarskii, *Dikkens v Rossii*.
65 Lotman, "Russkaia literatura na frantsuzskom iazyke," 368.
66 See Lary, *Dostoevsky and Dickens*, 18.
67 Dostoevskii, "Neskol'ko slov o Zhorzh Sand," in *PSS*, vol. 23, 33–4; Dostoevsky, "A Few Words about George Sand," trans. Lantz, 509.
68 Dostoevskii, "Neskol'ko slov o Zhorzh Sand," 33; Dostoevsky, "A Few Words about George Sand," 509.
69 See Catteau, *Dostoyevsky and the Process of Literary Creation*, 13.
70 Paperno, *Chernyshevsky and the Age of Realism*, 7.
71 Jenny, "The Strategy of Form," 39.

2. Gothic Transmutations in Pushkin and Gogol

1 Todorov, *The Fantastic*, 41–2.
2 Cornwell, "Russian Gothic: An Introduction," in *The Gothic-Fantastic in Nineteenth-Century Russian Literature*, 4.
3 Somoff, *The Imperative of Reliability*, 12.
4 See ibid., 3ff.
5 Franklin, "Novels without End," 373.
6 On genre repertoire, see Devitt, *Writing Genres*, 57.
7 Pushkin, *Evgenii Onegin*, in *Polnoe sobranie sochinenii* (*PSS*), vol. 6, 56.
8 On their significance in Russia, see M.P. Alekseev's scholarly commentary on *Melmoth the Wanderer*: Alekseev, "Ch.R. Met'iurin i ego 'Mel'mot skitalets.'" While *Melmoth* was not released in Russian translation until 1831, Pushkin is known to have read a copy imported from France in 1823 and was clearly reflecting on the novel while he was writing *Eugene Onegin*.
9 Tosi, *Waiting for Pushkin*, 346.
10 Pushkin, *Evgenii Onegin*, in *PSS*, vol. 6, 97; Pushkin, *Eugene Onegin*, trans. Falen, 106. Subsequent citations to the novel will first refer to the Russian edition, then the Falen translation, separated by a semicolon.
11 Nabokov, *Eugene Onegin: A Novel in Verse*, vol. 2, 330.
12 Walpole, Preface to the First Edition, *The Castle of Otranto*, vii–viii.
13 Mikhail Gershenzon argues that the dream has two parts – the initial descent into the dream state and its resolution in "prophetic" vision.

This pattern of buildup and deflation aligns with his reading. See Gershenzon, "Sny Pushkina."

14 Pushkin, *Evgenii Onegin*, 149; *Eugene Onegin*, 167.

15 Pushkin, *Evgenii Onegin*, 149; *Eugene Onegin*, 167.

16 "Does he play the outcast still? / In what new guise is he returning? / What role does he intend to fill? / Childe Harold? Melmoth for a while? / Cosmopolite? A Slavophile? / A Quaker? Bigot? – might one ask? / Or will he sport some other mask?" Pushkin, *Evgenii Onegin*, 168; *Eugene Onegin*, 188.

17 Pushkin, *Evgenii Onegin*, 56; *Eugene Onegin*, 62.

18 In a similar vein, Gershenzon observes, "All of *Eugene Onegin* is like a row of open, light rooms, through which we freely walk and examine their contents. But in the very centre of the building there is a crypt [тайник]; the door is locked, we look out the window and all the mysterious things [загадочные вещи] are inside; this is 'Tatyana's dream.'" See Gershenzon, "Sny Pushkina," 87.

19 Gogol', *Mertvye dushi*, in *Polnoe sobranie sochinenii*, vol. 1, 110; Gogol, *Dead Souls*, trans. R. Maguire, 120. Subsequent citations to *Dead Souls* will first refer to the Russian edition, then the Maguire translation, separated a semicolon.

20 R. Maguire, *Exploring Gogol*, 254.

21 See Fusso, *Designing Dead Souls*, 1 and passim.

22 Marianne Shapiro provides an overview of the development of this critical understanding. See Shapiro, "Gogol and Dante."

23 Gogol', *Mertvye dushi*, 111; Gogol, *Dead Souls*, 122.

24 Gogol', *Mertvye dushi*, 111; Gogol, *Dead Souls*, 123.

25 Gogol', *Mertvye dushi*, 111; Gogol, *Dead Souls*, 123.

26 Gogol', *Mertvye dushi*, 120; Gogol, *Dead Souls*, 133.

27 Gogol', *Mertvye dushi*, 111; Gogol, *Dead Souls*, 123.

28 See, for example, Shevyrev, "'Pokhozhdeniia Chichikova, ili Mertvye dushi.'" More recently, see Mann, *Poetika Gogolia*, 281.

29 Gogol', *Mertvye dushi*, 109; Gogol, *Dead Souls*, 119–20.

30 Gogol', *Mertvye dushi*, 112; Gogol, *Dead Souls*, 123–4.

31 See, for example, Vladislav Krivonos's reading of the image in Krivonos, *"Mertvye dushi" Gogolia*, 142–54.

32 Bakhtin, "Forms of Time and of the Chronotope in the Novel," in *The Dialogic Imagination*, 245–6.

33 Ibid., 246.

34 On the potential identities for Chichikov in this series, see Lotman, "Pushkin i 'Povest' o kapitane Kopeikine': (K istorii zamysla i kompozitsii 'Mertvykh dush')," in *Pushkin. Biografiia pisatelia, stat'i i zametki*, 277–8.

35 Weiner, *By Authors Possessed*, 77–8.

36 Porter, *Economies of Feeling*, 110.

37 Gogol', *Mertvye dushi*, 113; Gogol, *Dead Souls*, 124–5.
38 Gogol', *Mertvye dushi*, 113; Gogol, *Dead Souls*, 124–5.
39 Dante Alighieri, *Inferno*, 241.
40 Ibid., 629–31.
41 Gogol', *Mertvye dushi*, 116; Gogol, *Dead Souls*, 128–9.
42 See Mann, "Gogol's Poetics of Petrification."
43 Dante Alighieri, *Inferno*, 627.
44 Lotman, "Pushkin i 'Povest' o kapitane Kopeikine': (K istorii zamysla
     i kompozitsii 'Mertvykh dush')," in *Pushkin. Biografiia pisatelia, stat'i i
     zametki*, 279.
45 Radcliffe, *The Romance of the Forest*, 247–8.
46 Walpole, Preface to the Second Edition, *The Castle of Otranto*, xiv.
47 Walpole, Preface to the First Edition, *The Castle of Otranto*, vii.
48 Tynianov, *The Problem of Verse Language*, 33.

3. Russian Landscapes in a Gothic Frame

Parts of the analysis of Turgenev's "Bezhin Lea" presented in this
chapter have appeared in Katherine Bowers, "Through the Opaque Veil:
The Gothic and Death in Russian Realism," in *The Gothic and Death*, ed.
Carol Margaret Davison (Manchester: Manchester University Press, 2017),
157–73.

1 Allen, *Beyond Realism*, 140–1.
2 Belinskii, "Vzgliad na russkuiu literaturu 1874 goda: Stat'ia pervaia," in
    Polnoe sobranie sochinenii, vol. 10, 312.
3 Tarr, *Gothic Stories within Stories*, 2.
4 Ibid., 6.
5 Goncharov, *Oblomov*, in *Polnoe sobranie sochinenii i pisem*, vol. 4, 98;
    Goncharov, *Oblomov*, trans. Magarshack, 103. Subsequent citations to
    Oblomov will first refer to this edition, then this translation, separated by a
    semicolon.
6 Ely, *This Meager Nature*, 7.
7 Radcliffe, *The Mysteries of Udolpho*, 30.
8 Goncharov, *Oblomov*, 98–9; *Oblomov*, 103.
9 Tiutchev, "Kak khorosho ty, o more nochnoe …," in *Stikhotvoreniia*, 135.
    This poem was written in 1865, but is typical of Tyutchev's romantic
    nature writing throughout his poetic career.
10 Thomas Newlin notes, "The line separating Goncharov's Oblomovka
     from, say, Saltykov-Shchedrin's Golovlyovo is pretty thin; the Russian
     pastoral dream tends to veer easily into the realm of the squalid and the
     mundane or even into the realm of nightmare." See Newlin, *The Voice in
     the Garden*, 34.
11 Likhachev, *Poetika drevnerusskoi literatury*, 304.

12 Borowec, "Time after Time," 565.
13 Likhachev, *Poetika drevnerusskoi literatury*, 302.
14 Singleton, *No Place Like Home*, 77.
15 Likhachev, *Poetika drevnerusskoi literatury*, 304.
16 The *Petersburg Collection* (*Peterburgskii sbornik*, 1846), ed. Vissarion
    Belinsky and Nikolai Nekrasov, features four contributions from
    Turgenev, three of them lyric and typical of his early works. These
    include Russian translations of Goethe's twelfth "Roman Elegy" and
    Byron's "Darkness," as well as an original "story in verse" written in
    a humorous romantic style using a slightly modified "Onegin stanza."
    The fourth item is prose, but also written in a humorous light romantic
    style. This particular volume introduced Dostoevsky's *Poor Folk* (*Bednye
    liudi*) to the Russian reading public. Also included is a humorous gothic
    spoof by Vladimir Odoevsky called "Martingale: From the Notes of an
    Undertaker" ("Martingal: iz zapisok grabovshchika").
17 Turgenev, "Bezhin lug," in *Zapiski okhotnika*, in *Polnoe sobranie sochinenii i
    pisem*, vol. 3, 86.
18 Ibid., vol. 3, 87; Turgenev, "Bezhin Lea," in *Sketches from a Hunter's Album*,
    trans. Freeborn, 100. Subsequent citations to pieces from *Zapiski okhotnika*
    will refer to this edition, then this translation, separated by a semicolon.
19 Turgenev, "Bezhin lug," 87; "Bezhin Lea," 100.
20 Turgenev, "Bezhin lug," 88; "Bezhin Lea," 101.
21 Turgenev, "Bezhin lug," 88; "Bezhin Lea," 101.
22 Turgenev, "Bezhin lug," 97; "Bezhin Lea," 111.
23 Turgenev, "Bezhin lug," 104; "Bezhin Lea," 118.
24 Turgenev, "Bezhin lug," 101; "Bezhin Lea," 114.
25 Turgenev, "Bezhin lug," 101; "Bezhin Lea," 114.
26 Turgenev, "Bezhin lug," 101; "Bezhin Lea," 114–15.
27 Turgenev, "Bezhin lug," 105; "Bezhin Lea," 120.
28 Simpson, *The Russian Gothic Novel*, 87.
29 Turgenev, "Les i step'," 358; "Forest and Steppe," 387.
30 Turgenev, "Moi sosed Radilov," 55; "My Neighbour Radilov," 67–8.
31 Turgenev, "Biriuk," 155; "Loner," 173.
32 Costlow, "Who Holds the Axe?" 18.
33 Ibid., 19.
34 On Slavic place spirits, see Ivanits, *Russian Folk Belief*, 51–82, 169–89.
35 Botting, *Gothic*, 11.

4. *The Idiot*: Dostoevsky's Gothic Novel

1 Vatsuro, *Goticheskii roman v Rossii*, iii.
2 On the gothic narrative voice, see R. Miller, *Dostoevsky and "The Idiot,"*
   108–25. On the gothic narrative arcs and the gothic function of Holbein's

painting "The Dead Christ in the Tomb," see Bowers, "Under the Floorboards, Over the Door."

3 Dostoevskii, *Zimnye zametki o letnikh vpechetleniiakh*, in *Polnoe sobranie sochinenii* (*PSS*), vol. 5, 46; Dostoevsky, *Winter Notes on Summer Impressions*, trans. Patterson, 1–2.

4 Dostoevskii, *PSS*, vol. 28, 19.

5 See R. Miller, "Dostoevsky and the Tale of Terror." N.M. Lary also discusses Dostoevsky's British reading habits in *Dostoevsky and Dickens*, arguing that Dickens fascinated Dostoevsky because the English writer incorporated melodramatic and gothic plot elements into his work.

6 See L. Grossman, "Kompozitsiia v romane Dostoevskogo," in *Sobranie sochinenii*, vol. 2, 9–59; and R. Miller, *Dostoevsky's Unfinished Journey*, 128–47. Other critics who have discussed Dostoevsky's engagement with the gothic include Mikhail Bakhtin, Mario Praz, George Steiner, Donald Fanger, Joseph Frank, Malcolm V. Jones, Ignat Avsey, Leon Burnett, and Randi Gaustad, among others. Recently Boris Tikhomirov has argued that Dostoevsky thought he was reading Radcliffe but was actually reading other works published under Radcliffe's name. See Tikhomirov, "K probleme genezisa 'ital'ianskoi mechty' Dostoevskogo."

7 Nabokov, *Eugene Onegin: A Novel in Verse*, vol. 2, 191.

8 Nabokov, *Lectures on Russian Literature*, 96.

9 Frank, *Dostoevsky: The Seeds of Revolt*, 55.

10 R. Miller, *Dostoevsky and "The Idiot,"* 8.

11 Here I agree with Andrei Platonov's concept in "No odna dusha u cheloveka." Platonov's binary reading of the Myshkin-Rogozhin relationship goes against those who view *The Idiot*'s central relationship(s) as a simple love triangle between Myshkin, Rogozhin, and Nastasya Filippovna.

12 On the function of Myshkin's "compassionate realism," see Young, *Dostoevsky's "The Idiot" and the Ethical Foundations of Narrative*, 75–134; on its negative influence on other characters, see especially 124–6.

13 On Nastasya Filippovna's centrality in the final scenes, see ibid., 47–74.

14 Chard, introduction to *The Romance of the Forest*, ix.

15 Michasiw, introduction to *Zofloya, or The Moor*, xiv–xv.

16 Dostoevskii, *Idiot*, in *PSS*, vol. 8, 286–7; Dostoevsky, *The Idiot*, trans. Brailovsky, revising Garnett, 376–7. Subsequent citations to *The Idiot* will refer first to this edition, then this translation, separated by a semicolon.

17 Corrigan, *Dostoevsky and the Riddle of the Self*, 70.

18 Radcliffe, *The Mysteries of Udolpho*, 203.

19 Dostoevskii, *Idiot*, 50–1; Dostoevsky, *The Idiot*, 62–3. The Brailovsky-revised Garnett translation uses "restlessness" for беспокойства here, but

I have amended it to "anxiety," which seems like a closer meaning for the word in this passage.

20 Radcliffe, *Mysteries of Udolpho*, 165–6.
21 Dostoevskii, *PSS*, vol. 9, 204.
22 Dostoevskii, *Idiot*, 256; Dostoevsky, *The Idiot*, 333.
23 Butler, introduction to *Northanger Abbey*, xxviii.
24 Ibid.
25 Dostoevskii, *Idiot*, 170; Dostoevsky, *The Idiot*, 221.
26 An extended reading of this gothic narrative arc can be found in Bowers, "Under the Floorboards, Over the Door," 143–6.
27 Dostoevskii, *Idiot*, 170; Dostoevsky, *The Idiot*, 221.
28 Butler, introduction to *Northanger Abbey*, xxviii.
29 Dostoevskii, *Idiot*, 172; Dostoevsky, *The Idiot*, 224.
30 Malcolm Jones observes that "The gothic mode comes into its own" in the chapter immediately following these scenes in Rogozhin's house. Jones, *Dostoyevsky after Bakhtin*, 130.
31 For an extended gothic reading of this scene, see Bowers, "Under the Floorboards, Over the Door," 149–52.
32 On *The Idiot* and the Umetskaya case more specifically, see Bowers, "Ol'ga Umetskaia and *The Idiot*." On Dostoevsky's use of news items during this period, see Catteau, *Dostoyevsky and the Process of Literary Creation*, 180–2.
33 This paragraph and the one that follows it appear in a modified form in Bowers, "Ol'ga Umetskaia and *The Idiot*," 276.
34 Dostoevskii, *Idiot*, 65; Dostoevsky, *The Idiot*, 80.
35 On the journalistic origins of *Crime and Punishment*, see Klioutchkine, "The Rise of 'Crime and Punishment' from the Air of the Media."
36 McReynolds, *Murder Most Russian*, 117.
37 On the technical aspects of Dostoevsky's crime fiction, see Whitehead, "Shkliarevskii and Russian Detective Fiction.".
38 See Catteau, *Dostoyevsky and the Process of Literary Creation*, 224–9.
39 Dostoevskii, *PSS*, vol. 9, 176.
40 Ibid., 251.
41 R. Miller, "The Notebooks to *The Idiot*," 94.
42 Dostoevskii, *PSS*, vol. 9, 195.
43 Ibid., 252.
44 This reading of the text is supported by Bakhtin's concept of dialogue: "For himself Dostoevsky never retains any essential 'surplus' of *meaning*, but only that indispensable minimum of pragmatic, purely *information-bearing* 'surplus' necessary to carry forward the story. For if any essential surplus of meaning were available to the author, it would transform the great dialogue of the novel into a finalized and objectivized dialogue, or

into a dialogue rhetorically performed." Bakhtin, *Problems of Dostoevsky's Poetics*, 73.

45 Dostoevskii, *PSS*, vol. 28, book 2, 330.

46 See Dostoevsky's 11 (23) December 1868 letter to Maikov, in *PSS*, vol. 28, book 2, 327–33, especially 330.

47 Dostoevskii, *Idiot*, 272; Dostoevsky, *The Idiot*, 358.

48 Dostoevskii, *Idiot*, 308; Dostoevsky, *The Idiot*, 409.

49 Dostoevskii, *Idiot*, 315; Dostoevsky, *The Idiot*, 412.

50 R. Miller, *Dostoevsky and "The Idiot,"* 108.

51 Jones, *Dostoyevsky after Bakhtin*, 135.

52 Ibid., 114.

53 Ibid., 143.

54 Ibid., 143–4.

55 On voyeurism in *The Idiot* more broadly, see Johnson, "The Face of the Other in *The Idiot*." Gary Saul Morson writes about voyeurism in Dostoevsky's novels in relation to social space: "In Dostoevsky, the first sign of our essential sociality is that we are all voyeurs." Morson, "Misanthropology," 62.

56 Dostoevskii, *Idiot*, 158; Dostoevsky, *The Idiot*, 205.

57 Elsewhere I have identified these incidents of Rogozhin's disembodied gaze as markers that denote the beginning of gothic narrative force in the text. See Bowers, "Under the Floorboards, Over the Door," 146.

58 Dostoevskii, *Idiot*, 380; Dostoevsky, *The Idiot*, 493–4.

59 Dostoevskii, *Idiot*, 317; Dostoevsky, *The Idiot*, 414.

60 Dostoevskii, *Idiot*, 320; Dostoevsky, *The Idiot*, 418.

61 Dostoevskii, *Idiot*, 320–1; Dostoevsky, *The Idiot*, 419–20.

62 Dostoevskii, *Idiot*, 262; Dostoevsky, *The Idiot*, 342.

63 Zakharov, *Sistema zhanrov Dostoevskogo*, 155–6.

64 Dalton, *Unconscious Structure in "The Idiot,"* 65.

65 French, *Dostoevsky's "Idiot,"* 199.

66 On this paradox, see Holquist, *Dostoevsky and the Novel*, 104–17.

67 Dalton, *Unconscious Structure in "The Idiot,"* 65.

68 Robert Louis Jackson observes that beauty is the cornerstone of Dostoevsky's aesthetics; see Jackson, *Dostoevsky's Quest for Form*.

69 On the dual nature of beauty in *The Idiot*, and the irony of this question, see Blank, *Dostoevsky's Dialectics and the Problem of Sin*, 69–72.

5. Physiological Petersburg, Gothic Petersburg

This chapter originally appeared as Katherine Bowers, "The City through a Glass, Darkly: Use of the Gothic in Early Russian Realism," *Modern Language Review* 108, no. 4 (2013): 1237–53. It has been slightly revised and expanded.

1 P. Brooks, *Realist Vision*, 3.

2 Anonymous, "Raznye izvestiia i smeis'," 98.

3 P. Brooks, *Realist Vision*, 3.

4 Julie Buckler notes that nineteenth-century Petersburg writers maintain "a social-moral focus on city slums, a fact proudly cited by cultural chroniclers, who consider this pervasive theme a centrepiece of the literary tradition. Other vital aspects of urban life, most notably industry, however, are consigned to the literary margins." Her discussion goes beyond the 1840s to Vsevolod Krestovsky's novel *Petersburg Slums* (*Peterburgskie trushchoby*, 1864–7), but she addresses social concerns of 1840s writers and critics. Buckler, *Mapping St. Petersburg*, 159. On literary depictions of Petersburg slums, see ibid., 158–9, 170–9, 209. As writers and critics of the 1840s focused on reforming these injustices, the social problems addressed by texts analysed in this chapter all relate to urban poverty: overcrowding, squalor, domestic violence, alcoholism, despair, illness, inequality, and other such social ills.

5 Botting, *Gothic*, 11.

6 Roughly defined, the Petersburg Text represents a unifying metanarrative that is constructed out of specific physical and metaphysical elements. Those who incorporate St Petersburg into their works, literary and otherwise, each contribute to the overall mythopoesis of the city's image and, ultimately, to a better understanding – conscious or subconscious – of the Petersburg Text as such. The classic critical sources on the Petersburg Text are Vladimir Toporov's essays "Peterburg i Peterburgskii tekst russkoi literatury" and "Peterburgskie tektsty i Peterburgskie mify (Zametki iz serii)," both in Toporov, *Mif. Ritual. Simvol. Obraz*. See also Buckler, *Mapping St. Petersburg*, 17–26.

7 Vissarion Belinskii, "Moskva i Peterburg," in Nekrasov, *Fiziologiia Peterburga*, 37; Belinsky, "Petersburg and Moscow," in Nekrasov, *Petersburg: The Physiology of a City*, trans. Marullo, 23–4. Subsequent citations to pieces in Nekrasov's collection will first refer to the Russian edition, then the Marullo translation, separated a semicolon.

8 On Sue's reception in Europe, see Chevasco, *Mysterymania*.

9 Marullo, introduction to Nekrasov, *Petersburg*, li–lii.

10 Ibid., lii.

11 Buckler underscores this atmosphere as a key feature of Petersburg, beginning her study with the following statement: "According to cultural mythology, Petersburg is the capital of bad weather and dark moods that give rise to a[n awe inspiring] literary tradition." Buckler, *Mapping St. Petersburg*, 21.

12 Dmitrii Grigorovich, "Peterburgskie sharmanshchiki," in Nekrasov, *Fiziologiia Peterburga*, 190–1; "Petersburg Organ-Grinders," in *Petersburg*, 98.

13 Marullo himself describes them as vulgar in his analysis of Grigorovich's
    piece. According to Marullo, Grigorovich's sketch is a prime example
    of Bakhtin's carnival. See Marullo, introduction to Nekrasov, *Petersburg*,
    lxxxii–lxxxvi.
14 On Grigorovich's narrative development and the tension in this
    sketch between the real and the fantastic, see Matzner-Gore, "Dmitry
    Grigorovich and the Limits of Empiricism," especially 366–7.
15 Vladimir Dal', "Peterburgskii dvornik," in Nekrasov, *Fiziologiia
    Peterburga*, 113; "The Petersburg Yardkeeper," in *Petersburg*, 61.
16 Evgenii Grebenka, "Peterburgskaia storona," in Nekrasov, *Fiziologiia
    Peterburga*, 233–4; "Petersburg Quarter," in *Petersburg*, 121.
17 While Grebenka's trope does evoke Poe's "Tell-Tale Heart," it seems
    unlikely that Grebenka would have read the tale. Early essays about
    Poe's works were just beginning to emerge in French literary journals,
    spearheaded by Charles Baudelaire, in the mid-1840s. It was not until
    the 1860s and later that Poe's Russian influence became (relatively)
    widespread. However, sounds emerging from beneath the floorboards is
    a common gothic trope that appears in many works (e.g., *The Mysteries
    of Udolpho*, *The Monk*, etc.). I mention Poe's story here as it is the most
    famous example of this trope. For more information about Poe's reception
    in Russia, see J. Grossman, *Edgar Allan Poe in Russia*.
18 A fragment from Nekrasov's unfinished novel in the style of Sue, the full
    work would have depicted members of Petersburg's lower classes who
    had descended into a nightmare world of physical abusiveness, suicidal
    tendencies, alcoholism, and neglect. The sketch was so controversial
    in its depiction of St Petersburg life that Nekrasov had to seek special
    permission from the censors to publish it in the collection.
19 Nekrasov, "Peterburgskie ugly," in *Fiziologiia*, 261; my translation.
20 Nekrasov, "Peterburgskie ugly," in *Fiziologiia*, 261–2; Nekrasov,
    "Petersburg Corners," in *Petersburg*, 134.
21 Leonid Grossman first examined the influence of low genres on
    Dostoevsky's work in his seminal study "Kompozitsiia v romane
    Dostoevskogo," in *Sobranie sochinenii*, vol. 2, 9–59.
22 Dostoevskii, *Bednye liudi*, in *Polnoe sobranie sochinenii (PSS)*, vol. 1, 83–4;
    Dostoevsky, *Poor Folk and Other Stories*, trans. McDuff, 96.
23 See Carol Apollonio's chapter "The Body and the Book: *Poor Folk*" for
    a reading that argues that Devushkin himself is a negative and sinister
    character, in Apollonio, *Dostoevsky's Secrets*, 13–26.
24 In "The Living Corpse," written in the 1830s but published only in
    1844, a man dreams that he has died but retains consciousness and
    exists in a limbo-like state, which enables him to observe all the horrible
    consequences of his behaviour. Upon waking he is horrified by his
    dream and blames the novel he had been reading before bed (which we

understand to be in the gothic-fantastic style). Dostoevsky then uses this passage, with minor cuts, for the epigraph of *Poor Folk*. See Cornwell, *Vladimir Odoevsky and Romantic Poets*, 18–22, on Odoevsky's influence on Dostoevsky.

25 On reading *The Double* as a gothic text, see Bowers, "Gothic Doubling and *The Double*, Gothically."

26 Gaustad, "Rebuilding Gothic on Russian Soil."

27 The phrase is taken from a 1998–9 exhibition at the University of Virginia Library Special Collections, curated by Natalie Regensburg. On the use of the sublime in gothic novels, Alison Milbank notes: "[Radcliffe] grasps what is most interesting in [Edmund] Burke's analysis of the sublime – his recognition of the pleasure the seemingly painful can incite, and that what is most sublime is that which threatens our very sense of self-preservation." See Milbank, introduction to *A Sicilian Romance*, xi. Burke's essay explains, "Whatever is fitted in any sort to excite the ideas of pain, and danger, that is to say, whatever is in any sort terrible, or is conversant with terrible objects, or operates in a manner analogous to terror, is a source of the *sublime*; that is, it is productive of the strongest emotion which the mind is capable of feeling." See Burke, *A Philosophical Enquiry*, 51. As Mario Praz has theorized, "An Anxiety with no possibility of escape is the main theme of the gothic tales." Cited in Dryden, *The Modern Gothic and Literary Doubles*, 39. This archetypal anxiety becomes a source of the sublime in gothic fiction.

28 Cited in Fanger, *Dostoevsky and Romantic Realism*, 146. On the "dreamer" type in Dostoevsky's Petersburg fiction and his relationship to the romantic-fantastic, see ibid., 146–7, 166–70, 178–9.

29 The "Vision on the Neva" episode from "A Weak Heart" was republished in 1861 but without the framing narrative; Dostoevsky claimed the excerpt was an autobiographical sketch. On the episode's genesis, see the extensive discussion in Frank, *Dostoevsky: The Seeds of Revolt*, 133–6, 318–22.

30 Dostoevskii, "Slaboe serdtse," in *PSS*, vol. 2, 47–8; Dostoevsky, "A Weak Heart," in *Uncle's Dream and Other Stories*, trans. McDuff, 69. All subsequent quotations are from the same passage unless specified otherwise.

31 Dostoevskii, *Netochka Nezvanova*, in *PSS*, vol. 2, 161–2; Dostoevsky, *Netochka Nezvanova*, trans. Kentish, 34.

32 On this paradigm later in the novel, see Corrigan, *Dostoevsky and the Riddle of the Self*, 41–5.

6. Gothic Subjectivity and the Woman Question

1 On the gothic undercurrents of Chernyshevsky's novel, see Vaisman, "*Chto delat'?*."

2 Pettus, "Dostoevsky's Closed Threshold," 84.

3 Radcliffe, *The Italian*, 90.

4 Pavlova, *Dvoinaia zhizn'*, 52.

5 Khvoshchinskaia, *Povesti i rasskazy*, 114.

6 Hoeveler, "The Secularization of Suffering," 115.

7 Ayers, "Elena Gan and the Female Gothic in Russia," 179.

8 Published as a stand-alone work in *The Comet* (*Kometa*, 1851), but also as part 3 of Tur's four-part novel *The Niece* (*Plemiannitsa*, 1851). Part 1 of *The Niece* was serialized in *The Contemporary* in 1851 and the novel was published in full by Universitetskaia tipografiia later that year. Material cited in this chapter is from the section that appeared in *The Comet*.

9 See Costlow, "Love, Work, and the Woman Question in Mid Nineteenth-Century Women's Writing."

10 On the marginalization of women's criticism, see Gheith, *Finding the Middle Ground*, 85–7.

11 See Bowers, "The Gothic Novel Reader Comes to Russia."

12 Hoeveler, "Vindicating *Northanger Abbey*," 118.

13 For example, in works like Karamzin's stories "Bornholm Island" and "Sierra-Morena" (1793), Izvekova's novels *Emiliia* (1806) and *Milena* (1809), and Durova's novel *Gudishki* (1839) and story "Pavilion" ("Pavil'on," 1839).

14 See Moers, *Literary Women*, 90–8.

15 Ibid., 90.

16 Wilt, *Ghosts of the Gothic*, 3.

17 Wolstenholme, *Gothic (Re)Visions*, xi and passim.

18 Ellis, *The Contested Castle*, x.

19 Ibid., xiii.

20 On the Brontë sisters and the woman question, see Ambrose, *The Woman Question*, 26–30. On the history of the women's movement in Europe more broadly, see Fuchs and Thompson, *Women in Nineteenth-Century Europe*.

21 Engel, "Transformation versus Tradition," 137.

22 Rosenholm, *Gendering Awakening*, 8.

23 Ibid.

24 Stites, *The Women's Liberation Movement in Russia*, 11.

25 A history that centres women's lives in the eighteenth century is Pushkareva, *Chastnaia zhizn' russkoi zhenshchiny XVIII veka*; see especially 86–135. On the nineteenth century, see Engel, *Mothers and Daughters*, particularly part 1, which addresses the pre-reform period.

26 Anonymous, *Dzhenni Ir: Avtobiografiia*. This version is a literary narrative with some translated extracts by an anonymous author.

27 Anonymous, *Dzhenni Eir*, trans. Vvedenskii. This version is a more or less full translation of the novel by I.I. Vvedenskii.

28 Bell, *Dzhen Eir, roman Korrer Bellia*. This version is a literary narrative with some translated extracts by an anonymous author.

29 Anonymous, *Dzhenni Ir: Avtobiografiia*, 151.
30 Anonymous, *Dzhenni Eir*, n.p. Vvedenskii also translated *Vanity Fair*; his translation appeared in 1850.
31 Karamzin, in turn, contributed significantly to women's reading culture and the rise of the novel through publishing projects aimed at women readers. Olga Glagoleva calls Karamzin and his contemporary Nikolai Novikov the "founders of female reading in Russia." See Glagoleva, "Imaginary World," 132.
32 Khitrova, *Lyric Complicity*, 43.
33 Heldt, *Terrible Perfection*, 19.
34 Glagoleva, "Imaginary World," 140.
35 Turgenev, *Polnoe sobranie sochinenii i pisem* (*PSSiP*), *Sochineniia*, vol. 4, 486.
36 See Gilbert and Gubar's classic feminist literary critical text, *The Madwoman in the Attic*. Gilbert and Gubar attempt to reconstruct literary history by emphasizing the previously unremarked subversive potential implicit in women writers' texts. Their study was pathbreaking when it was published but has since undergone some revisionist interventions. See, for example, Federico, *Gilbert and Gubar's "The Madwoman in the Attic" after Thirty Years*. Of particular relevance to the present chapter is Carol R. Davison's chapter, "Ghosts in the Attic: Gilbert and Gubar's *The Madwoman in the Attic* and the Female Gothic," 203–16.
37 Tur, *Antonina*, 260–1; *Antonina*, trans. Katz, 2. Subsequent citations to *Antonina* will first refer to the Russian text, then this translation, separated by a semicolon.
38 On the link between the reading and red room scenes in *Jane Eyre* and the novel's central theme see Delamotte, *Perils of the Night*, 193–6.
39 On spatial imprisonment and subjective freedom in *Jane Eyre*, see Ambrose's reading of the red room scene in Ambrose, *The Woman Question*, 41–2.
40 Here my argument builds on Gheith's reading of Tur in Gheith, "The Superfluous Man and the Necessary Woman."
41 "Sal'ias, grafinia Elizaveta Vasil'evna," in Knizhnik, *Slovar' russkikh pisatel'nits*, 1454. On Tur's fame during this period more broadly, see Smirnova, "Evgeniia Tur," 1–6.
42 Cited in Gheith, *Finding the Middle Ground*, 133.
43 See Terts, *Chto takoe sotsialisticheskie realizm?*, 36–8.
44 Gheith, "The Superfluous Man and the Necessary Woman," 231–2.
45 Turgenev, *Diary of a Superfluous Man*, in *PSSiP*, *Sochineniia*, vol. 4, 168.
46 Ibid., 166.
47 Ibid.
48 Ibid., 168.
49 Ibid., 189.

50   Ibid., 191.
51   Ibid., 189.
52   Ibid., 191.
53   Ibid., 212–13.
54   Tur, *Antonina*, 343; *Antonina*, 74.
55   Tur, *Antonina*, 394; *Antonina*, 117.
56   Tur, *Antonina*, 277; *Antonina*, 17.
57   Tur, *Antonina*, 343; *Antonina*, 74.
58   Tur, *Antonina*, 282; *Antonina*, 21.
59   Tur, *Antonina*, 282; *Antonina*, 21.
60   Tur, *Antonina*, 296; *Antonina*, 33.
61   Tur, *Antonina*, 302; *Antonina*, 38.
62   Tur, *Antonina*, 347–8; *Antonina*, 77.
63   Tur, *Antonina*, 412; *Antonina*, 133.
64   Turgenev, *Diary of a Superfluous Man*, in *PSSiP, Sochineniia*, vol. 4, 205.
65   Ibid., 168.
66   Costlow, "Speaking the Sorrow of Women," 328ff.
67   Ibid., 330.
68   Turgenev, "Neschastnaia," in *PSSiP, Sochineniia*, vol. 8, 70.
69   Ibid., 121.
70   See, for example, Costlow, "Speaking the Sorrow of Women," 333.
71   Turgenev, "Neschastnaia," in *PSSiP, Sochineniia*, vol. 8, 125, 132, 137.
72   Ibid., 125.
73   Ibid., 132.
74   Ibid., 137.
75   Ibid.
76   Soare, "The Female Gothic Connoisseur," 22.
77   Tur, "Miss Bronte, ee zhizn' i sochineniia."
78   Turgenev, "Plemiannitsa," in *PSSiP, Sochineniia*, vol. 4, 486.
79   Ibid., 478.
80   Ibid., 474.
81   Ibid., 478.
82   Ibid., 489.
83   Turgenev, "163. Poline Viardo," in *PSSiP, Pis'ma*, vol. 2, 372.
84   Turgenev, "164. Poline Viardo," in *PSSiP, Pis'ma*, vol. 2, 373.
85   Turgenev, *PSSiP, Sochineniia*, vol. 4, 491.
86   On the role of women in Russian salon culture, see Bernstein, "Women on the Verge of a New Language."
87   Andrew, "'A Crocodile in Flannel or a Dancing Monkey,'" 55.
88   Cited in ibid., 52.
89   See Stroganova, "The Writing Experience as Emotional Trauma." Stroganova's study details Gan's challenges in getting her work published

without significant editorial intervention from her publishers and the extreme differences evident in her drafts and final published versions.

90 Jane Costlow's analysis of Turgenev's intertextual dialogue with Tur's *Antonina* in *Unhappy Woman* (*Neschastnaia*, 1868) supports this position. See Costlow, "Speaking the Sorrow of Women."

91 Tur, "Miss Bronte, ee zhizn' i sochineniia," 503.

92 Ibid., 575.

93 Mikhailov, "Zhenshchiny, ikh vospitanie i znachenie v sem'e i obshchestve."

94 On the the critical debate surrounding the novel, see Gheith, *Finding the Middle Ground*, 88–9.

95 Tur, "Neskol'ko slov po povodu stat'i Russkoi Zhenshchiny," 665.

7. Political Terror and the School of Horror

1 Cited in Radzinsky, *Alexander II*, 415–16.

2 See Pavlov, "Rossiiskie liberaly i revoliutsionnye demokraty o iakobintsakh," 43–4ff.

3 Cited in Izmozik, "Politicheskii rozysk vedet Tret'e Otdelenie," 266.

4 Beer, "Decembrists, Rebels, and Martyrs in Siberian Exile," 530.

5 See Lacôte, "Gothic and the French Revolution."

6 See Davison, *History of the Gothic*, chap. 4.

7 Crawford, *Gothic Fiction and the Invention of Terrorism*, x.

8 A Jacobin Novelist (anon.), letter to the editor.

9 Ibid.

10 Sade, "Idée sur les romans," 35.

11 For the extension of this argument, see Paulson, "Gothic Fiction and the French Revolution."

12 Lewis, *The Monk*, 405.

13 Davison, *History of the Gothic*, chap. 4.

14 Radcliffe, "On the Supernatural in Poetry," 150.

15 Schiller, "Vom Erhabenen," 508.

16 Robespierre, "On the Principles of Political Morality," n.p.

17 Belinskii, "199. V.P. Botkinu," in *Polnoe sobranie sochinenii*, vol. 12, 105.

18 See Bergman, *The French Revolutionary Tradition*, 21–2.

19 All citations of Nechaev's text are from Nechaev, "Katekhizis revoliutionera," n.p. The English translation is mine, adapted from Nechayev, "The Revolutionary Catechism," n.p.

20 Dostoevskii, *Besy*, in *Polnoe Sobranie Sochinenii* (*PSS*), vol. 10, 33; Dostoevsky, *Demons*, trans. R. Maguire, 64. Subsequent citations to the novel will first refer to this edition, then this translation, separated by a semicolon.

21 Saraskina, *Besy: Roman – preduprezhdenie*, 10.
22 Lounsbery, "Dostoevskii's Geography," 229.
23 Scherr, "The Topography of Terror," 74.
24 Ibid., 85.
25 Bagby, *First Words: On Dostoevsky's Introductions*, 92.
26 Holland, *The Novel in the Age of Disintegration*, 5.
27 Dostoevskii, *Besy*, 395; Dostoevsky, *Demons*, 576.
28 Dostoevskii, *Besy*, 395; Dostoevsky, *Demons*, 576.
29 Dostoevskii, *Besy*, 396–7; Dostoevsky, *Demons*, 578–9.
30 Dostoevskii, *Besy*, 394; Dostoevsky, *Demons*, 575.
31 Dostoevskii, *Besy*, 453; Dostoevsky, *Demons*, 660.
32 Dostoevskii, *Besy*, 454; Dostoevsky, *Demons*, 661.
33 Dostoevskii, *Besy*, 437; Dostoevsky, *Demons*, 636.
34 Dostoevskii, *Besy*, 456; Dostoevsky, *Demons*, 662.
35 Dostoevskii, *Besy*, 461; Dostoevsky, *Demons*, 669.
36 Dostoevskii, *Besy*, 461; Dostoevsky, *Demons*, 669.
37 Dostoevskii, *Besy*, 461; Dostoevsky, *Demons*, 669.
38 Dostoevskii, *Besy*, 461; Dostoevsky, *Demons*, 669.
39 Dostoevskii, *Besy*, 475; Dostoevsky, *Demons*, 691.
40 Dostoevskii, *Besy*, 476; Dostoevsky, *Demons*, 692.
41 Dostoevskii, *Besy*, 504; Dostoevsky, *Demons*, 732.
42 Dostoevskii, *Besy*, 506; Dostoevsky, *Demons*, 734.
43 David Patterson, introduction to Dostoevsky, *Winter Notes on Summer Impressions*, viii.
44 Dostoevskii, *Besy*, 499; Dostoevsky, *Demons*, 724.
45 Dostoevskii, *Besy*, 37; Dostoevsky, *Demons*, 73.
46 Dostoevskii, *Besy*, 37; Dostoevsky, *Demons*, 73.
47 Dostoevskii, *Besy*, 164; Dostoevsky, *Demons*, 247.
48 Dostoevskii, *Besy*, 165; Dostoevsky, *Demons*, 248.
49 Dostoevskii, *Brat'ia Karamazovy*, in *PSS*, vol. 14, 100.
50 Dostoevskii, *Besy*, 513; my translation.
51 Dostoevskii, *Besy*, 402; Dostoevsky, *Demons*, 585.
52 Dostoevskii, *Besy*, 513; Dostoevsky, *Demons*, 745.
53 Dostoevskii, *Besy*, 498; Dostoevsky, *Demons*, 722.
54 Dostoevskii, *Besy*, 508; Dostoevsky, *Demons*, 738.
55 Susan K. Morrissey provides an overview of the two prominent waves of assassination and political terrorism in Russia from 1877–81 and 1902–16, with figures detailing the number of victims. See Morrissey, "The 'Apparel of Innocence,'" especially 613–18.
56 Savinkov, *Kon' blednyi, Izbrannoe*, 367.
57 Ibid., 357.
58 Ibid., 374.

59 Gippius, *Dmitrii Merezhkovskii*, 162.
60 See Patyk, "The Byronic Terrorist," 166–9.
61 Nechaev, "Katekhizis revoliutionera," n.p.; trans. adapted from Nechayev, "The Revolutionary Catechism," n.p.
62 Ibid.
63 See Drozd, *Chernyshevskii's "What Is to Be Done?": A Reevaluation*, 114.
64 Patyk, *Written in Blood*, 100.
65 On the nuances of this usage, see Goodwin, *Confronting Dostoevsky's Demons*, 17–23. Recently Boris Tikhomirov has argued that Nechaev's "Catechism" played a substantial role in shaping parts 2 and 3 of *Demons*. See Tikhomirov, "'Katekhizis revoliutsionera' Sergeia Nechaeva."
66 Cited in Patyk, *Written in Blood*, 99.
67 Brower, "Nihilists and Terrorists," 93.
68 Patyk, *Written in Blood*, 6.

8. The Fall of the House on the Russian Estate

An earlier version of this chapter appeared as "The Fall of the House: Gothic Narrative and the Decline of the Russian Estate," in *Russian Writers and the Fin de Siècle: The Twilight of Realism*, ed. Katherine Bowers and Ani Kokobobo (Cambridge: Cambridge University Press, 2015), 145–61. The chapter has been revised and expanded here.

 1 Saltykov-Shchedrin, *Gospoda Golovlevy*, *Sobranie sochinenii*, vol. 13, 251; Saltykov-Shchedrin, *The Golovlyov Family*, trans. Cioran, 237–8. Unless otherwise noted, subsequent citations will first refer to this edition, then this translation, separated by a semicolon.
 2 Joost van Baak discusses the "house myth" in *The House in Russian Literature*, including numerous examples of families in decline (69–75, 164–5). According to van Baak, "fall of the house" narratives depict cyclic routine and order "disrupted by catastrophic or fatal plot developments, especially where a family disintegrates or dies out, bringing their house to an end – the Death of the House" (261).
 3 The "fall of the house" topos appears in the first gothic novel, Horace Walpole's *Castle of Otranto* (1764) and reoccurs frequently in the genre. For more information about the "fall of the house" plot in gothic fiction, see Williams, *Art of Darkness*, 38–48 (on houses and patriarchal systems), and 87–96 (on families and legacies). For an in-depth look at the "fall of the house" plot and domestic space, see Ellis, *The Contested Castle*, especially 3–17, 33–52.
 4 Steinberg, *Petersburg* Fin de Siècle, 157.
 5 Max Nordau's discussion of the decline of culture in *Degeneration* (1892), citing works by Turgenev and Tolstoy, points to this trend, as do the

works of scholars such as Thomas Newlin, who concludes his study *The Voice in the Garden* with a discussion about the anxiety of disillusionment in the pastoral by later writers such as Tolstoy, Chekhov, and Blok (187–90). In *This Meager Nature*, Christopher Ely claims that the combination of "the abiding negation of the Russian landscape" (compared to Europe) and an "emerging tendency to celebrate a special, even virtuous, Russian misery" "paradoxically made attractive an image of the Russian land as a uniquely grim and unappealing space" (135). This aesthetic view translates into anxiety in Russian novels chronicling gentry life. See, for example, Amy Singleton's discussion of *Oblomov* (1859) in *No Place Like Home*. Singleton argues that Oblomov's family estate becomes "an anxiety-provoking land of the dead" (77–9).

6 On the correlation between fin-de-siècle degeneration and gothic themes, see Hurley, *The Gothic Body*; and Smith, *Victorian Demons*.

7 See Aksakov, "Istoriia moego znakomstva s Gogolem, s vkliucheniem vsei perepiski, c 1832 po 1852," in *Sobranie sochinenii* (*SS*), vol. 3, 384–5.

8 van Baak, *The House in Russian Literature*, 155.

9 Gogol', *Mertvye dushi*, in *Polnoe sobranie sochinenii*, vol. 7, 111–12.

10 For example, in *The Castle of Otranto*, the main action of the novel is dictated by the family's curse but sparked by the patriarch's obsession with building his legacy. *The Old English Baron* has a similar focus on legacy and heredity. For more information about the perils of legacy building in gothic fiction and an overview of this theme in gothic literature, see Hepburn, *Troubled Legacies*, 8–11.

11 Aksakov, *Semeinaia khronika*, in *SS*, vol. 1, 100–1; Aksakov, *The Family Chronicle*, trans. Beverley, 51–2. Subsequent citations will first refer to this edition, then this translation, separated by a semicolon.

12 Aksakov, *Semeinaia khronika*, 104; *The Family Chronicle*, 54–5.

13 In contrast, Richard Gregg claims that while Stepan Mikhailych's terrible temper establishes him as a gothic villain, the family's ability to come together in the end neutralizes his anger and prevents his decline. See Gregg, "The Decline of a Dynast."

14 Andrew Durkin presents Praskovya Ivanovna as an oppressed gothic heroine. Aksakov's fascination with the gothic does not extend to its obsession with psychologies such as fear, Durkin notes; instead, this gothic episode serves to bring the work's inherent moral judgment into sharper focus. See Durkin, *Sergei Aksakov and Russian Pastoral*, 114–68.

15 Aksakov, *Semeinaia khronika*, 114; *The Family Chronicle*, 65.

16 Although Aksakov was writing within a largely conservative Slavophile tradition, his critical depiction of violence against women within marriage bears certain similarities to the critique of marriage emerging in Western Europe among his socialist contemporaries, such as Charles

Fourier and Robert Owen, who rejected the family unit as a significant hindrance to their visions of a socially equal society.

17 Marx and Engels, *Manifesto of the Communist Party and Selected Essays*, 19. For more information, see Weikart, "Marx, Engels, and the Abolition of the Family."

18 See Stites, *The Women's Liberation Movement in Russia*, especially 29–115.

19 See Holland, "The Russian Rougon-Macquart."

20 Jenny Kaminer has analysed Arina Petrovna's maternal instincts (and lack thereof) in "A Mother's Land."

21 As Ilya Vinitsky argues, Saltykov-Shchedrin forges a "realist-gothic" aesthetic, and his novel operates within the gothic's realm. Vinitsky uses his gothic interpretation of *The Golovlyov Family* as a way into the work's resonance with spiritualism. See Vinitsky, *Ghostly Paradoxes*, 113–16.

22 Saltykov-Shchedrin, *Gospoda Golovlevy*, 67; *The Golovlyov Family*, 61.

23 Saltykov-Shchedrin, *Gospoda Golovlevy*, 249; my translation.

24 Saltykov-Shchedrin, *Gospoda Golovlevy*, 118–19; *The Golovlyov Family*, 111.

25 See Steinberg, *Petersburg* Fin de Siècle, 252.

26 Saltykov-Shchedrin, *Gospoda Golovlevy*, 256; *The Golovlyov Family*, 242.

27 See Praz, *The Romantic Agony*. Praz catalogues romantic tendencies, such as Byronism, that grew into widespread ennui and emptiness in decadence.

28 Vinitsky, *Ghostly Paradoxes*, 114.

29 Ehre, "A Classic of Russian Realism," 107.

30 For a gothic reading of Bunin's novella, see Peterson, "Russian Gothic."

31 Bunin, *Sukhodol*, in *Sobranie sochinenii*, vol. 2, 111; Bunin, *Dry Valley*, in *Ivan Bunin: Collected Stories*, trans. Hettlinger, 19–20. Subsequent citations will first refer to this edition, then this translation, separated by a semicolon.

32 Bunin, *Sukhodol*, 113; *Dry Valley*, 22.

33 van Baak, *The House in Russian Literature*, 244–5.

34 Bunin, *Sukhodol*, 153–4; Bunin, *Dry Valley*, 72–3.

35 Bunin, *Sukhodol*, 152; Bunin, *Dry Valley*, 71.

36 Tsvetaeva, *Dom u starogo Pimena*, in *Sobranie sochinenii*, vol. 5, 135; Tsvetaeva, *The House at Old Pimen*, in *Marina Tsvetaeva: A Captive Spirit*, trans. King, 264. Subsequent citations will first refer to this edition, then this translation, separated by a semicolon.

37 Tsvetaeva, *Dom u starogo Pimena*, 117; *The House at Old Pimen*, 240.

38 Tsvetaeva, *Dom u starogo Pimena*, 110–11; *The House at Old Pimen*, 233.

39 Tsvetaeva, *Dom u starogo Pimena*, 140; *The House at Old Pimen*, 270.

40 Lenin, *Polnoe sobranie sochinenii*, vol. 36, 409. Furthermore, *The Golovlyov Family* clearly had a major influence on the early Soviets, and Lenin in particular, as an ideological text. Lenin would refer to his enemies as "Иудушки" – "Little Judases" – directly referring to the novel. See Foote,

"Introduction: Saltykov and 'The Golovlyovs,'" in *Saltykov-Shchedrin's "The Golovlyovs,"* 21–2.

41 Eric Naiman discusses the correlations between the gothic and early Soviet political rhetoric in *Sex in Public*, 158–60.

Conclusion

1 Chekhov, "Chernyi monakh," in *Polnoe sobranie sochinenii i pisem (PSSiP)*, *Sochineniia*, vol. 8, 226.

2 Ibid., 234–5.

3 Shneyder, *Russia's Capitalist Realism*, 149. See also Shneyder's concise summary of *byt*, 149–53, and Vladimir Kataev's more expansive discussion in Kataev, "Chekhov i ego literaturnoe okruzhenie."

4 Many scholars have analysed the story's gothic or gothic fantastic theme. Some of these include Mantual, "Chekhov's 'Black Monk' and Byron's 'Black Friar'"; Shchipachaeva, "Zagadochnoe i tainstvennoe v povesti A.P. Chekhova 'Chernyi monakh'"; and Poliakova and Tamarchenko, "'Chernyi monakh' A.P. Chekhova i sud'by goticheskoi traditsii," in *Goticheskaia traditsiia v russkoi literature*, 239–49. Poliakova and Tamarchenko's study also provides a comprehensive overview of scholarship on the subject.

5 Shestov, "Tvorchestvo iz nichego (A.P. Chekhov)," 595.

6 Whitehead, "Anton Chekhov's *The Black Monk*," 619.

7 Komaromi, "Unknown Force," 259.

8 For example: on reading "The Black Monk" as a symbolist text, see Debreczeny, "The Black Monk"; on Freud and "The Black Monk," see Finke, *Seeing Chekhov*, 139–41; on Darwin and "The Black Monk," see Finke, *Seeing Chekhov*, 120–8.

9 Komaromi, "Unknown Force," 259.

10 Chekhov, "Chernyi monakh," in *PSSiP*, *Sochineniia*, vol. 8, 227.

11 Ibid., 241.

12 Chekhov, "Nervy," in *PSSiP*, *Sochineniia*, vol. 4, 12.

13 Ibid., 12–13.

14 Chekhov, "Tainyi sovetnik," in *PSSiP*, *Sochineniia*, vol. 5, 128.

15 Chekhov, "Gusev," in *PSSiP*, *Sochineniia*, vol. 7, 333.

16 Chekhov, "Palata No. 6," in *PSSiP*, *Sochineniia*, vol. 8, 121.

17 Vinitsky, *Ghostly Paradoxes*, viii.

18 Chekhov, "Sosedi," in *PSSiP*, *Sochineniia*, vol. 8, 71.

19 Ibid.

20 Ibid.

21 Chekhov, *Zapisnaia knizhka I*, in *PSSiP*, *Sochineniia*, vol. 17, 10.

22 Ibid.

23 Chekhov, "Strakh," in *PSSiP, Sochineniia*, vol. 8, 131.
24 Shneyder, *Russia's Capitalist Realism*, 153.
25 Pan'kov, "'Everything else depends,'" 52–3.
26 Ibid., 46.
27 On Russian modernist and later incarnations of gothic, see Naiman, "Behind the Red Door: An Introduction to NEP Gothic," in *Sex in Public*, 148–80; Khapaeva, *Goticheskoe obshchestvo*; Khapaeva, *Koshmar: literatura i zhizn'*; M. Maguire, *Stalin's Ghosts*; Platt and Khapaeva, "Russian Gothic"; and Romanets, "Postcoloniality and Neo-Gothic Fictions in the Post-Soviet Space."
28 Platt, Emerson, and Khapaeva, "Introduction: The Russian Gothic," 3.
29 See Vatsuro, *Goticheskii roman v Rossii*; Sobol, "Forum: Rethinking the Gothic in Ukraine"; and Sobol, *Haunted Empire.*

Works Cited

Aksakov, Sergei. *The Family Chronicle.* Translated by M.T. Beverley. Westport, CT: Greenwood Press, 1985.

– *Sobranie sochinenii.* 5 vols. Moscow: Izdatel'stvo "Pravda," 1966.

Alekseev, M.P. "Ch.R. Met'iurin i ego 'Mel'mot skitalets.'" In Ch.R. Met'iurin, *Mel'mot skitalets,* edited by M.P. Alekseev and A.M. Shadrin, 563–674. Moscow: Nauka, 1983.

Alighieri, Dante. *Inferno.* Translated by Robert Hollander and Jean Hollander. New York: Anchor Books, 2002.

Allen, Elizabeth Cheresh. *Beyond Realism: Turgenev's Poetics of Secular Salvation.* Stanford, CA: Stanford University Press, 1992.

Ambrose, Kathryn. *The Woman Question in Nineteenth-Century English, German and Russian Literature: (En)gendering Barriers.* Leiden: Brill, 2016.

Andrew, Joe. "'A Crocodile in Flannel or a Dancing Monkey': The Image of the Russian Woman Writer, 1790–1850." In *Gender in Russian History and Culture,* edited by Linda Edmondson, 52–72. Basingstoke: Palgrave, 2001.

Andriopoulos, Stefan. *Ghostly Apparitions: German Idealism, the Gothic Novel, and Optical Media.* New York: Zone Books, 2013.

Anonymous. *Dzhenni Eir.* Translated by I.I. Vvedenskii. *Otechestvennye zapiski* 6–10 (1849).

– *Dzhenni Ir: Avtobiografiia. Biblioteka dlia chteniia* 94 (1849): 151–72.

– "Raznye izvestiia i smeis'." *Syn otechestva* 11 (1839): 98.

– "Terrorist Novel Writing." In *Spirit of the Public Journals for 1797,* vol. 1, 223–5. London, 1798.

Apollonio, Carol. *Dostoevsky's Secrets: Reading against the Grain.* Evanston, IL: Northwestern University Press, 2009.

Armstrong, Nancy. *How Novels Think.* New York: Columbia University Press, 2005.

Arndt, Christiane. "Theodor Sturm's *Der Schimmelreiter*: Schauerrealismus or Gothic Realism in the Family Periodical." In *The German Bestseller in the Late Nineteenth Century,* edited by Charlotte Woodford and Benedict Schofield, 144–64. Rochester, NY: Camden House, 2012.

Austen, Jane. *Northanger Abbey.* London: Penguin Books, 2006.

Ayers, Carolyn Jursa. "Elena Gan and the Female Gothic in Russia." In *The Gothic-Fantastic in Nineteenth-Century Russian Literature,* edited by Neil Cornwell, 171–88. Amsterdam: Rodopi, 1999.

Backus, Margot Gayle. "Irish Gothic Realism and the Great War." In *The Gothic Family Romance: Heterosexuality, Child Sacrifice, and the Anglo-Irish Colonial Order,* 144–70. Durham, NC: Duke University Press, 1999.

Baer, Brian James. Introduction to *No Good without Reward: Selected Writings.* Toronto: University of Toronto Press, 2011.

Bagby, Lewis. *First Words: On Dostoevsky's Introductions.* Boston: Academic Studies Press, 2016.

Bakhtin, Mikhail. *The Dialogic Imagination: Four Essays.* Edited by Michael Holquist. Translated by Caryl Emerson and Michael Holquist. Austin: University of Texas Press, 1981.

– *Problems of Dostoevsky's Poetics.* Edited and translated by Caryl Emerson. Minneapolis: University of Minnesota Press, 1984.

Baldick, Chris. Introduction to *Melmoth the Wanderer,* by Charles Maturin, vii–xix. Oxford: Oxford University Press, 1998.

Barkhoff, Jürgen. "'The echo of the question as if it had merely resounded in a tomb': The Dark Anthropology of the *Schauerroman* in Schiller's *Der Geisterseher.*" In *Popular Revenants: The German Gothic and Its International Reception, 1800–2000,* edited by Andrew Cusack and Barry Murnane, 44–59. Rochester, NY: Camden House, 2012.

Beer, Daniel. "Decembrists, Rebels, and Martyrs in Siberian Exile: The 'Zerentui Conspiracy' of 1828 and the Fashioning of a Revolutionary Genealogy." *Slavic Review* 72, no. 3 (2013): 528–51.

Belinskii, Vissarion. *Polnoe sobranie sochinenii.* 13 vols. Moscow: Izdatel'stvo akademii nauk, 1953–9.

Bell, Korrer. *Dzhen Eir, roman Korrer Bellia. Sovremennik* 21 (1850): 31–8.

Bergman, Jay. *The French Revolutionary Tradition in Russian and Soviet Politics, Political Thought, and Culture.* Oxford: Oxford University Press, 2019.

Bernstein, Lina. "Women on the Verge of a New Language: Russian Salon Hostesses in the First Half of the Nineteenth Century." In *Russia Women Culture,* edited by Helena Goscilo and Beth Holmgren, 209–24. Bloomington: Indiana University Press, 1996.

Bestuzhev-Marlinskii, A.A. *Sochinenii.* 2 vols. Edited by P. Kochurin. Moscow: Khudozhestvennaia literatura, 1958.

Biblioteka dlia chteniia. St Petersburg: Tipografii vdovy Pliushar s synom, 1834–65.

Blank, Ksana. *Dostoevsky's Dialectics and the Problem of Sin.* Evanston, IL: Northwestern University Press, 2010.

Borowec, Christine. "Time after Time: The Temporal Ideology of Oblomov." *Slavic and East European Journal* 38, no. 4 (1994): 561–73.

Botting, Fred. *Gothic*. London: Routledge, 2006.

Bour, Isabelle. "The Reception of Jane Austen's Novels in France and Switzerland: The Early Years, 1813–1828." In *The Reception of Jane Austen in Europe*, edited by Anthony Mandal and Brian Southam, 12–33. London: Continuum, 2007.

Bowers, Katherine. "The City through a Glass, Darkly: Use of the Gothic in Early Russian Realism." *Modern Language Review* 108, no. 4 (2013): 1237–53.

– "The Fall of the House: Gothic Narrative and the Decline of the Russian Estate." In *Russian Writers and the* Fin de Siècle*: The Twilight of Realism*, edited by Katherine Bowers and Ani Kokobobo, 145–61. Cambridge: Cambridge University Press, 2015.

– "Ghost Writing: Radcliffiana and the Russian Gothic Wave." *Victorian Popular Fictions Journal* 3, no. 2 (2021): 153–79.

– "Gothic Doubling and *The Double*, Gothically." *All the Russias' Blog*. NYU Jordan Center, 6 November 2015. https://jordanrussiacenter.org/news /gothic-doubling-double-gothically/.

– "The Gothic Novel Reader Comes to Russia." In *Reading Russia: A History of Reading in Modern Russia*, edited by Damiano Rebecchini and Raffaella Vassena, vol. 2, 377–408. Milan: Ledizioni, 2020.

– "Ol'ga Umetskaia and *The Idiot*." In *A Dostoevskii Companion: Texts and Contexts*, edited by Katherine Bowers, Connor Doak, and Kate Holland, 274–8. Boston: Academic Studies Press, 2018.

– "Through the Opaque Veil: The Gothic and Death in Russian Realism." *The Gothic and Death*, edited by Carol Margaret Davison, 157–73. Manchester: Manchester University Press, 2017.

– "Under the Floorboards, Over the Door: The Gothic Corpse and Writing Fear in *The Idiot*." In *Dostoevsky at 200: The Novel in Modernity*, edited by Katherine Bowers and Kate Holland, 137–58. Toronto: University of Toronto Press, 2021.

Brontë, Charlotte. *Jane Eyre: An Autobiography*. London: Smith, Elder & Co., 1869.

Brooks, Jeffrey. *When Russia Learned to Read: Literacy and Popular Literature, 1861–1917*. Evanston, IL: Northwestern University Press, 2003.

Brooks, Peter. *The Melodramatic Imagination: Balzac, Henry James, Melodrama, and the Mode of Excess*. New Haven, CT: Yale University Press, 1995.

– *Realist Vision*. New Haven, CT: Yale University Press, 2005.

Brower, Daniel. "Nihilists and Terrorists." In *Times of Trouble: Violence in Russian Literature and Culture*, edited by Marcus C. Levitt and Tatyana Novikov, 91–102. Madison: University of Wisconsin Press, 2007.

Brown, Marshall. "A Philosophical View of the Gothic Novel." *Studies in Romanticism* 26, no. 2 (1987): 275–301.

Brunson, Molly. *Russian Realisms: Art and Literature, 1840–1890*. DeKalb: Northern Illinois University Press, 2016.

Buckler, Julie. *Mapping St. Petersburg: Literary Text and Cityshape*. Princeton, NJ: Princeton University Press, 2005.

Bunin, Ivan. *Ivan Bunin: Collected Stories*. Translated by Graham Hettlinger. Chicago: Ivan R. Dee, 2007.

– *Sobranie sochinenii*. 5 vols. Moscow: Izdatel'stvo "Pravda," 1956.

Burke, Edmund. *A Philosophical Enquiry into the Origin of Our Ideas of the Sublime and Beautiful*. London: Oxford University Press, 1998.

Butler, Marilyn. Introduction to *Northanger Abbey*, by Jane Austen. London: Penguin Books, 2006.

Byron, George Gordon, Lord. *Lord Byron: The Major Works*, edited by Jerome J. McGann. Oxford: Oxford University Press, 2008.

Castle, Terry. "Ann Radcliffe's *The Mysteries of Udolpho*." In *Boss Ladies, Watch Out! Essays on Women, Sex and Writing*, 55–72. London: Routledge, 2002.

Catteau, Jacques. *Dostoyevsky and the Process of Literary Creation*. Translated by Audrey Littlewood. Cambridge: Cambridge University Press, 1989.

Ceron, Cristina. "Manfred, the Brontes, and the Byronic Gothic Hero." In *The Gothic Byron*, edited by Peter Cochran, 165–77. Newcastle: Cambridge Scholars Publishing, 2009.

Chard, Chloe. Introduction to *The Romance of the Forest*, by Ann Radcliffe. Oxford: Oxford University Press, 1999.

Chekhov, A.P. *Polnoe sobranie sochinenii i pisem*. 30 vols. Moscow: AN SSSR, 1974–83.

Chevasco, Berry Palmer. *Mysterymania: The Reception of Eugene Sue in Britain, 1838–1860*. London: Peter Lang, 2003.

Cochran, Peter, ed. *The Gothic Byron*. Newcastle: Cambridge Scholars Publishing, 2009.

Cornwell, Neil, ed. *The Gothic-Fantastic in Nineteenth-Century Russian Literature*. Amsterdam: Rodopi, 1999.

– *The Life, Times and Milieu of V.F. Odoyevsky*. London: Athlone Press, 1986.

– *Vladimir Odoevsky and Romantic Poets*. Oxford and New York: Berghahn Books, 1998.

Corrigan, Yuri. *Dostoevsky and the Riddle of the Self*. Evanston, IL: Northwestern University Press, 2017.

Costlow, Jane T. "Love, Work, and the Woman Question in Mid Nineteenth-Century Women's Writing." In *Women Writers in Russian Literature*, edited by Toby W. Clyman and Diana Greene, 61–75. Westport, CT: Greenwood Press, 1994.

– "Speaking the Sorrow of Women: Turgenev's 'Neschastnaia' and Evgeniia Tur's 'Antonina.'" *Slavic Review* 50, no. 2 (1991): 328–35.

– "Who Holds the Axe? Violence and Peasants in Nineteenth-Century Russian Depictions of the Forest." *Slavic Review* 68, no. 1 (2009): 10–30.

Crawford, Joseph. *Gothic Fiction and the Invention of Terrorism: The Politics and Aesthetics of Fear in the Age of the Reign of Terror.* New York: Bloomsbury, 2013.

Cross, Anthony. *N.M. Karamzin: A Study of His Literary Career, 1783–1803.* Carbondale: Southern Illinois University Press, 1969.

Dalton, Elizabeth. *Unconscious Structure in "The Idiot": A Study in Literature and Psychoanalysis.* Princeton, NJ: Princeton University Press, 1979.

Davison, Carol Margaret. *History of the Gothic: Gothic Literature, 1764–1824.* Cardiff: University of Wales Press, 2009.

Debreczeny, Paul. "The Black Monk: Chekhov's Version of Symbolism." In *Reading Chekhov's Text*, edited by Robert Louis Jackson, 179–88. Evanston, IL: Northwestern University Press, 1993.

Delamotte, Eugenia C. *Perils of the Night: A Feminist Study of Nineteenth-Century Gothic.* Oxford: Oxford University Press, 1990.

Devitt, Amy J. *Writing Genres.* Carbondale: Southern Illinois University Press, 2004.

Diakonova, Nina, and Vadim Vatsuro. "'No Great Mind and Generous Heart Could Avoid Byronism': Russia and Byron." In *The Reception of Byron in Europe*, edited by Richard A. Cardwell, 333–52. London: Continuum, 2004.

Dickens, Charles. *Oliver Twist.* London: Penguin Classics, 2003.

Dostoevskii, F.M. *Polnoe sobranie sochinenii.* 30 vols. Leningrad: Nauka, 1972–90.

Dostoevsky, Fyodor. *Demons.* Translated by Robert A. Maguire. Edited by Ronald Meyer. London: Penguin Books, 2008.

– "A Few Words about George Sand." In *A Writer's Diary, Volume 1: 1873–1876*, 507–14. Translated by Kenneth Lantz. Evanston, IL: Northwestern University Press, 1997.

– *The Idiot.* Translated by Anna Brailovsky, revising Constance Garnett. New York: Random House, 2003.

– *Netochka Nezvanova.* Translated by Jane Kentish. London: Penguin Group, 1985.

– *Poor Folk and Other Stories.* Translated by David McDuff. London: Penguin Group, 1988.

– *Uncle's Dream and Other Stories.* Translated by David McDuff. London: Penguin Group, 1989.

– *Winter Notes on Summer Impressions.* Translated by David Patterson. Evanston, IL: Northwestern University Press, 1997.

Drews, Peter. *Die Rezeption deutscher Belletristik in Russland, 1750–1850.* Munich: Otto Sagner, 2007.

Drozd, Andrew M. *Chernyshevskii's "What is to Be Done?": A Reevaluation.* Evanston, IL: Northwestern University Press, 2001.

Dryden, Linda. *The Modern Gothic and Literary Doubles: Stevenson, Wilde and Wells.* London: Palgrave Macmillan, 2003.

Durkin, Andrew. *Sergei Aksakov and Russian Pastoral*. New Brunswick, NJ: Rutgers University Press, 1983.

Ehre, Milton. "A Classic of Russian Realism: Form and Meaning in *The Golovlyovs*." In *Saltykov-Shchedrin's "The Golovlyovs": A Critical Companion*, edited by I.P. Foote, 101–18. Evanston, IL: Northwestern University Press, 1998.

Elbert, Monika, and Wendy Ryden. "American Gothic Realism and Naturalism." In *The Cambridge Companion to American Gothic*, edited by Jeffrey Andrew Weinstock, 44–56. Cambridge: Cambridge University Press, 2017.

Ellis, Kate Ferguson. *The Contested Castle: Gothic Novels and the Subversion of Domestic Ideology*. Urbana: University of Illinois Press, 1989.

Ely, Christopher. *This Meager Nature: Landscape and National Identity in Imperial Russia*. Dekalb: Northern Illinois University Press, 2002.

Engel, Barbara Alpern. *Mothers and Daughters: Women of the Intelligentsia in Nineteenth-Century Russia*. Cambridge: Cambridge University Press, 1983.

– "Transformation versus Tradition." In *Russia's Women: Accommodation, Resistance, Transformation*, edited by Barbara Evans Clements, Barbara Alpern Engel, and Christine D. Worobec, 135–47. Berkeley: University of California Press, 1991.

Erickson, T. "Making Sense of Computer-Mediated Communication (CMC): Conversations as Genres, CMC Systems as Genre Ecologies." *Proceedings of the 33rd Hawaii International Conference on System Sciences*, edited by R.H. Sprague, Jr, n.p. Maui: IEEE Computer Society Press, 2000. https://www.mediensprache.net/archiv/pubs/2862.pdf.

Fanger, Donald. *Dostoevsky and Romantic Realism: A Study of Dostoevsky in Relation to Balzac, Dickens, and Gogol*. Cambridge, MA: Harvard University Press, 1967.

Federico Annette R., ed. *Gilbert and Gubar's "The Madwoman in the Attic" after Thirty Years*. Foreword by Sandra M. Gilbert. Columbia: University of Missouri Press, 2011.

Finke, Michael. *Seeing Chekhov: Life and Art*. Ithaca, NY: Cornell University Press, 2005.

Foote, I.P., ed. *Saltykov-Shchedrin's "The Golovlyovs": A Critical Companion*. Evanston, IL: Northwestern University Press, 1998.

Frank, Joseph. *Dostoevsky: The Seeds of Revolt, 1821–1849*. Princeton, NJ: Princeton University Press, 1979.

Franklin, Simon. "Novels without End: Notes on 'Eugene Onegin' and 'Dead Souls.'" *Modern Language Review* 79, no. 2 (1984): 372–83.

Frazier, Melissa. *Frames of the Imagination: Gogol's* Arabesques *and the Romantic Question of Genre*. New York: Peter Lang, 2000.

– *Romantic Encounters: Writers, Readers, and the Library for Reading*. Stanford, CA: Stanford University Press, 2007.

French, Bruce A. *Dostoevsky's "Idiot": Dialogue and the Spiritually Good Life.* Evanston, IL: Northwestern University Press, 2001.

Fuchs, Rachel G., and Victoria E. Thompson. *Women in Nineteenth-Century Europe.* Basingstoke: Palgrave Macmillan, 2005.

Fusso, Susanne. *Designing Dead Souls: An Anatomy of Disorder in Gogol.* Stanford, CA: Stanford University Press, 1993.

Garrett, Peter K. *Gothic Reflections: Narrative Force in Nineteenth-Century Fiction.* Ithaca, NY: Cornell University Press, 2003.

Gaustad, Randi. "Rebuilding Gothic on Russian Soil: The Roles of Religion and Intertwining of Minds in Dostoevskii's *The Landlady.*" In *Celebrating Creativity: Essays in Honor of Jostein Børtnes*, edited by Jostein Børtnes, Knut Grimstad, and Ingunn Lunde, 205–15. Bergen: University of Bergen, 1997.

Gershenzon, O.M. "Sny Pushkina." In *Pushkin. Sbornik pervyi*, edited by N.K. Piksanov, 79–96. Moscow: Gosudarstvennoe izdatel'stvo, 1924.

Gheith, Jehanne M. *Finding the Middle Ground: Krestovskii, Tur, and the Power of Ambivalence in Nineteenth-Century Women's Prose.* Evanston, IL: Northwestern University Press, 2004.

– "The Superfluous Man and the Necessary Woman: A 'Re-vision.'" *Russian Review* 55, no. 2 (1996): 226–44.

Gilbert, Sandra, and Susan Gubar. *The Madwoman in the Attic.* New Haven, CT: Yale University Press, 1979.

Gippius, Z.N. *Dmitrii Merezhkovskii.* Paris: YMCA Press, 1951.

Glagoleva, Olga E. "Imaginary World: Reading in the Lives of Russian Provincial Noblewomen (1750–1825)." In *Women and Gender in 18th-Century Russia*, edited by Wendy Rosslyn, 129–45. Aldershot: Ashgate, 2003.

Gogol, Nikolay V. *Dead Souls.* Translated by Robert A. Maguire. London: Penguin Books, 2004.

Gogol', N.V. *Polnoe sobranie sochinenii.* 14 vols. Moscow: AN SSSR, 1937–52.

Golburt, Luba. *The First Epoch: The Eighteenth Century and the Russian Cultural Imagination.* Madison: University of Wisconsin Press, 2014.

Goncharov, I.A. *Oblomov.* Translated by David Magarshack. London: Penguin Group, 1981.

– *Polnoe sobranie sochinenii i pisem.* 20 vols. St Petersburg: Nauka, 1997.

Goodwin, James. *Confronting Dostoevsky's Demons: Anarchism and the Specter of Bakunin in Twentieth-Century Russia.* New York: Peter Lang, 2010.

Gregg, Richard. "The Decline of a Dynast: From Power to Love in Aksakov's *Family Chronicle.*" *Russian Review* 50, no. 1 (1991): 35–47.

Grossman, Joan Delaney. *Edgar Allan Poe in Russia: A Study in Legend and Literary Influence.* Wurzburg: Jal-Verlag, 1973.

Grossman, Leonid. *Sobranie sochinenii.* 2 vols. Moscow: Sovremmenye problemy, 1928.

Gubskaia, T.V. "F. Shiller v russkoi literature XIX veka: proza, poeziia." Kand. diss., Orskii gumanitarno-tekhnologicheskii institut, 2004.

Gutsche, George. "Dinner at Smirdin's: Forces in Russian Print Culture in the Early Reign of Nicholas I." In *The Space of the Book: Print Culture in the Russian Social Imagination*, edited by Miranda Remnek, 54–81. Toronto: University of Toronto Press, 2011.

Hammarberg, Gitta. *From the Idyll to the Novel: Karamzin's Sentimentalist Prose.* Cambridge: Cambridge University Press, 1991.

Heldt, Barbara. *Terrible Perfection: Women and Russian Literature.* Bloomington: Indiana University Press, 1987.

Hepburn, Allan. *Troubled Legacies: Narrative and Inheritance.* Toronto: University of Toronto Press, 2007.

Hoeveler, Diane Long. "The Secularization of Suffering: Toward a Theory of Gothic Subjectivity." *Wordsworth Circle* 35, no. 3 (2004): 113–17.

– "Vindicating *Northanger Abbey*: Mary Wollstonecraft, Jane Austen, and Gothic Feminism." In *Jane Austen and Discourses of Feminism*, edited by Devoney Looser, 117–35. New York: St Martin's Press, 1995.

Holland, Kate. *The Novel in the Age of Disintegration: Dostoevsky and the Problem of Genre in the 1870s.* Evanston, IL: Northwestern University Press, 2013.

– "The Russian Rougon-Macquart: Degeneration and Biological Determinism in the Golovlev Family." In *Russian Writers and the* Fin de Siècle: *The Twilight of Realism*, edited by Katherine Bowers and Ani Kokobobo, 15–32. Cambridge: Cambridge University Press, 2015.

Holquist, Michael. *Dostoevsky and the Novel.* Princeton, NJ: Princeton University Press, 1977.

Hoogenboom, Hilde. "Sentimental Novels and Pushkin: European Literary Markets and Russian Readers." *Slavic Review* 74, no. 3 (2015): 553–74.

Hurley, Kelly. *The Gothic Body: Sexuality, Materialism, and Degeneration at the* Fin de Siècle. Cambridge: Cambridge University Press, 2004.

Hutcheon, Linda. *A Theory of Parody: The Teachings of Twentieth-Century Art Forms.* Urbana: University of Illinois Press, 2000.

Ivanits, Linda. *Russian Folk Belief.* New York: M.E. Sharpe, 1989.

Izmailov, N.V. "Fantasticheskaia povest'." In *Russkaia povest' XIX veka: Istoriia i problematika zhanra*, edited by B.S. Meilakh, 134–69. Leningrad, 1973.

Izmozik, V.S. "Politicheskii rozysk vedet Tret'e Otdelenie (1826–1880 gody)." In *Zhandarmy Rossii*, edited by V.S. Izmozik, 248–77. St Petersburg: Neva, 2002.

Jackson, Robert Louis. *Dostoevsky's Quest for Form.* Bloomington, IN: Physsardt, 1966.

A Jacobin Novelist (anon.). Letter to the editor. *Monthly Magazine*, 19 August 1797.

Jakobson, Roman. "On Realism in Art." In *Readings in Russian Poetics: Formalist and Structuralist Views*, edited by Ladislav Matejka and Krystyna Pomorska, 38–46. Chicago: Dalkey Archive Press, 2001.

James, Henry. "Preface to Vol. 7: The Tragic Muse." In *Literary Criticism*. Vol. 2, *French Writers, Other European Writers, Prefaces to the New York Edition*. New York: Library of America, 1984.

Jenny, Laurent. "The Strategy of Form." In *French Literary Theory Today*, edited by Tzvetan Todorov, 34–63. Cambridge: Cambridge University Press, 1982.

Johnson, Leslie. "The Face of the Other in *The Idiot*." *Slavic Review* 50, no. 4 (1991): 867–78.

Jones, Malcolm. *Dostoyevsky after Bakhtin: Readings in Dostoyevsky's Fantastic Realism*. Cambridge: Cambridge University Press, 1990.

Kaminer, Jenny. "A Mother's Land: Arina Petrovna Golovlyova and the Economic Restructuring of the Golovlyov Family." *Slavic and East European Journal* 53, no. 4 (2009): 545–65.

Karamzin, N.M. *Izbrannye sochineniia*. 2 vols. Moscow: Khudozhestvennaia literatura, 1964.

Kataev, V.B. "Chekhov i ego literaturnoe okruzhenie (80-e gody XIX veka)." In *Sputniki Chekhova*, edited by V.B. Kataev, 5–47. Moscow: Izdatel'stvo Moskovskogo universiteta, 1982.

Katarskii, Igor'. *Dikkens v Rossii*. Moscow: Nauka, 1966.

Khapaeva, Dina. *Goticheskoe obshchestvo: Morfologiia koshmara*. Moscow: Novoe literaturnoe obozrenie, 2007.

– *Koshmar: literatura i zhizn'*. Moscow: Text, 2010.

Khitrova, Daria. *Lyric Complicity: Poetry and Readers in the Golden Age of Russian Literature*. Madison: University of Wisconsin Press, 2019.

Khvoshchinskaia, N.D. *Povesti i rasskazy*. Edited by M.S. Goriachkina. Moscow: Gos. Izd. Khudozhestvennaia literatura, 1963.

Kilgour, Maggie. *The Rise of the Gothic Novel*. New York: Routledge, 1995.

Klioutchkine, Konstantine. "The Rise of 'Crime and Punishment' from the Air of the Media." *Slavic Review* 61, no. 1 (2002): 88–108.

Knizhnik, Nikolai, ed. *Slovar' russkikh pisatel'nits (1759–1859)*. *Russkii arkhiv* 11–12 (1865).

Komaromi, Ann. "Unknown Force: Gothic Realism in Chekhov's *The Black Monk*." In *The Gothic-Fantastic in Nineteenth-Century Russian Literature*, edited by Neil Cornwell, 257–76. Amsterdam: Rodopi, 1999.

Kristeva, Julia. *Powers of Horror: An Essay on Abjection*. Translated by Leon S. Roudiez. New York: Columbia University Press, 1982.

Krivonos, V.Sh. *"Mertvye dushi" Gogolia. Prostranstvo smysla*. Moscow: Flinta, 2015.

Lacôte, Fanny. "Gothic and the French Revolution, 1789–1804." In *The Cambridge History of the Gothic*, edited by Angela Wright and Dale Townshend, vol. 1, 262–83. Cambridge: Cambridge University Press, 2020.

Lary, N.M. *Dostoevsky and Dickens*. London and Boston: Routledge and Kegan Paul, 1973.

Lenin, V.I. *Polnoe sobranie sochinenii*. 55 vols. Moscow: Izd-vo politecheskoi literatury, 1967–70.

Lermontov, M. Iu. *Sobranie sochinenii*. 4 vols. Leningrad: Nauka, 1979–81.

Lewis, M.G. *The Monk*. Richmond, VA: Valancourt Books, 2013.

Likhachev, D.S. *Poetika drevnerusskoi literatury*. Moscow: Nauka, 1979.

Lotman, Iurii M. *Pushkin. Biografiia pisatelia, stat'i i zametki. 1960–1990, "Evgenii Onegin." Kommentarii*. St Petersburg: Iskusstvo-SPB, 1995.

– "Russkaia literatura na frantsuzskom iazyke." In *Izbrannye stat'i*, vol. 2, 350–68. Tallinn: Aleksandra, 1992.

Lounsbery, Anne. "Dostoevskii's Geography: Centers, Peripheries, and Networks in Demons." *Slavic Review* 66, no. 2 (2007): 211–29.

Mahawatte, Royce. *George Eliot and the Gothic Novel: Genres, Gender, Feeling*. Cardiff: University of Wales Press, 2013.

Maguire, Muireann. *Stalin's Ghosts: Gothic Themes in Early Soviet Literature*. Oxford: Peter Lang, 2012.

Maguire, Robert A. *Exploring Gogol*. Stanford, CA: Stanford University Press, 1994.

Mann, Iurii. "Gogol's Poetics of Petrification." In *Essays on Gogol: Logos and the Russian Word*, edited by Susanne Fusso and Priscilla Meyer, 75–88. Evanston, IL: Northwestern University Press, 1994.

Mann, Iu. V. *Poetika Gogolia. Variatsii k teme*. Moscow: Coda, 1996.

Mantual, D. "Chekhov's 'Black Monk' and Byron's 'Black Friar.'" *International Fiction Review* 5, no. 1 (1978): 46–51.

Marker, Gary S. *Publishing, Printing and the Origins of the Intellectual Life in Russia, 1700–1800*. Princeton, NJ: Princeton University Press, 1985.

Marx, Karl, and Friedrich Engels. *Manifesto of the Communist Party and Selected Essays*. Rockville, MD: Arc Manor, 2008.

Met'iurin, Ch.R. *Mel'mot skitalets*. Edited by M.P. Alekseev and A.M. Shadrin. Moscow: Nauka, 1983.

Matveeva, Irina G. "Immigration and the Book: Foreigners as the Founders of the First Libraries in Russia." *Libraries and Culture* 33, no. 1 (1998): 62–8.

Matzner-Gore, Greta. "Dmitry Grigorovich and the Limits of Empiricism." *Russian Review* 77, no. 3 (2018): 359–77.

McReynolds, Louise. *Murder Most Russian: True Crime and Punishment in Late Imperial Russia*. Ithaca, NY: Cornell University Press, 2013.

Michasiw, Kim Ian. Introduction to *Zofloya, or The Moor*, by Charlotte Dacre. Oxford: Oxford University Press, 1997.

Mikhailov, M.L. "Zhenshchiny, ikh vospitanie i znachenie v sem'e i obshchestve." In *Muzhskie otvety na zhenskii vopros v Rossii. Antologiia*, edited by Valentina Uspenskaia, vol. 1, 35–100. Tver': Feminist-Press, 2005.

Milbank, Alison. Introduction to *A Sicilian Romance*, by Ann Radcliffe. Oxford: Oxford University Press, 1993.

Miller, Carolyn R. "Genre as Social Action." In *Genre and the New Rhetoric*, edited by Aviva Freedman and Peter Medway, 20–36. London: Taylor & Francis, 2005.

Miller, Robin Feuer. *Dostoevsky and "The Idiot": Author, Narrator and Reader*. Cambridge, MA: Harvard University Press, 1981.

– "Dostoevsky and the Tale of Terror." In *Dostoevskii and Britain*, edited by W.J. Leatherbarrow, 139–58. Oxford: Berg, 1995.

– *Dostoevsky's Unfinished Journey*. New Haven, CT: Yale University Press, 2007.

– "The Notebooks to *The Idiot*." In *Dostoevsky's "Idiot": A Critical Companion*, edited by Liza Knapp, 53–104. Evanston, IL: Northwestern University Press, 1998.

Moers, Ellen. *Literary Women: The Great Writers*. New York: Doubleday, 1976.

Morrissey, Susan K. "The 'Apparel of Innocence': Toward a Moral Economy of Terror in Late Imperial Russia." *Journal of Modern History* 84 (2012): 607–42.

Morson, Gary Saul. "Misanthropology." *New Literary History* 27, no. 1 (1996): 57–72.

Nabokov, Vladimir, trans. *Eugene Onegin: A Novel in Verse*. Princeton, NJ: Princeton University Press, 1991.

– *Lectures on Russian Literature*. New York and San Diego: Harcourt, Inc., 1981.

– "On a Book Entitled *Lolita*." In *The Annotated Lolita: Revised and Updated*, 207–11. New York: Vintage, 1991.

Naiman, Eric. "'Husband and Wife': An Approach to the Gothic in *Anna Karenina*." In *Critical Insights: Anna Karenina*, edited by Robert C. Evans, 39–57. Ipswich, MA: Grey House Publishing, 2021.

– *Sex in Public: The Incarnation of Early Soviet Ideology*. Princeton, NJ: Princeton University Press, 1997.

Nechaev, S.G. "Katekhizis revoliutionera." *Elektronnaia biblioteka Istoricheskogo fakul'teta MGU im. M V. Lomonosova*. n.p. Moscow: Moscow State University History Faculty, 2010. http://www.hist.msu.ru/ER/Etext/nechaev.htm.

Nechayev, Sergey. "The Revolutionary Catechism." *Marxists Internet Archive Library*. n.p. https://www.marxists.org/subject/anarchism/nechayev /catechism.htm.

Nekrasov, Nikolai, ed. *Fiziologiia Peterburga*. St Petersburg: A. Ivanov, 1845.

– ed. *Petersburg: The Physiology of a City*. Translated by Thomas Gaiton Marullo. Evanston, IL: Northwestern University Press, 2009.

Newlin, Thomas. *The Voice in the Garden: Andrei Bolotov and the Anxieties of Russian Pastoral, 1738–1833*. Evanston, IL: Northwestern University Press, 2001.

Odoevskii, Vladimir. *Povesti i rasskazy*. Moscow: Khudozhestvennaia literatura, 1988.

Offord, Derek. "Karamzin's Gothic Tale: *The Island of Bornholm*." In *The Gothic-Fantastic in Nineteenth-Century Russian Literature*, edited by Neil Cornwell, 37–58. Amsterdam: Rodopi, 1999.

Pan'kov, Nikolai. "'Everything else depends on how this business turns out':
    Mikhail Bakhtin's Dissertation Defence as Real Event, as High Drama
    and as Academic Comedy." In *Bakhtin and Cultural Theory*, edited by Ken
    Hirschkop and David Shepherd, 26–61. Manchester: Manchester University
    Press, 2001.
Paperno, Irina. *Chernyshevsky and the Age of Realism*. Stanford, CA: Stanford
    University Press, 1988.
Passage, Charles. *The Russian Hoffmannists*. The Hague: Mouton, 1963.
Patyk, Lynn Ellen. "The Byronic Terrorist: Boris Savinkov's Literary Self-
    Mythologization." In *Just Assassins: The Culture of Terrorism in Russia*, edited
    by Anthony Anemone, 163–90. Evanston, IL: Northwestern University
    Press, 2010.
– *Written in Blood: Revolutionary Terrorism and Russian Literary Culture,
1861–1881*. Madison: University of Wisconsin Press, 2017.
Paulson, Ronald. "Gothic Fiction and the French Revolution," *ELH* 48, no. 3
    (1981): 532–54.
Pavlov, A.V. "Rossiiskie liberaly i revoliutsionnye demokraty o iakobintsakh."
    Metamorfozy istorii, no. 2 (2002): 43–54.
Pavlova, K. *Dvoinaia zhizn'. Ocherk*. Moscow: Tipografiia Got'e i Monigetti, 1848.
Peterson, Dale. "Russian Gothic: The Deathless Paradoxes of Bunin's Dry
    Valley." *Slavic and East European Journal* 31, no. 1 (1987): 36–49.
Pettus, Mark. "Dostoevsky's Closed Threshold in the Construction of the
    Existential Novel." PhD diss., Princeton University, 2009.
Platonov, Andrei. "No odna dusha u cheloveka." In *Sobranie sochinenii*, vol. 3,
    519–21. Moscow: Sovetskaia Rossiia, 1985.
Platt, Kevin M.F., Caryl Emerson, and Dina Khapaeva. "Introduction: The
    Russian Gothic." *Russian Literature* 106 (2019): 1–9.
Platt, Kevin M.F., and Dina Khapaeva, eds. "Russian Gothic." Special issue,
    Russian Literature 106 (May–June 2019): 1–116.
Poe, Edgar Allan. "The Fall of the House of Usher." In *The Collected Tales and
    Poems of Edgar Allan Poe*, 231–45. New York: Vintage Books, 1975.
Poliakova, A.A., and N.D. Tamarchenko, eds. *Goticheskaia traditsiia v russkoi
    literature*. Moscow: Rossiiskii gosudarstvennyi gumanitarnyi
    universitet, 2008.
Porter, Jillian. *Economies of Feeling: Russian Literature under Nicholas I*.
    Evanston, IL: Northwestern University Press, 2017.
Potter, Franz J. *The History of Gothic Publishing, 1800–1835: Exhuming the Trade*.
    London: Palgrave Macmillan, 2005.
Praz, Mario. *The Romantic Agony*. Oxford: Oxford University Press, 1978.
Punter, David. *The Literature of Terror*. Vol. 2, *The Modern Gothic*. London:
    Longman Group, 1996.

Pursglove, Michael. "Does Gothic Verse Exist? The Case of Vasilii Zhukovskii." In *The Gothic-Fantastic in Nineteenth-Century Russian Literature*, edited by Neil Cornwell, 83–101. Amsterdam: Rodopi, 1999.

Pushkareva, Natal'ia. *Chastnaia zhizn' russkoi zhenshchiny XVIII veka*. Moscow: Izdatel'stvo "Lomonosov," 2012.

Pushkin, Aleksandr. *Eugene Onegin*. Translated by James Falen. Oxford: Oxford University Press, 2009.

– *Polnoe sobranie sochinenii*. 16 vols. Moscow: Akademiia Nauk SSSR, 1937.

Radcliffe, Ann. *The Italian, or the Confession of the Black Penitents*. Oxford: Oxford University Press, 1998.

– *The Mysteries of Udolpho*. Oxford: Oxford University Press, 1998.

– "On the Supernatural in Poetry." *New Monthly Magazine* 16, no. 1 (1826): 145–52.

– *The Romance of the Forest*. Oxford: Oxford University Press, 1998.

Radzinsky, Edvard. *Alexander II: The Last Great Tsar*. Translated by Antonina W. Bouis. New York: Free Press, 2005.

Robespierre, Maximilien. "On the Principles of Political Morality." In *Internet Modern History Sourcebook*, edited by Paul Halsall, n.p. New York: Fordham University History Department, 1997. https://sourcebooks.fordham.edu /mod/1794robespierre.asp.

Romanets, Maryna, ed. "Postcoloniality and Neo-Gothic Fictions in the Post-Soviet Space." Special issue, *Canadian Slavonic Papers* 61, no. 4 (2019): 373–438.

Rosenholm, Arja. *Gendering Awakening: Femininity and the Russian Woman Question of the 1860s*. Helsinki: Kikimora Publications, 1999.

Sade, Marquis de. *The Gothic Tales*. Translated by Margaret Crossland. London: Peter Owen, 1990.

– "Idée sur les romans." In *Les Crimes de l'Amour*, edited by Michel Delon, 27–51. Paris: Gallimard, 1987.

Sage, Victor. *Horror Fiction in the Protestant Tradition*. New York: St Martin's Press, 1988.

Saltykov-Shchedrin, M.E. *The Golovlyov Family*. Translated by Samuel Cioran. Dana Point: Ardis, 1977.

– *Gospoda Golovlevy*. In *Sobranie sochinenii*, vol. 13, 5–262. Moscow: Izdatel'stvo khudozh. literatura, 1972.

Saraskina, Liudmila. *Besy: Roman – preduprezhdenie*. Moscow: Sovetskii pisatel', 1990.

Savinkov, Boris. *Kon' blednyi, Izbrannoe*. Moscow: Khudozhestvennaia literatura, 1990.

Scherr, Barry P. "The Topography of Terror: The Real and Imagined City in Dostoevsky's *Besy*." *Dostoevsky Studies*, n.s., 18 (2014): 59–86.

Schiller, Friedrich. "Vom Erhabenen." In *Sämtliche Werke*, vol. 5, 489–513. Munich: Carl Hanser Verlag, 1962.

Schroder, Anne. "Voodoo and Conjure as Gothic Realism." In *The Palgrave Handbook of the Southern Gothic*, edited by Susan Castillo Street and Charles L. Crow, 421–33. London: Palgrave Macmillan, 2016.

Scott, Walter, Sir. "Horace Walpole." In *Sir Walter Scott on Novelists and Fiction*, edited by Ioan Williams, 84–93. London: Routledge, 1968.

Shapiro, Marianne. "Gogol and Dante." *Modern Language Studies* 17, no. 2 (1987): 37–54.

Shchipachaeva, N.A. "Zagadochnoe i tainstvennoe v povesti A.P. Chekhova 'Chernyi monakh.'" In *Tvorchestvo A.P. Chekhova: poetika, istoki, vliianie*, 117–24. Taganrog: 2000.

Shestov, Lev. "Tvorchestvo iz nichego (A.P. Chekhov)." In *A.P. Chekhov: Pro et contra*, edited by I.N. Sukhikh, 566–98. St Petersburg: Izdatel'stvo Russkogo Khristianskogo gumanitarnogo instituta, 2002.

Shevyrev, Stepan. "'Pokhozhdeniia Chichikova, ili Mertvye dushi,' poema N.V. Gogolia." *Moskvitianin* 4, nos. 7–8 (1842): 205–28 and 346–76.

Shneyder, Vadim. *Russia's Capitalist Realism: Tolstoy, Dostoevsky, and Chekhov*. Evanston, IL: Northwestern University Press, 2020.

Simpson, Mark S. *The Russian Gothic Novel and Its British Antecedents*. Columbus: Slavica, 1986

Singleton, Amy C. *No Place Like Home: The Literary Artist and Russia's Search for Cultural Identity*. Albany: SUNY Press, 1997.

Smirnova, O.V. "Evgeniia Tur: Sud'ba zhenshchiny-pisatel'nitsy v Rossii XIX veka." Kand. diss., Tver' Gosudarstvennyi Universitet, 2010.

Smith, Andrew. *Victorian Demons: Medicine, Masculinity, and the Gothic at the Fin-de-Siècle*. Manchester: Manchester University Press, 2004.

Soare, Monica Cristina. "The Female Gothic Connoisseur: Reading, Subjectivity, and the Feminist Uses of Gothic Fiction." PhD diss., University of California, Berkeley, 2013.

Sobol, Valeria, ed. "Forum: Rethinking the Gothic in Ukraine." *Slavic and East European Journal* 62, no. 2 (2018): 246–317.

– *Haunted Empire: Gothic and the Imperial Russian Uncanny*. Ithaca, NY: Cornell University Press, 2020.

Sobol', Valeriia. "Monakh v Madride: Otzvuki goticheskogo romana Met'iu G. L'iuisa 'Monakh' v p'ese A.S. Pushkina 'Kammenyi gost'" *Filologicheskie nauki* 5 (2015): 75–84.

Somoff, Victoria. *The Imperative of Reliability: Russian Prose on the Eve of the Novel, 1820s–1850s*. Evanston, IL: Northwestern University Press, 2015.

Somov, Orest M. "Matushka i synok." In *Byli i nebylitsy*, 327–49. Moscow: Sovetskaia Rossiia, 1984.

– "Mommy and Sonny." Translated by John Mersereau, Jr. In *Russian Romantic Prose: An Anthology*, edited by Carl R. Proffer, 212–30. Ann Arbor, MI: Translation Press, 1979.

Steinberg, Mark. *Petersburg* Fin de Siècle. New Haven, CT: Yale University Press, 2011.

Stites, Richard. *The Women's Liberation Movement in Russia: Feminism, Nihilism, and Bolshevism, 1860–1930*. Princeton, NJ: Princeton University Press, 1978.

Stroganova, Evgeniia. "The Writing Experience as Emotional Trauma: The Case of Elena Andreevna Gan." In *Mapping Experience in Polish and Russian Women's Writing*, edited by Marja Rytkönen, Kirsi Kurkijärvi, Urszula Chowaniec, and Ursula Phillips, 50–64. Newcastle upon Tyne: Cambridge Scholars Publishing, 2010.

Tarr, Clayton Carlyle. *Gothic Stories within Stories: Frame Narratives and Realism in the Genre, 1790–1900*. Jefferson, NC: McFarland & Company, 2017.

Terts, Abram. *Chto takoe sotsialisticheskie realizm?* Paris: Syntaxis, 1988.

Tikhomirov, B.N. "'Katekhizis revoliutsionera' Sergeia Nechaeva. Istoricheskii dokument i ego rol' v tvorcheskoi istorii romana 'Besy.'" *Dostoevskii i mirovaia kul'tura* 7, no. 3 (2019): 162–78.

– "K probleme genezisa 'ital'ianskoi mechty' Dostoevskogo: Radklif ili psevdo-Radklif?" *Dostoevskii i mirovaia kul'tura* 10, no. 2 (2020): 128–52.

Tiutchev, F.I. *Stikhotvoreniia, 1850–1873*. In *Polnoe sobranie sochinenii i pisem*, vol. 2. Moscow: Klassika, 2003.

Todd, William Mills, III. "Periodicals in Literary Life of the Early Nineteenth Century." In *Literary Journals in Imperial Russia*, edited by Deborah A. Martinsen, 37–63. Cambridge: Cambridge University Press, 1997.

Todorov, Tzvetan. *The Fantastic: A Structural Approach to a Literary Genre*. Translated by Richard Howard. Ithaca, NY: Cornell University Press, 1975.

Tolstoi, L.N. *Polnoe sobranie sochinenii*. 90 vols. Moscow: Gos. Izd-vo Khudozh. Lit-ry, 1928–64.

Toporov, Vladimir. *Mif. Ritual. Simvol. Obraz: Issledovaniia v oblasti mifopoeticheskogo*. Moscow: Progress, 1995.

– *Peterburgskii tekst russkoi literatury: Izbrannye trudy*. St Petersburg: Iskusstvo-SPB, 2003.

Tosi, Alessandra. *Waiting for Pushkin: Russian Fiction in the Reign of Alexander I (1801–1825)*. Amsterdam: Rodopi, 2006.

Tsvetaeva, Marina. *Marina Tsvetaeva: A Captive Spirit: Selected Prose*. Translated by J. Marin King. London: Virago Press, 1983.

– *Sobranie sochinenii*. 7 vols. Moscow: Ellis Lak, 1994.

Tur, Evgeniia. *Antonina*. Translated by Michael R. Katz. Evanston, IL: Northwestern University Press, 1996.

– *Antonina. Epizod iz romana, Kometa. Ucheno-literaturnyi almanakh.* Moscow: tip. Aleksandra Semena, 1851.

– "Miss Bronte, ee zhizn' i sochineniia." *Russkii vestnik* 18 (1858): 501–75.

– "Neskol'ko slov po povodu stat'i Russkoi Zhenshchiny." *Moskovskie vedomosti,* no. 85 (17 April 1860): 665–7.

Turgenev, Ivan S. *Sketches from a Hunter's Album.* Translated by Richard Freeborn. London: Penguin Books, 1990.

– *Polnoe sobranie sochinenii i pisem.* 30 vols. Moscow: Nauka, 1978–2014.

Tynianov, Yuri. *The Problem of Verse Language.* Translated by Michael Sosa and Brent Harvey. Ann Arbor, MI: Ardis, 1981.

Vaisman, Margarita. "*Chto delat'?* N.G. Chernyshevskogo i *Kaleb Vil'iams* U. Godvina: Tipologicheskie parallely." *Vestnik Permskogo Universiteta* 5, no. 11 (2010): 104–10.

Vaisman, M., A. Vdovin, I. Kliger, and K. Ospovat, eds. *Russkii realizm XIX veka: Mimesis, politika, ekonomika.* Moscow: Novoe literaturnoe obozrenie, 2020.

van Baak, Joost. *The House in Russian Literature: A Mythopoeic Exploration.* Amsterdam: Rodopi, 2009.

Vatsuro, V.E. *Goticheskii roman v Rossii.* Edited by T.F. Selezneva. Moscow: Novoe literaturnoe obozrenie, 2002.

Vigel', F.F. *Zapiski.* Moscow: Artel' pisatelei "Krug," 1928.

Vinitsky, Ilya. *Ghostly Paradoxes: Modern Spiritualism and Russian Culture in the Age of Realism.* Toronto: University of Toronto Press, 2009.

Walpole, Horace. *The Castle of Otranto.* 3rd ed. London, 1769.

Watt, Ian. *The Rise of the Novel: Studies in Defoe, Richardson, and Fielding.* Oakland: University of California Press, 1957.

Weikart, Richard. "Marx, Engels, and the Abolition of the Family." *History of European Ideas* 18, no. 5 (1994): 657–72.

Weiner, Adam. *By Authors Possessed: The Demonic Novel in Russia.* Evanston, IL: Northwestern University Press, 1998.

Wellek, René. *Concepts of Criticism.* New Haven, CT: Yale University Press, 1963.

Whitehead, Claire. "Anton Chekhov's *The Black Monk*: An Example of the Fantastic?" *The Slavonic and East European Review* 85, no. 4 (2007): 601–28.

– *The Fantastic in France and Russia in the Nineteenth Century: In Pursuit of Hesitation.* London: Legenda, 2006.

– "Shkliarevskii and Russian Detective Fiction." In *Dostoevskii's Overcoat: Influence, Comparison, and Transposition,* edited by Joe Andrew and Robert Reid, 101–22. Amsterdam: Rodolpi, 2013.

Williams, Anne. *Art of Darkness: A Poetics of Gothic.* Chicago: University of Chicago Press, 1995.

Wilt, Judith. *Ghosts of the Gothic: Austen, Eliot, and Lawrence.* Princeton, NJ: Princeton University Press, 1980.

Wolstenholme, Susan. *Gothic (Re)Visions: Writing Women as Readers.* Albany: State University of New York Press, 1993.

Young, Sarah J. *Dostoevsky's "The Idiot" and the Ethical Foundations of Narrative: Reading, Narrating, Scripting.* London: Anthem Press, 2004.

Zakharov, V.N. *Sistema zhanrov Dostoevskogo.* Leningrad: Izdatel'stvo Leningradskogo Universiteta, 1985.

Index

Page numbers in *italics* indicate illustrations.

abjection, 8–10, 149–50, 173

affective engagement: of early realism, 37; of gothic, 7–8, 10, 18, 27–8; and gothic landscapes, 65–6; and gothic subjectivity, 127–31; in *Idiot*, 88–91; vacillations in, 42–4, 46, 56–7, 88–90, 126–7, 144–8

Age of Assassinations, 154

Aksakov, Sergei, 183; *Family Chronicle, The (Semeinaia khronika)*, 15, 160–5, 167, 169, 171–2

alchemy, 33, 36, 38–9

Alexander II, 137–8, 157–8, 160

Alexandrovich, Sergei, 154

Allen, Elizabeth Cheresh, 58

ambivalence and ambiguity, 45, 53, 55–6, 64, 68, 130, 144–6, 152–6, 171

Andrew, Joe, 133

Antonina (Tur): gothic subjectivity in, 14, 117–18, 127–31; and *Jane Eyre*, 122–4; publication history of, 122, 200n8; and Turgenev's texts, 124–31, 203n90; and women's consciousness, 115, 121, 135–6

anxiety: at decay and degeneration, 159–61, 169–71; as defining element of gothic, 4, 6–7, 18, 32–3; of Dostoevsky's urban spaces, 79–80, 108–14; and female gothic tradition, 117–21; of future cataclysm, 144; ghosts as manifestations of, 177–82; and gothic landscape, 62–3, 65; and gothic trappings, 87–93, 100–1; of heredity and legacy, 161–4; historical, 34–5, 172–4; at modernity, 176–82; and moral questioning, 143, 149–51, 153–6; of Petersburg Text, 103–7, 114; in structure of *Demons*, 144–5; sublime, 77–8, 109–12; of upheaval in traditional family, 164–8. *See also* fear

Apollonio, Carol, 198n23

Aristotle, 42–3

Armstrong, Nancy, 185n15, 186n42

Austen, Jane, *Northanger Abbey*, 25, 27–8

Ayers, Carolyn Jursa, 117

Baer, Brian James, 188n20

Bagby, Lewis, 145

Bakhtin, Mikhail, 3, 15–17, 51–2, 182, 195n44, 198n13

Bakunin, Mikhail, 157

193n16; and Russian heroines, 135; Tatyana's dream in, 12, 41–5, 191n18

Falconet, Étienne, 34
"fall of the house" narratives: and anxiety at cultural decline, 159–61, 183; and degeneration, 164–8; and heredity and legacy, 161–4; introduced, 15, 36–7; as lens on vanished past, 172–4; and nostalgia, 168–71
fantastic: gothic-, 33–6, 39–40; vs realism, 5, 99, 103–4, 114, 177; Todorov on, 39
Fatherland Notes (journal), 121
Faust, 32
fear: affective capacity of, 3–4, 7, 27–8, 91–3, 126–7; and folk belief systems, 66–8, 70–1, 169–70; and foreboding, 79; and historical anxiety, 34–5; and horrors of revolution, 139–40; and imagination, 142, 178–9; as isolating, 165–7; and machinery of terror, 42–3, 46; and poetics of petrification, 55, 80, 92, 128; in retrospect, 107–8. *See also* anxiety
feuilletons. *See* physiological sketch
fin de siècle, 161, 164, 167–8, 171, 174
folklore, 29, 33–4, 39, 66–8, 70–1, 169–70
Fonvizin, Denis, 159
Fourier, Charles, 206n16
framing devices. *See* narrative frames
Frank, Joseph, 74
Franklin, Simon, 40
Frazier, Melissa, 24, 35
French, Bruce, 94
French influence, 23, 29, 35–7, 39–40, 102, 107, 138. *See also individual authors*

French Revolution, 138–43, 145, 158
Fusso, Susanne, 47

Gan, Elena, 117, 132–3
Garrett, Peter K., 11
Gaskell, Elizabeth, *Life of Charlotte Brontë*, 131–4
Gaustad, Randi, 109
generational sagas. *See* "fall of the house" narratives
genre: ecology of, 30–7; and formula vs feeling, 42; and hybridity, 57; and parody, 25–6; theorized, 7, 10, 12, 22. *See also* gothic; gothic realism; realism
German influence, 23, 29, 33–5, 37, 64, 141–2. *See also individual authors*
German Theatre (St Petersburg), 23
Gershenzon, Mikhail, 190n2, 191n18
Gheith, Jehanne, 125
Gilbert, Sandra, 201n36
Gippius, Zinaida, 155
Glagoleva, Olga, 122, 201n31
Gnedich, Nikolai, 28, 39
Goethe, Johann Wolfgang von, 193n16
Gogol, Nikolai, 12, 47, 55, 72, 74, 107, 114; *Arabesques (Arabeski)*, 34–5; *Evenings on a Farm near Dikanka (Vechera na khutore bliz Dikan'ki)*, 34; *Mirgorod*, 34; "Nevsky Prospect" ("Nevskii Prospekt"), 33–4, 103; "The Nose" ("Nos"), 33, 103; "The Overcoat" ("Shinel'"), 34, 37; "The Portrait" ("Portret"), 34, 39, 176; "Viy" ("Vii"), 34, 39. See also *Dead Souls (Mertvye dushi)*
Golovlyov Family, The (Gospoda Golovlevy) (Saltykov-Shchedrin): degeneration in, 15, 160–1, 164–8, 174, 207n40; fatalism of, 159–60,